Experience Design

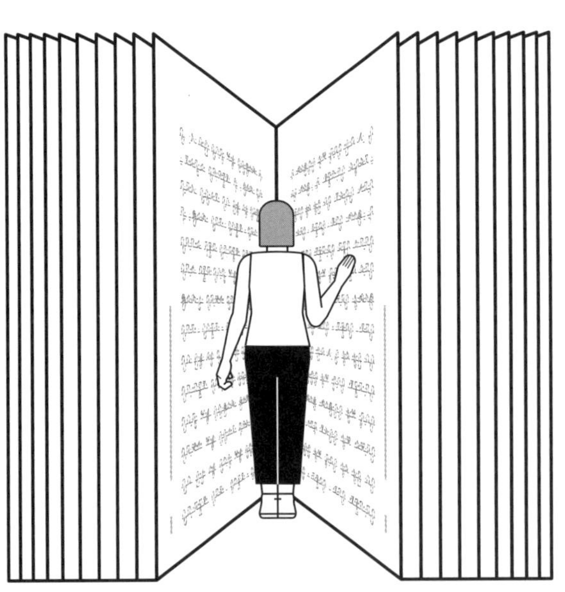

EXPERIENCE DESIGN

A PARTICIPATORY MANIFESTO

Abraham Burickson

Foreword by Ellen Lupton
Design by Erica Holeman

Yale University Press
New Haven and London

yalebooks.com/art

Layout and cover design by Erica Holeman
Set in Neue Haas Unica and Space Mono by Erica Holeman
Neue Haas Unica was designed by Toshi Omagari
Space Mono was designed by Colophon Foundry
Siliconian was designed by Pragun Agarwal, Misha Gomez, and Katie Mancher

Printed in Malaysia

Library of Congress Control Number: 2023935201
ISBN 978-0-300-26947-5
e-book ISBN 978-0-300-27252-9

A catalogue record for this book is available from the British Library.

This paper meets the requirements of ANSI/NISO Z39.48–1992 (Permanence of Paper).

10 9 8 7 6 5 4 3 2 1

Front cover: photograph by Abraham Burickson

Contents

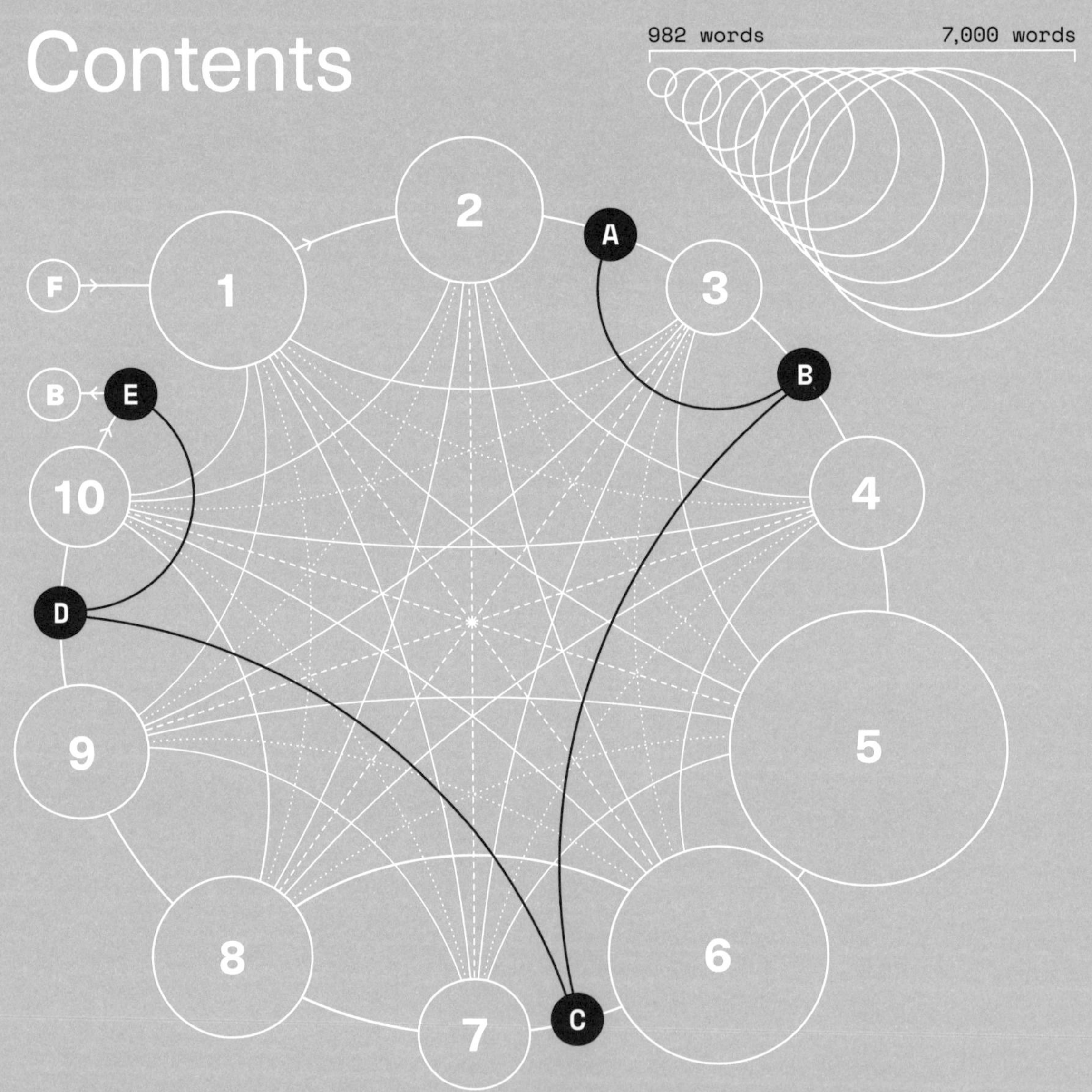

Front Matter

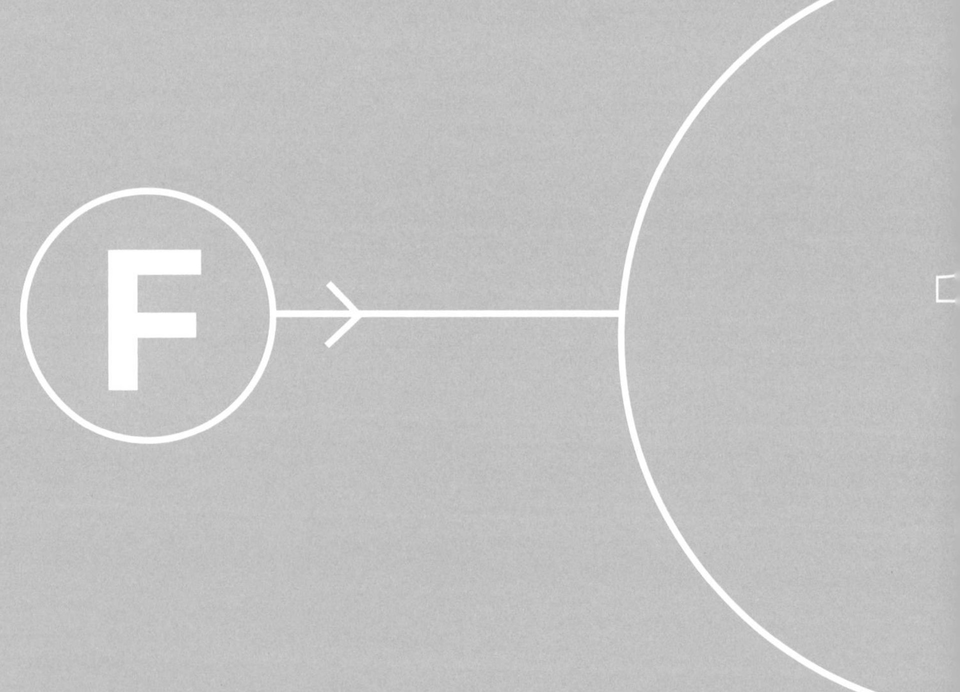

Foreword

Ellen Lupton

Experience is a booming buzzword for museums, tourist boards, fast-food restaurants, digital product designers, and brands of every scope and purpose. A wool sock, a carryout salad, or a flight to Cleveland is now an experience. Brands desperately attempt to turn every consumer into an ambassador of happy vibes. Yet if it's true that we are witnessing an ever-expanding experience economy, why do so many efforts at engagement feel so empty? The word *immersion* makes it sound easy to engage people. Put stuff on the walls, floors, and ceilings and make it move—that's immersion. Take a hot shower with good shampoo—that's immersion, too, and possibly more satisfying than many ticketed events. A museum exhibition that is little more than a light show or an Instagram backdrop leaves visitors feeling drained of time, energy, and the price of admission.

Abraham Burickson takes us deeper by showing how to connect with people on an emotional and physical level. The insights in this book come from centuries of artistic practice (novels, operas, Vatican City) and new and emerging genres (street theater, interactive fiction, group therapy). This book also draws on Burickson's own extraordinary work in the field of experience design—a practice that had no name when he first got started.

Burickson is best known for his work with the performance group Odyssey Works (cofounded with Matthew Purdon in 2001 and directed with Ayden LeRoux since 2012). To create intimate journeys for just one person, the Odyssey Works team researches their singular audience member to discover what matters to them. That person (chosen from a list of applicants) completes a long-form written interview describing their hopes, histories, values, social ties, and connections to works of art, literature, and music. This knowledge helps Odyssey Works craft a unique set of artifacts, places, and actions, divulged over time through phone calls, hidden rooms, chance meetings on the street, unexpected airline tickets, and more. One participant (the novelist Rick Moody) completed his multiweek Odyssey in a tiny hut on a prairie in Saskatchewan, listening to a live performance by a cellist he had read about in a notebook left in a secret room near his home in Brooklyn. The revelatory power of that afternoon on a Canadian prairie built on dozens of smaller encounters with Odyssey Works. These handcrafted, deeply personal journeys touch participants to their very core.

Burickson's Long Architecture practice is a natural extension of his work as an experience designer. Trained as an architect, Burickson spent his early career designing private homes and renovations. Back then, he focused on the usual subjects of architecture: the site, the budget, and the basic requirements of living. Interacting with clients meant sorting through floor plans, bathroom tiles, and lighting fixtures to create spaces that functioned well and looked good. Twenty years later, Burickson returned to architecture from the perspective of experience design. Creating a home should be as personal as staging an Odyssey Works performance. He started to ask, how could a home help one become the person one wants to be? How does architecture change behavior and build relationships? Closets could be designed to discourage buying too much. A living room stripped of its customary couches and side tables could become a place for children to dance and play. Rainwater could enter the home in the form of a small fountain, connecting the domestic interior to natural rhythms.

Such experiences require concrete objects and physical settings. What about the design of digital experiences? During the COVID-19 pandemic, Burickson created *The Book of Separation*, a performance that connects two people digitally. During the pandemic, many people relied on constant screen time to communicate. Weddings, funerals, classrooms, and comedy shows migrated online. To blast past the deadening grid of Zoom, Burickson invited pairs of friends—

separated during the pandemic—to reconnect through physical things and actions. Bodies, feelings, and objects punctured the skin of the screen. How? Instructions sent by phone asked participants to mine their own homes for artifacts of love and care (such as a book that reminds one of the other person) and to spin, jump, or dance in their distant rooms. The tasks, according to Burickson, helped break down Zoom's relentless focus on the torso. The tasks were easy to complete. They wrought joy and surprise. They helped people connect with each other while also finding peace in being alone.

Personal connection is what makes an experience memorable. It's hard to touch someone's soul with a vat of plastic bubbles in a room that smells like ice cream. Many artists are able to make deeper connections more easily than designers. Artists embrace friction, ambiguity, and specificity instead of highly formatted user flows. The joy triggered by the environmental light show *Beyond Van Gogh* may derive not from the details of its experience design but from the deep human bond that people feel with van Gogh's personal story.

Novelists have always been world builders, transporting readers into other minds with the almost-nothing of ink and paper. Empathy, the feeling of entering someone else's mind or body, is triggered by literature and film. Experience design expands the fundamental act of storytelling, pulling the audience into the plot as active players who—in the best of circumstances—change the outcome and are changed by it. Empathy, a key component of meaningful experiences, is explored in the second chapter of this book. Other chapters explore frames (and how to break them), people (and how to know them), worlds (and how to build them), and much more. Theories of narrative, performance, and behavior come to life through examples created by leading artists, designers, and producers. Erica Holeman's delightful instructional diagrams emphasize the fun of playing along and doing it yourself. This book distills Burickson's thoughtful, bespoke approach to experience design, imparting a rich set of principles and practices that any designer or maker can put into play.

Introduction

I love books. Don't you? They're elegant and compact experiential frameworks within which so much is possible. The weight, the size, the carefully considered balance between image and text, the satisfying sound of turning a page, the single purpose of it, honed by so many centuries of development. When I was young, I loved the way opening a book meant crossing a threshold into a new world and how, once there, I could live a different life, be a different person, one imagined into existence by the designer of that world.

From a very young age I knew I wanted to write, or, rather, I knew I wanted to make books. I also knew I wanted to be an architect. Are books and buildings so different, after all? The threshold of a great piece of architecture, like that of a book, offers a view onto another world, one with entirely new possibilities for who I might be. A school, a cathedral, a train station:

each of these is its own world, filled with people who somehow belong there, each with a story to tell and something to do. And, by entering, I was a part of that room, each threshold a portal into another possibility.

But architecture and writing are, in our world, treated as entirely separate practices; it took many years and a great deal of schooling for me to remember that what interested me in them was the same—each is a means of crafting experience. It turned out that the architects and the writers I loved seemed already to understand this; when they spoke about their work, their interest was not in how faithful they had been to their job titles but how they had expanded the experiential potential of their disciplines. Why was nobody talking about this? Did this open secret practice have a name?

In recent years, the term *experience design* has been finding its way into the conversations of designers and artists and makers in an unexpected array of disciplines. It's not always clear what people mean when they use the term, but it's often met with an *ah ha!* look in their listeners. *This is what I've been trying to do*, they seem to be thinking. The idea of designing experience is exciting because it promises more sensory engagement, more liveness, more connection. It promises beautiful moments rather than just beautiful objects, relational engagement rather than demographic targeting. It promises long-term thinking, wonder, awe.

This promise is real, as is its broad application, because experience design is not so much a design methodology (like, say, Human-Centered Design) or an artistic discipline as it is an approach to making. All we have is experience. Experience design comprehends the things we make, the systems we develop, the communities we facilitate as vessels for experience. Experience designers begin with the experience they wish to create and work backward from there. Once on this path, it's hard to turn back, to think just about the stage directions rather than the anticipation of the lights going down in the theater, to think about the kitchen appliances rather than the joy of cooking together, to think about the book jacket rather than the thrill of page one.

If you know what to look for you find experience designers everywhere. These are folks working in immersive theater or immersive technology who find themselves thrilled by the experiential potential of what they are doing. These are also artists in a wide variety of fields for whom the audience is more than just a consumer. These are the social designers, the makers of community, the leaders of organizations seeking a more holistic, human approach to their work. These are the designers of things and images, of digital interfaces and modes of communication, who wish to think about what they make outside the mere moment of contact with the user. These are doctors and teachers, creators of theme parks and creators of city parks, curators of museums and curators of conversations, all of them looking to engage their work more fully with the lives of those they serve. These are the individuals with an idea about some unexpected thing they can do to make their world a little more fair or a little more magical or a little more fun. Their discoveries speak to each other, together developing a practice whose tools are at once very new and as old as humanity. This practice is experience design. It connects these disciplines and erodes the lines between them.

The books I love most are the ones that have immersed me in a way of seeing, escorting me on a journey through a territory of ideas that become a part of me. I'd like to invite you on just such a journey. This is a book designed for active engagement, not just in the explicitly participatory elements but in the very process of reading. It is a partnership: you and me, exploring ideas, wrestling with them, imagining how they might be applied in new ways, to new practices, for new experiences.

You'll notice that I use the words *artist* and *designer* interchangeably in this book. Much work has been done over the years policing the borders of these terms, but experience design is not particularly interested in the divide, or many other divides, because its focus is not so much on the thing being made as on the person who beholds it: you, standing at the threshold of the experience that is this book.

Come, then.
Let us begin.

Manifesto:

All designs are experiences.

All we have are experiences.

CHAPTER ONE

All We Have Are Experiences

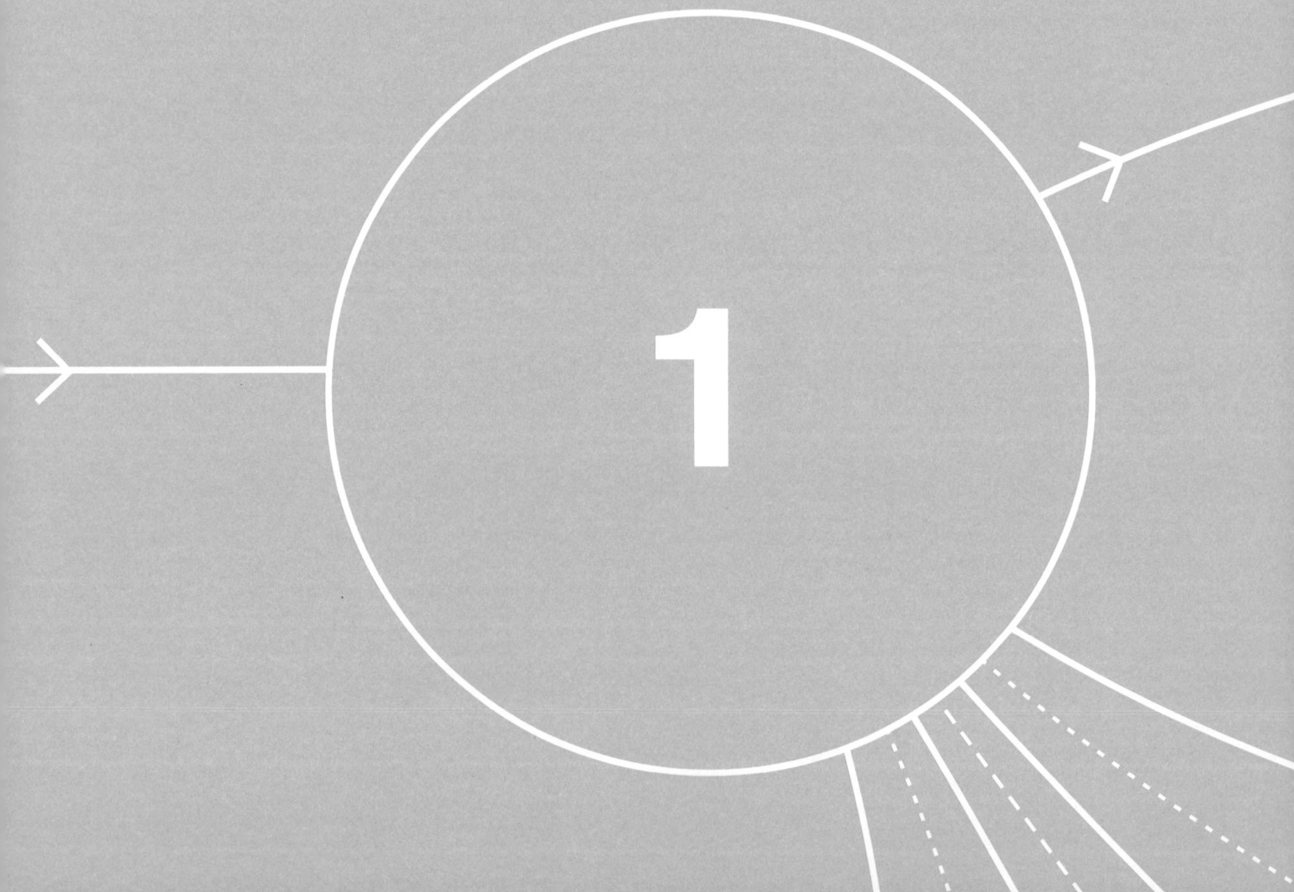

We begin here, with these words. On this page. With you reading, focusing on what is being said while words project themselves into your mind. A little mind control, perhaps. At the same time, pay attention to the way the words look, how they are arranged on the page. The aesthetics tell you something about what is being said, as do the graphics. The aesthetics say this is a designed book, one where the layout matters, and perhaps that's the idea. It's an unusual shape—clearly not the shape, say, of a novel, though not as unusual as some children's books you've seen. The title, of course, did a lot of work to prepare you for this page, but perhaps you're still wondering how the title and the text are going to reconcile. Or maybe the image on the cover was more suggestive than the title. Suggestive of what? Do the thing that is said and the way that thing looks agree?

How can we create a beginning here, one that opens up a way of thinking? This is the aim of this book. Is it your aim? Did you open the book because you were already excited by the idea of experience design and wanted to know more? Or are you looking forward to having an argument because you have your own ideas about experience design, ready to exclaim aloud, *Are you kidding me?*, even though no one can hear? Maybe your designer friend took a call and you're poking through their library? Or someone—a professor or a friend or your kid—told you to read it and you're giving it a try?

It all matters, of course, if we're going to make a good beginning. The book is already written but the experience has just begun, so we need to work together. Let's mark the moment. Look at the date and time. Write it down here:

DATE TIME

Are you well rested? Are you relaxed? Do you feel excited? Impatient? Insecure? Intrigued? Are you trying to read these words but really thinking about that email you're supposed to send? Take a moment to consider the state you're in. Maybe make some notes in the margins, you know, to mark the beginning.

Now, before you turn to the next page, hold your breath. No one will know. Just for thirty seconds. Or pinch yourself. While you are doing so, recognize that anyone else who has read this book has been asked to do so as well. You may be alone reading this book, but this little action weaves you into a web of other readers. Do you know anyone who has read the book? Or who is reading it now? Do you think they held their breath too, or resisted, impatient to get on with it? Why would a book slow you down, anyway?

Hold your breath. Just a few more seconds . . .

That's what we're here to talk about: you as you read, not the book. The experience, not the thing.

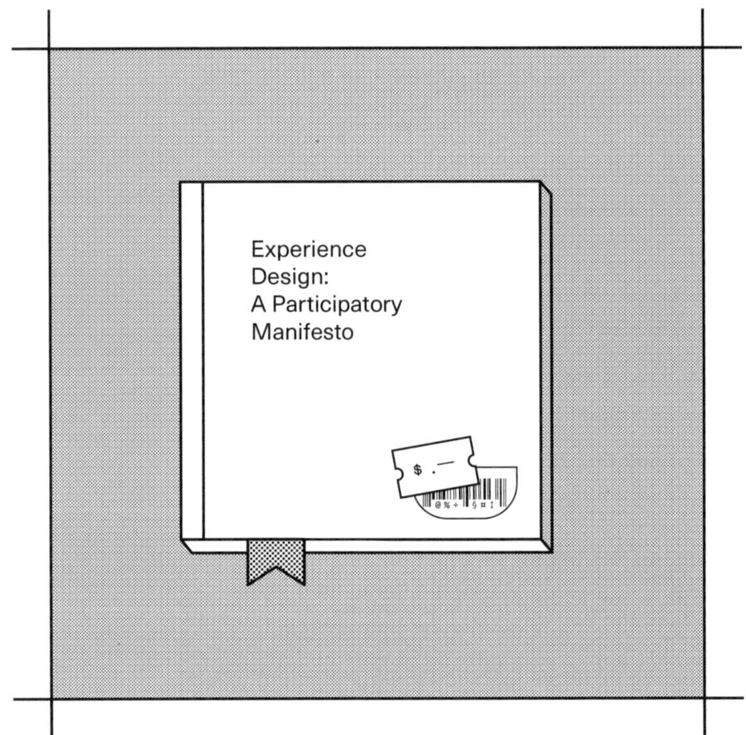

Thing

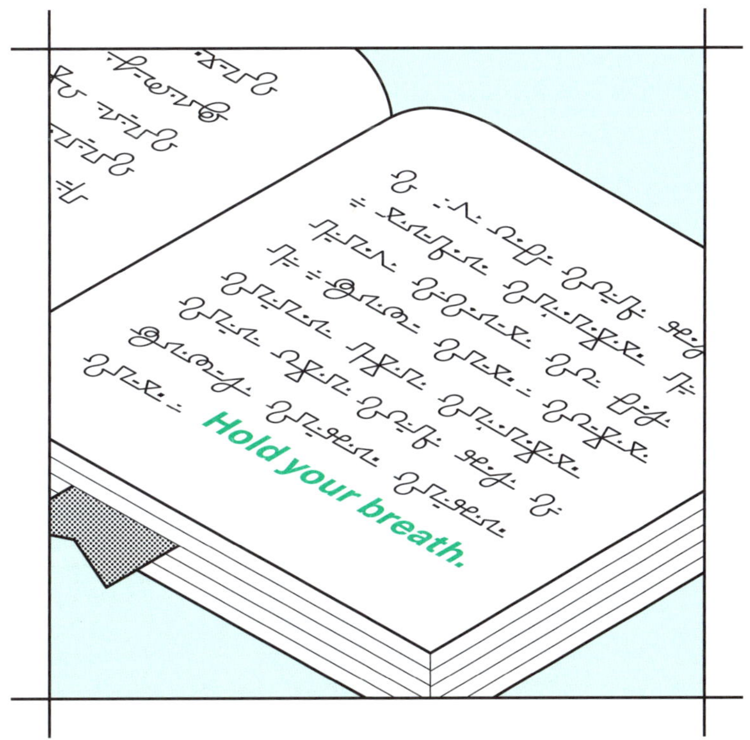

Experience

In the middle of the New Mexico desert, one hundred miles from the dusty intersection of Route 60 and I-25, and another seventy-five miles from Albuquerque, sits *The Lightning Field*. It consists of a grid of four hundred lightning rods, filling an area one mile long by one kilometer wide. Each rod is at least twice as tall as a human, and the tips of them are all at exactly the same altitude, despite the rolling terrain. If you were to place a pane of glass over the top of the installation, it would touch the tip of every rod.

When a low storm comes and lightning strikes, it dances across the rods, producing a natural light show that can exist nowhere else in the world. It is more spectacular than the light show on the Egyptian pyramids, more immersive than any virtual reality film. It is a show worth the long trip away from civilization.

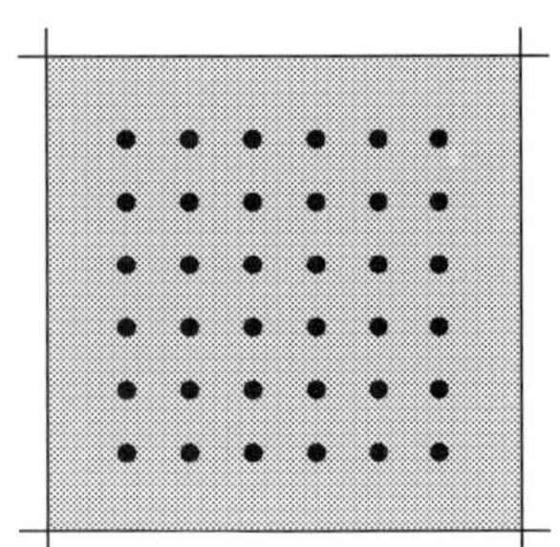

It is also a show that is dependent on the weather. Hardly anyone who makes the journey ever sees it. This is not a secret, yet reservations are booked months and even years in advance. So why do people keep coming?

Because the *experience* of visiting the field, which was created by the artist Walter de Maria in 1977, is exquisitely and uniquely designed. Other famous land art installations in the American West have visitor centers offering guided tours; the installations are like outdoor sculpture gardens, variably busy or thronged with people depending on the weather and the time of year. But *The Lightning Field* has no parking lot and no visitor center. There isn't even a proper road, and to see the installation, you have to commit to spending the night, with strangers, in a log cabin whose porch opens onto the lightning rods.

When you make your reservation, you are told what time to arrive in the nearest town, Quemado, New Mexico. It's a tiny town, and it seems no one else is there. You park your car and wait, taking the time to breathe in the desert air after the long drive and to wonder, again, if you're in the right place. Eventually a man arrives in a pickup truck. He's rugged and wears a hat and you can't help calling him a cowboy, at least in your mind. He's friendly, but he doesn't say a lot as he drives you off the main road and then off the dirt road through the desert for what seems like way too long. Eventually you find yourself asking him questions: Did he help build the field? *Yes, he's been here ferrying people to see it for decades.* Why so far out in the middle of nowhere? *Well, there's more lightning here, and it's hard to find a spot in this country where you can see so far to the horizon without any man-made structures.* Does he ever get tired of answering the same questions about it? *Oh, no. Glad people get to see it. Hope you enjoy the enchiladas.*

Then, after an hour, the truck stops in front of a dusty log cabin. The cowboy drives off, saying he'll see you tomorrow. There's a tiny wraparound porch, several bedrooms, and enchiladas with cooking instructions in the fridge. There are also a couple of people you've never met staying in the other bedrooms. And there are the lightning rods, glimmering in the field like alien artifacts. The sky is clear, the desert is cooling under the evening sun, and the distance from other human infrastructure is otherworldly.

And there you remain until the next day, in the curious circumstance of having traveled so far to see something you know will not happen. The titular lightning of the field is nowhere on the horizon, and you are left to witness where you are and ask yourself how to be. You are Dorothy discovering what you knew all along: that there is no wizard. What you have now is yourself, some strangers to meet, a living desert to behold, four hundred exquisitely crafted stainless steel rods to wonder at, and a tray of enchiladas. So you wander through the lightning rods, follow a jackrabbit for an hour, watch the sunset, get to know the other guests, and learn about neuroscience and art in Germany (that's where they're from). When the sun sets, you heat up the dinner, which is delicious. You were advertised natural spectacle, but you were given unstructured time in a beautiful place.

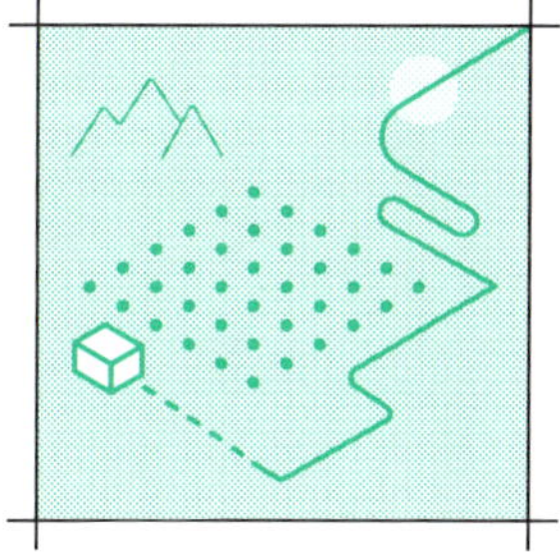

When was the last time you had unstructured time? I mean time when you're not waiting for something to happen, for something to finish and something else to start; I mean time when you don't even have to worry about what to eat. At *The Lightning Field*, your only role is to attend to the place, and yourself, and relate to the strangers you meet there, who are in the same circumstance as you. Everything that led up to your being here primed you to seek beauty: traveling all day, paying for the reservation, gazing at unbelievable images of lightning, setting aside a whole weekend. When you arrive, you're prepared to see things differently.

For the land artist, steel rods and concrete are the materials. For the experience designer, the steel rods and concrete are the tools, and modes of attention and ways of being are the materials. The design of *The Lightning Field* is the rods in the field, against a backdrop of exquisite natural beauty, and on land more likely to have lightning strikes. The experience design of *The Lightning Field* is the drive to Quemado, the ride in the pickup truck with the cowboy, the specific and unusual social situation of spending the night in the middle of nowhere with strangers, the engagement with the landscape and the rods, the slight but expected disappointment of not seeing lightning, the enchiladas. The aim of the design of *The Lightning Field*, from an ordinary, thing-based perspective, is the field of rods and their function as attractors of lightning, facilitating a unique spectacle. The aim of the *experience design* of *The Lightning Field* is akin, in some ways, to a pilgrimage: a transformative experience of nature, other people, and self, activated not just by the design of the physical objects but by the specifically curated stages of approach, arrival, being in the space, sleeping, waking up, and leaving. In the experience design of *The Lightning Field*, time speeds up and slows down as attention and anticipation rise and fall.

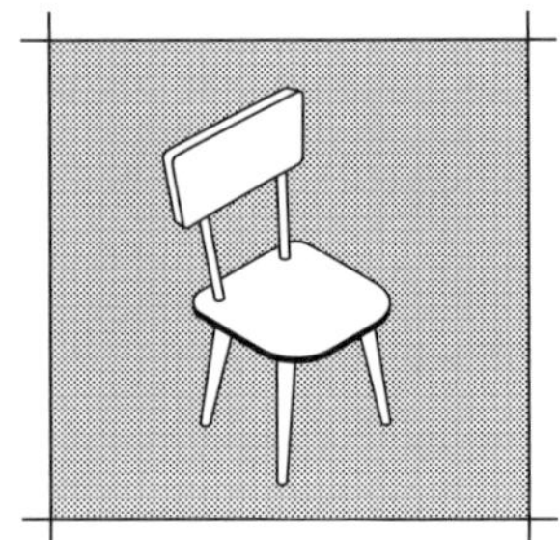

In a traditional design process, predictability is key: it eliminates the unknown and specifies use in a reliable way. Design seeks to control for the chaos that is human unpredictability; luxuriously designed cars get big enough to be as comfortable as home, so people start eating in them. This eating becomes a problem: people keep spilling their drinks all over the upholstery, so designers create the cup holder. Problem solved. And solving problems is the mania of design, so much so that the most celebrated designs—the iPhone, say, or HDTV—solve for problems we didn't even know we had.

But experience is not a problem to be solved; it is life. Experience designers engage with unpredictability and the unknown, partnering with their audiences to generate possibility and relationality. All designs are experiences, but thing-based design tends to forget this, narrowing in on specific mechanics and functions, continually trying to fix problems. The designers of things speak of *affordances*: the activities that a design allows. A cup holder affords the holding of a cup. A chair affords sitting. A book affords reading. But a cup holder also affords bringing your coffee with you to the car, which affords a sense of comfort and a willingness to take longer drives, which affords time to listen to audiobooks about design. The book affords reading, but it also affords something to shake as you make your point, causing your friend to offer a concessionary nod as the two of you carpool to work, well-caffeinated and dreaming about how you might change your careers.

Experiential affordances consider the design element within the broader context of a user's life, focused not so much on predicting discrete actions as considering experiential possibilities. Experience design is, therefore, a much broader practice than ordinary design. The design of a chair is discrete, beginning with the wood and ending with the upholstery; the experience design of the chair is connected to the relative softness of its seat compared to others, the incipient arthritis in the user's hips, the way that chair reminds the user of a chair grandmother had, which, despite its ersatz hand finish, felt expensive. The experience is also connected to how the chair is offered to a dinner guest: with pride, just as the drinks are brought out. The experience design of a chair is never complete in itself and must, therefore, be thought of as an intervention in the continuity of a user's life, realized in partnership with them.

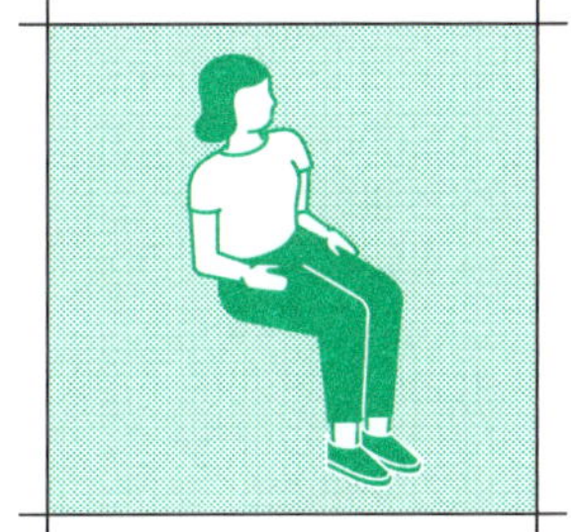

To design experience seems a grandiose idea; it is to design a portion of the life of another person. But when we recognize that each experience design can be only a tiny intervention in the ongoing experience of a person's life, the design must become both a partnership between designer and audience and an honest engagement with the unknown. Humility is, therefore, the first necessary tool. An experience designer knows it's impossible to fully determine how a design will be received, but with an attention to the narratives, the frames of attention, the worldbuilding, and the subjective position of the audience, that experience designer may more skillfully craft an offering.

Possibly the most common engagement with experience design is the gift. From a *thing* point of view, gifts make little sense. Why waste your time or money on an object for someone else that they might not want or wouldn't buy for themselves? Better to give money, say the economists, who lament the inefficiency. Why spend thirty-five dollars on a book for your friend when you could just give them the cash and let them pick out a book they really wanted?

But the gift, of course, is not the book but the experience of the gift of the book. It is fundamentally a relational moment: it reflects the fact that you have thought about your friend, have considered their interests and what books are already on their shelf. The gift is wrapped, presented upon your entry to the house, or mailed in carefully designed packaging. Usually, gifts are surprises, and the moment of revelation is carefully considered; you think about what you will say to your friend, how you will demonstrate that it represents an empathetic understanding of them, or how it ties into a story the two of you share. The book is both testament and proof of the validity of such claims; when your friend reads it, they know right away if you actually considered them, if your claims to understand them are true. A book can be a high-risk gift, for it asks the recipient to invest time reading and then to measure the claims of the gift giver against the object itself. If you're way off base, it's clear. If you get just the right book, the one that changes the way your friend thinks, they will always credit you. And they will be charged with doing the same for you, because a gift demands reciprocity, becoming both bonding agent and symbol of your relationship.

To really go deep into the idea of the gift, pick up a copy of Lewis Hyde's *The Gift*, which looks at mythology, anthropology, and the arts as a window onto the power and function of gift giving.

How did you
come into
possession of
this book?

How has that
experience
colored the way
you are reading
it thus far?

Phase Zero

But how do we begin such a design process? The first step is to determine the experiential scope and potential of a project. Most traditional thing-based practice begins with form and proceeds to content. Let us say you are a playwright; therefore, you will write a play. This play will be about mortality. Because it is a play, it will probably last between one and three hours, and it will have a delimited relationship between actors and audience, and between cast and crew. It will or it will not have a set. It will or it will not take place in a theater. The choices the designer (in this case, the playwright) makes in the piece, in short, will be determined by the potentials and traditions of the form. The experience the audience may have is limited by the experiential affordances of the form of a play.

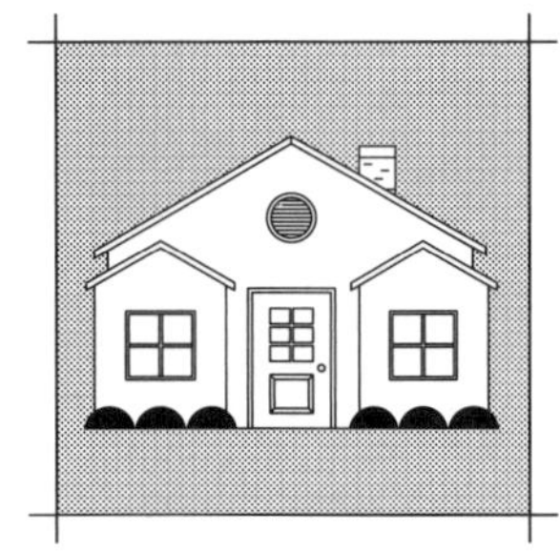

But if I set out to create a narrative experience of a confrontation with mortality, the field of my work is much broader. It may involve a play, yes, possibly a piece of immersive theater, or it may involve several plays, or it may involve the development of a community of individuals exploring their mortality together. It may begin with theater, but then pass into poetry, funerary practice, pilgrimage, asceticism, divination, cooking, epistolary communication, psychedelics, historical research, meditation, or countless other forms. It may last for a few minutes or many lifetimes. The determination of this experiential aim, as well as the search for the best way in which to achieve that aim, is the purpose of Phase Zero.

Consider a typical approach to the design of a new home. Clients and Architect meet and discuss scope—Clients want a three-bedroom home, with sustainable features but without the coldness of so much modern design. Clients love the pictures they saw of Architect's work. Clients also like what Architect wrote on his website: a focus on sustainability, human-scaled space, pattern languages. Clients would love a sauna but know they probably can't afford it. Architect suggests passive cooling, a visit to the site. Do Clients cook a lot? Will they be having more kids? (Awkward silence.) Are there other homes Clients have seen and loved? What were their features?

It's a good interaction; ultimately a scope is agreed on. A cost estimate is signed. Schemes are developed. The investment is huge, a financial commitment beyond even what Clients paid for their college degrees. The emotional investment is huge as well. The new home will define the family. The children's life paths will start there. Communities will cohere there. Relationships with nature and self will be developed there. The home will be the center of the social, aesthetic, and ethical development not just of Clients, but of their family, even of those who live in the house after they move on.

The contrast between the thing and the experience here is stark. The thing that is the house is limited to the structure and finishes of the building. The experience that is the home includes a whole life for which the house is the stage. It includes the people who live there, the values and sense of community that exist there, the aesthetics of comfort and safety. A house is a spot on a map. A home is an orientation in the world. A house is finished when the certificate of occupancy is issued. A home is never finished so long as humans occupy it.

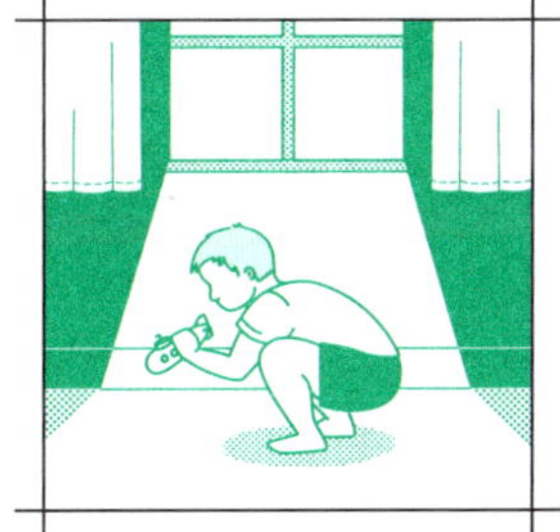

In Phase Zero, Architect and Clients work together to understand designing the house as an intervention in the larger project of designing the experience of home. Phase Zero asks not *What kind of house are you hoping to build* but *What kind of **life** are you hoping to build?* It is a question for Architect and Clients: both parties will be investing enormously in its development, although in different ways. In Phase Zero, the overall aim of the project is laid out, as is the physical and temporal scope. Perhaps Clients, wishing to have a positive effect on the environment, will opt for a net-zero, off-grid structure. But the design may also be such that the home is understood not as a way of protecting Clients from the ravages of nature but of connecting them in a better way with nature. Are Clients lovers of storytelling, wishing to raise children with this same love? Perhaps the house should be embedded with a mystery, or the design of the house should accompany the commission of a novel, or the concurrent construction of a writer's residence. Or maybe Clients and Architect wish to be part of the development of a more economically equitable local community. How might not just the design and construction, but all the ongoing functions of the home, be harnessed to build such a community? In Phase Zero, participants both imagine and research, then identify what collaborations will be needed to realize the design.

An experience designer tosses out the traditional form-then-content process in favor of an experience-then-content-then-form process. Phase Zero does not ask, *What kind of VR film will we make?* but, simply, *What experience are we trying to create?* It is a question that precedes form. Then the answer may be, for instance, *An embodied, narrative experience of the trials of an illegal border crossing*. From here, form is found. Yes, there will be a VR film, but the deep multisensory immersion in a narrative may also require a room filled with sand, the reading of news clips about the trials of border crossings, thirst, discomfort, perhaps even an ongoing conversation between audience members and people who have made similar border crossings through the desert. Perhaps those conversations will need to last weeks, even months. Each Phase Zero decision is not so much a solution to a problem as an opening to experiential possibility.

In the Wachowski siblings' film *The Matrix: Reloaded*, the hero, Neo, makes his way to the spotless, TV-encircled office of The Architect, who is the designer of the artificial world in which most humans live. It seems a beautiful world, but the audience is aware that inhabitants are, in fact, unknowingly stuck inside a computer program. The Architect—an artificial intelligence—is the omnipresent, all-controlling god of his world and has designed not just its landscape but the totality of its inhabitants' experiences and actions. He boasts that the world he designed was "quite naturally perfect, flawless, sublime," but we know not to celebrate this because his totally designed world is clearly devoid of life. He is a designer of the experiences of those inside the Matrix, but he designs experiences as if they are things, without empathy, without relationality, without the unknown. This perfect world, like any totalitarian regime, will ultimately collapse. "The problem," says Neo, before setting out to destroy the Matrix, "is choice." The Matrix is a thing-based approach to worldbuilding. We feel a revulsion for its absolute control in our gut. A world with no unprogrammed choices, no true unknown, is not a human world.

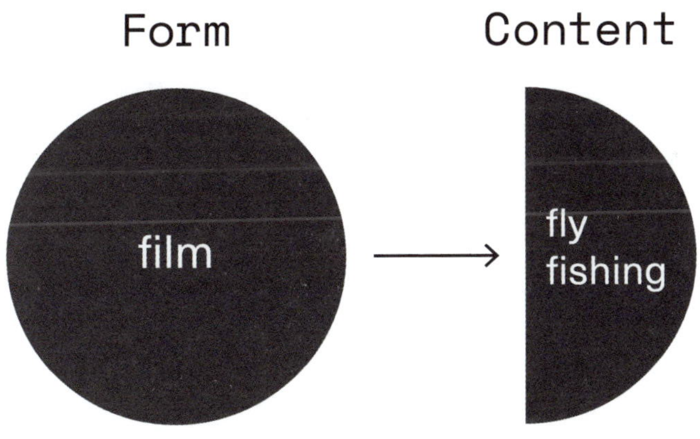
Form
Content
film
fly
fishing

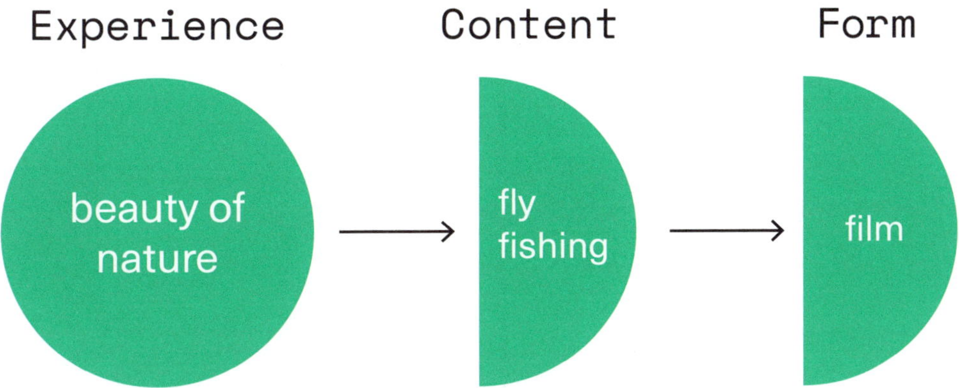
Experience
Content
Form
beauty of
nature
fly
fishing
film

Experience design is, at its core, a fundamentally human approach to design, enfolding both risk and possibility within the scope of its intention. The term *experience design* may be relatively new, but many of its practices are as old as human history. They are rooted in telling stories around the campfire, in religious practices, in how we build families and communities, and how we collectively act on what is meaningful. Experience design makes one practice of immersive theater and architecture, the design of a community

Until recently, most designers who used the term *experience design* were probably referring to user experience design (UX), a practice focused on designing interfaces and services with attention to the behaviors such designs provoke. In *Change by Design: How Design Thinking Transforms Organizations and Inspires Innovation* (2009), IDEO's Tim Brown lays out an experience design practice as a stage in a design thinking research and prototyping practice. These and other precedent uses of the term offer much to learn from, but they are generally used as design thinking research phases, ultimately in the service of thing-based design.

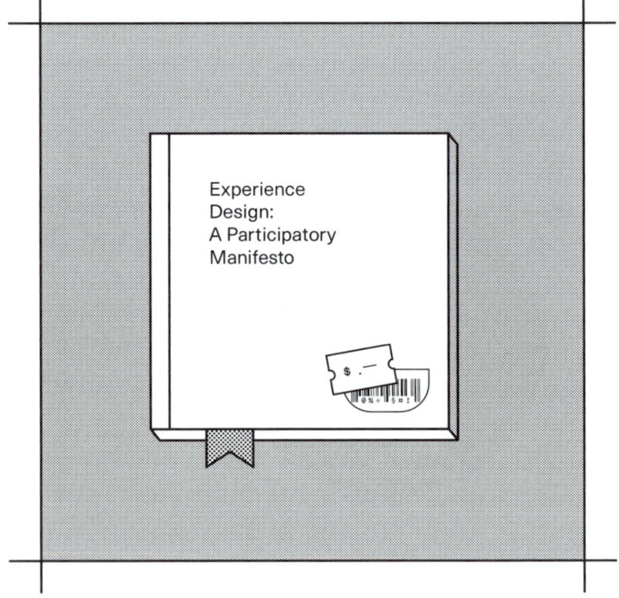

and the design of a dinner party, the design of a field of lightning rods and the design of a book.

When we stop making things and offer, instead, to craft the minutes or hours of another person's life, we must step out of ourselves and be open to the perspectives of others. It is a bold proposition: a fundamentally relational mode of making. It runs counter to our cultural habit of looking inward for our material. The best tool we have for this is *empathy*.

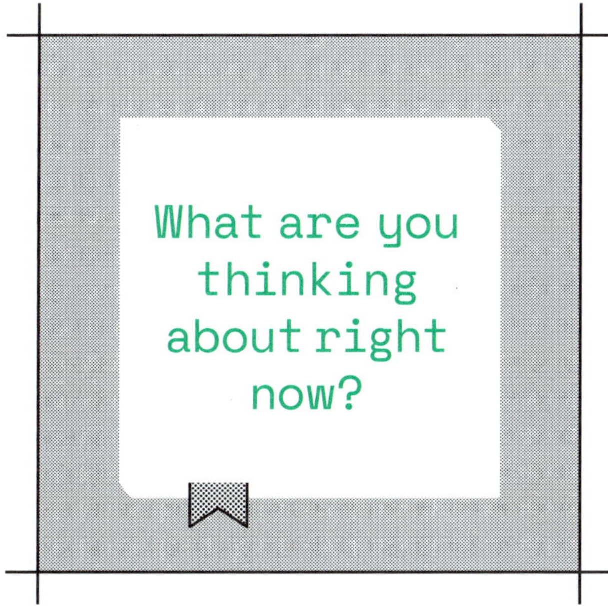

CHAPTER TWO

Employ Empathy Rigorously

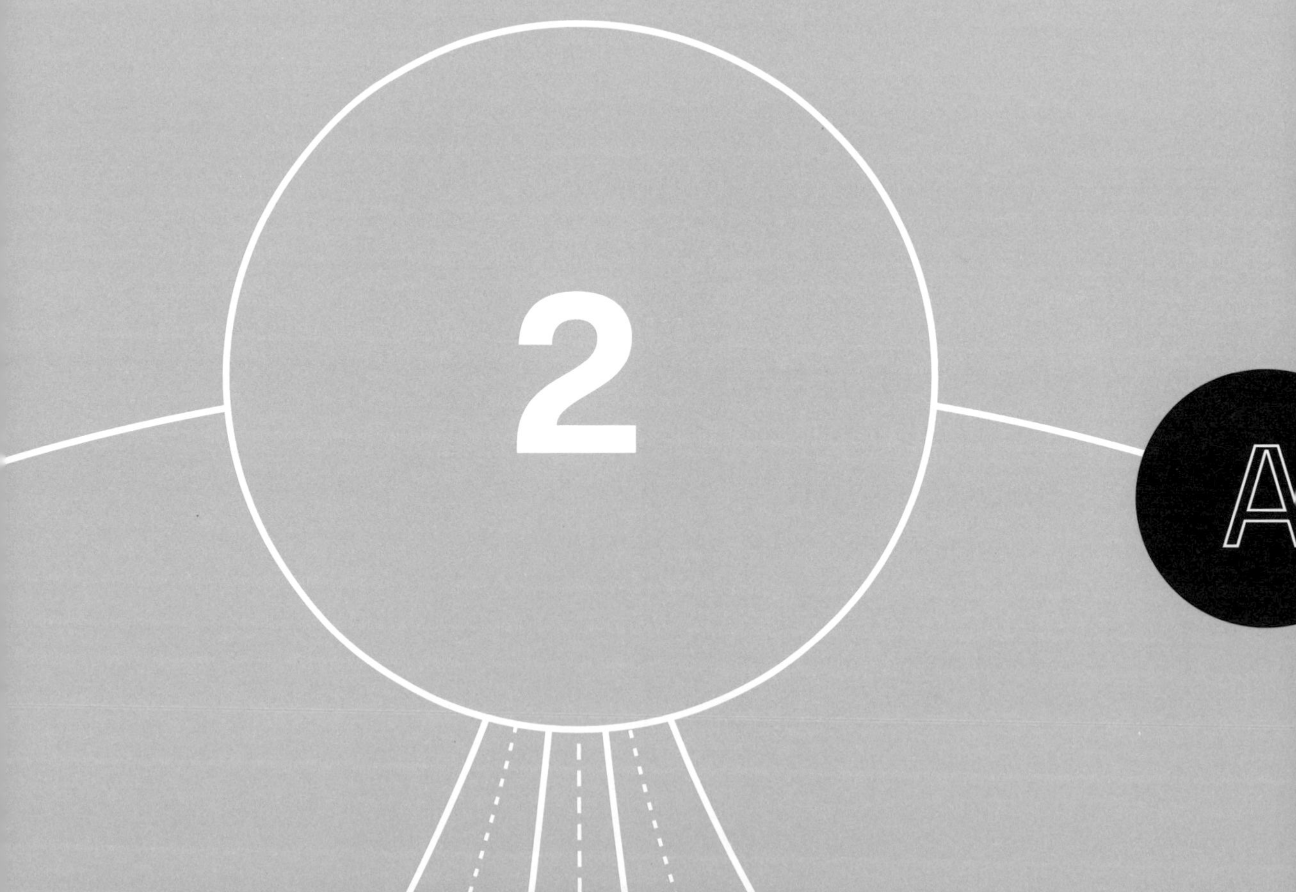

There is something incredibly moving about a successful experience design; you have created something that, for a minute or an hour or a lifetime, has offered someone a new experience of life. To witness this is to affirm our connectedness. Though the minds and hearts of others are invisible to us, their subjective inner experiences impossible to fully communicate, we try. We are built to try. Our brains and our hearts and even our bodies are complex tools designed to help us empathetically understand others. It is the effort at the core of successful relationships and strong communities, at the core, in many ways, of being human. To design with empathy is to remember that we are not demographics, not entities operating in isolation. It is a risky activity, at once challenging our sense of self and tempting us to believe that we understand more than we do, but to design with empathy is to strive to make work that is interrelational rather than didactic, dynamic rather than prescriptive.

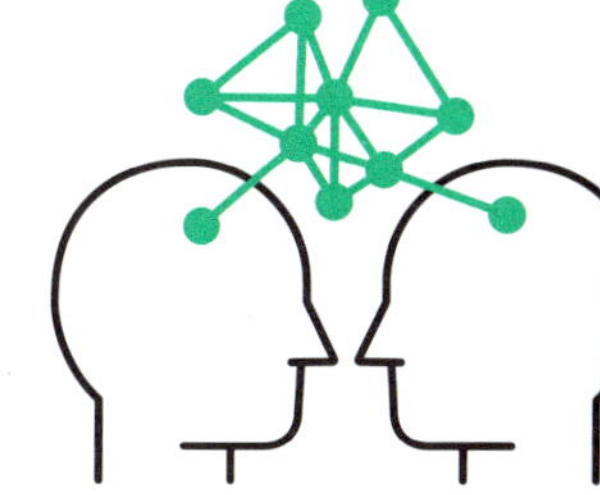

But empathetic research is not just a feeling one has about another; it is the process of integrating traditional research, embodiment, relationality, inclusion, and intuition into making. It is needed because making for others is a project that begins in our own consciousness, our own subjectivity, and navigates the avenues of similarity and difference that lead to the consciousness of another. This navigation is the realm of *empathy*. It is an active process, at once intuitive and intellectually rigorous. Empathy is both a tool and an aim in itself, reminding designers of why they chose to design and keeping them aligned with their purpose.

But how do we intentionally develop empathy for another? We must walk a mile, the saying goes, in another person's shoes. In 2015 the UK-based Empathy Museum decided to invite people to do just that. Their *A Mile in My Shoes* project was a pop-up shoe store where you could pick up a pair of shoes and walk around in them while listening to a recording of the shoes' owner talking about their life.[1] Passersby could try walking in the shoes of a Syrian refugee, a war veteran, a neurosurgeon, or scores of others. Doing so was challenging; they didn't always fit right, even if they were the right size, having been worn in over time by their owner's gait and environment. And walking in a new way while listening to headphones increased cognitive load. Nevertheless, people reported being deeply moved. "It just made me feel really inspired," said one visitor. "I just love the fact that they've taken the concept of empathy and made it tangible."[2] Such efforts, which challenge how we inhabit the world, are key to what makes empathy possible. Walking in the shoes of another implies the changing of physical and corresponding mental habits, rearranging your physical and psychological approach to the world to mimic those of another person. In doing so, you absorb a different physicality, a different mode of thinking. There is a liberation here, a sense of wonder: you can engage the world differently and in so doing you can broaden your sense of self.

Recognizing what you experience when walking in the shoes of another as *empathy* is so obvious that it may come as a surprise

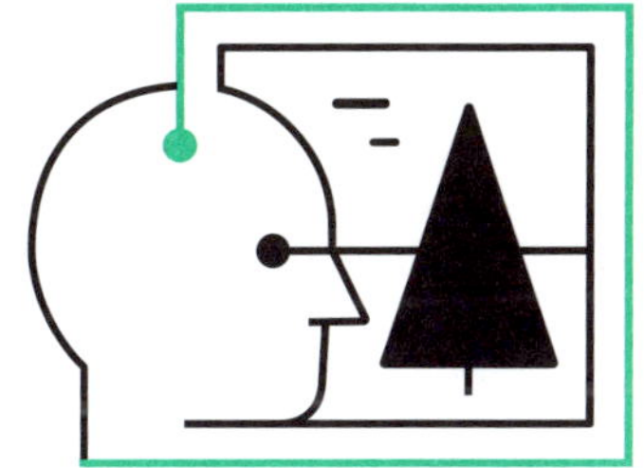

to discover that before 1908 there was no such thing as *empathy*, at least not in the English language. There was *sympathy*, and *compassion*, but even the German word that preceded *empathy* was a far cry from the word we use today. That word, *Einfühlung*, meant, literally, *in-feeling*. One *felt-in* not to fellow humans but to art. You would project your feeling into a sculpture, a landscape, a piece of music.[3] *Einfühlung* is related to being *moved* by a piece of work, being *transported*, or feeling *immersed*. It brings to mind transcendent experiences, like wonder and awe, which many today seek in live, immersive, and technologically innovative experiences. *Einfühlung*, however, is particular in the participation required of the viewer. One must actively *feel-in* to a painting or a landscape.

Here we are speaking about empathy between humans. It is similarly connected to awe and wonder, and similarly transcendent. To feel-in to another person is a process as magical-sounding as it is to feel-in to a painting. Were it not a process innate to humans, it would be impossible to describe. Most design processes understandably have little space for such an abstract, hard-to-quantify tool. Playtesting and A/B testing and focus-grouping can generally cover your bases because, for most design, understanding how users *respond* to a design is enough. Do they actually take the pills? Do they click the *Donate* link? Do they applaud when the curtain goes down? These are functional, behavioral measures. They are actions and reactions, and though they may be the result of the internal experience the user has had of a design, they do not measure that internal experience. Human-Centered Design, for instance, invites designers to engage stakeholders throughout development, but nowhere in its clearly articulated process does it require the same empathetic *in-feeling* that experience design demands. For most design, the internal experience of the user is a tool in the generation of a desired response. If the goal is to get patients to take their pills, do you terrify them about the risks of not taking them, or do you show them happy pictures of people who did take their pills? If the goal is to raise donations for an NGO supporting Ukrainian refugees, do you write a story about one refugee's journey or do you stage a dark comedy about war? The choice, of course, will be determined by what works.

Human-Centered Design is well articulated by the double diamond diagram, which, in its various iterations, lays out an ordered set of steps of identifying problems and researching solutions, and of convergent and divergent thinking.

Experience design, by contrast, is concerned with the *internal* experience of an audience. We are interested in how the work we do connects to our audience's understanding of self, the stories of their lives, their comfort, their joy, their awe. The actions they take as a result of our work may be indicators of what they've experienced, but they are not the goal. Are they applauding because it was a great show or because it is finally over? Are they sharing that article because it amplifies their anxiety or offers them insight? It's a radical notion: to value how a person receives the world more than how they respond to it.

But how can you hope to understand how another person receives the world?

The answer is: you can't, not completely, and that, in some way, is the point. There is something deeply moving in being seen, but there is also something moving in the effort to empathize, to bridge the gap between one person and another. It reveals as much about the person making the effort as about the person being seen, putting both into relationship, elevating both, allowing each to be affected by the other. In-feeling into another person may be risky; you wouldn't want to try to empathize with someone who wishes you harm, or someone whose experience may be too traumatic for you. But it may also be incalculably rewarding. We may not become another person when we walk a mile in their shoes, but we see them a little better, and, in doing so, we understand ourselves in a new light.

From 2010 to 2017, Conflict Kitchen served lunch to the public in downtown Pittsburgh.[4] The kernel of the idea was simple: serve the foods of the cuisines of countries in conflict with the United States. The aim: to build understanding and empathy between Americans and citizens of those countries. It functioned primarily like any other lunch joint, offering up now Cuban cuisine, now Iranian, now Palestinian. Menus included information about the different cultures and the conflicts, and how they affected individuals in those countries. Passersby would grab lunch and sit down to read the menu, associating what they were consuming with what they were learning, simultaneously engaging mind and body in witnessing another way of being, another culture. If they

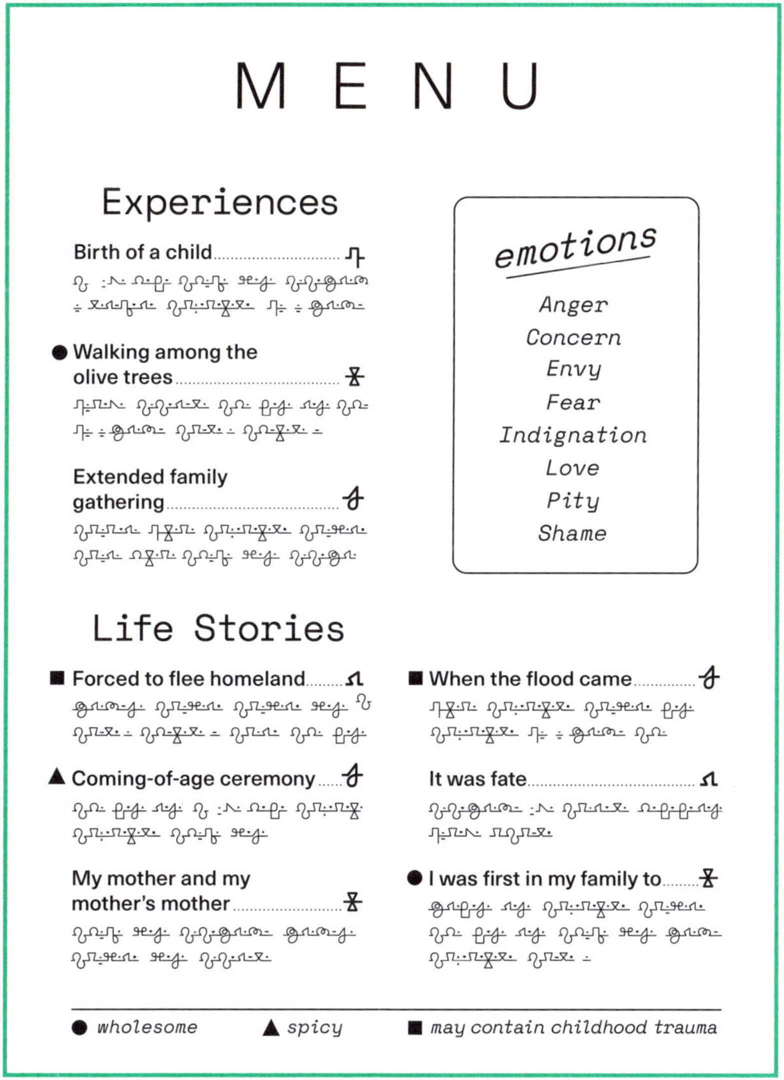

MENU

Experiences

Birth of a child

● Walking among the olive trees

Extended family gathering

emotions

Anger
Concern
Envy
Fear
Indignation
Love
Pity
Shame

Life Stories

■ Forced to flee homeland

▲ Coming-of-age ceremony

My mother and my mother's mother

■ When the flood came

It was fate

● I was first in my family to

● *wholesome* ▲ *spicy* ■ *may contain childhood trauma*

came at the right time, customers might be able to catch something more experimental—they could eat their lunch at a long table that extended into a screen on which was a live image of a similar table in another country, creating the sense that they were sharing lunch with companions half a world away. Or they might have a conversation with an actor who was channeling, through a phone call in their earbuds, an old man living in Pakistan.[5]

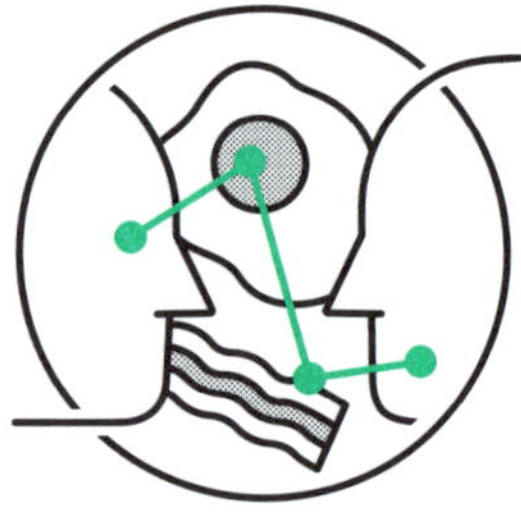

What better entry point into empathy than food? We all eat, and the making and consuming of food constitute a communal and relational staple. Visitors to the restaurant were able to encounter those who might have seemed strange to them on the common ground of lunch. Unlike a book or a documentary, lunch is an embodied aesthetic engagement with the world of another, an opportunity to—in the hands, in the mouth, in the belly—*feel-in* to another person's world.

Empathy, as it is commonly understood today, is more than just emotional understanding. We build empathy by holding hands with a person as they speak, by working together, by walking a mile in their shoes rather than just looking at those shoes. Empathy is physical, intentional, and often challenging. While sympathy is something that may appear after learning about a person's situation, empathy is something we actively develop, with our bodies, our minds, our emotions.

It is also an integral springboard moving us from a thing-based mode of design to an experience-based mode of design because experiences live in the subjectivities of our audience. Where the engineer's research may involve studying tectonics and taking soil samples, the experience designer's research must involve empathy. When I speak of empathetic research, I am referring to a multilayered, full-bodied, rigorous practice. Treating it as a passive, intuitive process runs the risk of fooling us into thinking we fully understand another person with a different life experience. Empathetic research must be as rigorous as any other kind of research and should identify not only commonalities and sites of in-feeling but differences, comprehension of the limits of understanding, and directions for growth. Beginning with empathy means beginning with a search for the bounds of our in-feeling.

The risks of not being rigorous with empathy are not small. Critics such as the Yale University psychologist Paul Bloom would like to do away with empathy altogether, pointing out that we are more likely to have empathy for those who look and act like us, which reinforces bias in our decision making.[6] A moving empathetic experience that offers us an understanding of another person's life may also fool us into believing we know more than we know, or we have really experienced what others have experienced. When we see another person smiling or dancing or crying, mirror neurons fire in our brains, and it is as if the experience we are learning about is our own experience.[7] But it is not. Empathetic experiences are powerful; they begin to bridge the gap between our experience and that of another. But a sighted person wearing a blindfold does not have the same experience as a blind person.[8] A simulated Virtual Reality border crossing offers the viewer merely a slice of what a refugee endures in the search for safety.

Empathetic research must, therefore, situate our emotional capacities within an intentional process of **experiential research**, **relational engagement**, and **inclusion**.

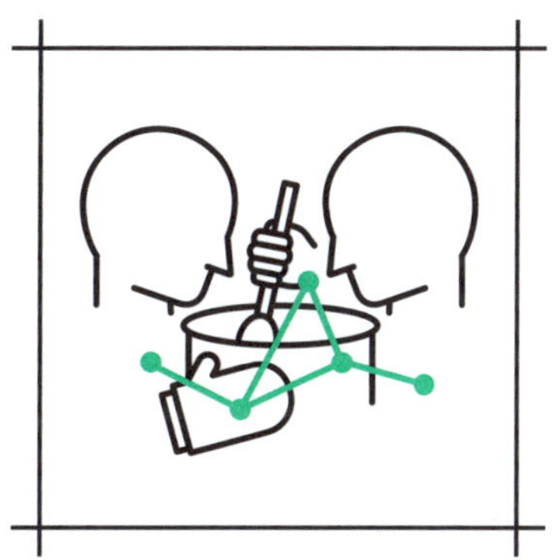

Experiential Research

If you care about someone, you'll want to learn as much about their situation as possible. This includes what you might normally think of as research—books, online resources, archives, and so on—but, since we're talking about experience, it's experiential research as well. Reading about the harrowing challenges of living in a refugee camp is one thing, interviewing someone about their personal experience there is another, and visiting a camp, or being walked through a simulation of being in one, is something else entirely. As is the case with traditional forms of research, there is a qualitative difference between primary and secondary sources, between firsthand experience and interpretive experience. You learn from experiential research much as you learn from your life; you recall it, come back to it, orbit the memory in your mind. You must, of course, pursue traditional forms of research as well. You must read books, conduct studies, develop experiments; this is the qualitative and quantitative research necessary to contextualize and analyze our experiential research. But it is experiential research that makes this other research really matter, just as it is the actual meal that makes the dinner menu worth reading.

Experiential research is putting yourself in the conditions the other person has been in, visiting their childhood home, listening to the music they like, studying up on what they do for a living. We generally say we can empathize with someone when we have had an experience similar to theirs; research can fill in the gaps between our experience and theirs. The main tool for such research is ourselves, in our bodies, willing to experience life in a different way, to confront the perimeters of our own world and think about how another body moves through theirs. Often, this means placing ourselves in new contexts with individuals who will invite us to embody different ways of being. It means spending time with people, walking with them, listening to their stories, digging deep into their self-expression, listening to the music they listen to, eating the food they eat, allowing ourselves to be changed by them, to see the world anew.

The artists behind San Francisco–based *For You*—Erika Chong Shuch, Rowena Richie, and Ryan Tacata—do just such a deep dive. They create experiences for small audiences that are emergent from the time they spend with their audience members. "How do we build a work that does not assume audiences enter into our worlds," wonders Shuch, "but rather we, the creators, enter into theirs?" They then proceed to spend time with their audiences; they visit them at home and talk to them about their lives, their hopes, their shames, their fears.[9] The visits both build trust and immerse the artists in the audience's world. What results from this research is entirely emergent from the research itself. In one case, the group noticed the relationship between an audience member (Helen Paris) and the music the neighbors played, which drifted in through the windows often enough that Paris had come to see it as a piece of home, calling the neighbors "the Jazzies." Later, during the For You performance, the Jazzies performed their music as the Jazzies. The experience at once built comfort for Paris and elevated and celebrated this aspect of home. "In the end, *For You* was for me in ways I could never have predicted, ways that are perhaps more myself than I," she said after her experience. "The commitment of the *For You* artists was there full force in the quality of the attention that was paid, in the deepness of the listening."[10]

Experiential research is important even if you count yourself a member of the community you are studying. The designer Denise Shanté Brown wanted to address the issue of depression among black women. It was a problem she had herself encountered, and

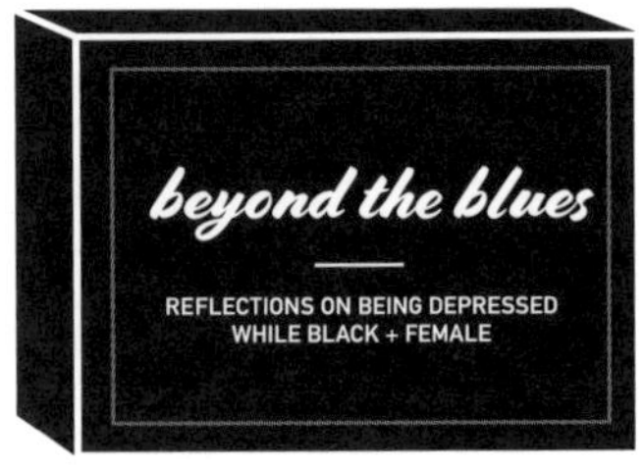

so she felt empathy for others in the situation. Still, she set out to do some research. She sat down with scores of black women facing similar issues and identified three communities she wanted to speak with—church groups, mental health professionals, and other Baltimore-based black women facing depression. Putting herself in these contexts expanded her comprehension of this topic beyond her own experience. This is essential to a rigorous mode of empathetic design—not just saying, *I get it, I've been there*, but exploring nuance and difference. "It illuminated the conditions that create mental health challenges among Black women," she said, "and why it's culturally hard for us to discuss and heal from."[11] Her interviews revealed that silence and shame were primary barriers to recovery, and she decided to create experiences that would remove the silence, end the shame, and connect people through the development of empathy. She found a deeper purpose beyond just looking at the theme of depression. Her research redefined the issue to focus on how silence and shame stood in the way of healing.

The end product was *Beyond the Blues: Reflections on Being Depressed While Black + Female*, a folio of prompts and stories that would be used to facilitate discussions in groups. The process, for her, was based in inclusive, relational research and became the basis of her ongoing practice.

Relational Engagement

Brown's work is rooted in research, but it is fundamentally relational. And this is the second aspect of empathy: relational engagement. People all over the world suffer and die, just as they experience great joys and triumphs. We read about war, disease, and exploitation in the news, but they don't affect us nearly as readily as the perhaps less dramatic daily distress of those with whom we are in relationship. This is, in part, because we care about people we feel close to and, in part, because it is in our bones to empathize with whoever is in front of us. When sitting across the table from someone, we absorb much more than information—we gather rhythms of attentiveness, ways of talking, a sense of wholeness. The same is true in communities. Being in relationship with a group of people attunes us to collective experience, collective practice, collective understanding. We feel-in to a group as much as to another person. You may research the work of a dance company, but unless you dance with them, you will never understand them. You may read about the practices of a religious group, but unless you pray with them, none if it will make much sense. So much information, so much of our experience, exists relationally. Experience designs cannot help existing in relational spaces. This is because so much of our experience—in the moment of engagement, in the telling later, in how we think about them and measure their value—is relational. What we design engages the relationships between our users and their communities and between our users and us. We are all implicated. Relationality means that we take in what we witness, allowing it to change how we see and think about the world. It is reciprocal rather than extractive: not just in-feeling but co-feeling as well.

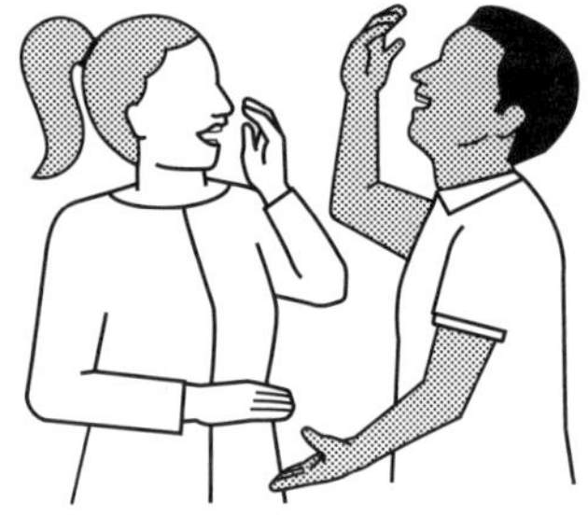

Inclusion

Finally, because empathy is an impossible task, one that, when engaged with honestly, shows us as much about the limitations of our own experience as it does about the other person, inclusion is essential. Much that is designed with the aim of benefiting others but without inclusion may, in the end, do more harm than good. For Denise Shanté Brown, this became a driving force behind her research. The interviews, she said, "showed how imperative it is for research to begin with deep listening—it was so important to resist being extractive, especially with so much mistrust around health in the Black community and in Baltimore because of historical trauma."[12]

Depending on the project, inclusion may mean bringing members of your selected audience to play some role in your development process, or to partner with them. Such inclusion challenges the traditional separation of designer and user, as well as the notion that the connection between the artist and the audience is entirely mediated by the artwork.

This may take different forms, such as inviting community members to collaborate or to workshop ideas with the design team. It may mean that the design is, to a certain extent, responsive to the user's inputs, that it is participatory and interactive in a way that folds the audience's worldview into the piece. Or it may mean that—as in the case of *Beyond the Blues*—the designer is a member of the community for whom the piece is intended.

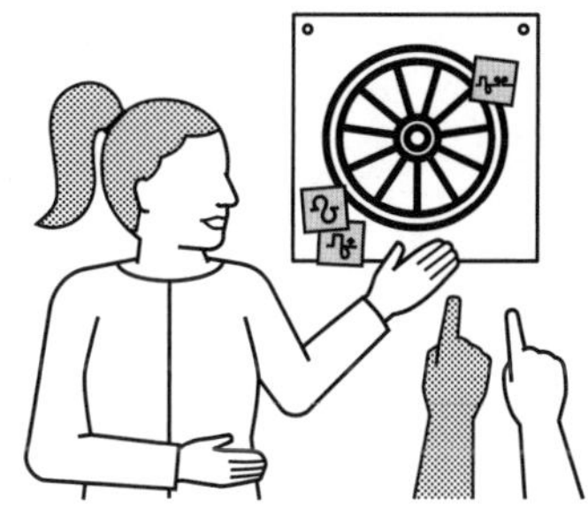

It may seem excessive to demand this level of rigor from what might have otherwise been a simple *I feel you*, but to make effective work, this rigor is essential. Empathetic research steps beyond the interest of ordinary research to a place of caring, of wanting to learn for the benefit of both self and other. Empathetic research functions in some ways like falling in love, kicking off a desire to read books about the person's interests, try out the food they love, visit their childhood home. Empathy is, in many ways, a far grander project than falling in love, as it asks us to engage in the same activities without the precedent endorphin rush, to look at a person with a different life experience, different politics, different priorities, and to value that person's inner experience per se, as much as our own.

EXPERIMENT PART A

The Atom of the Experience

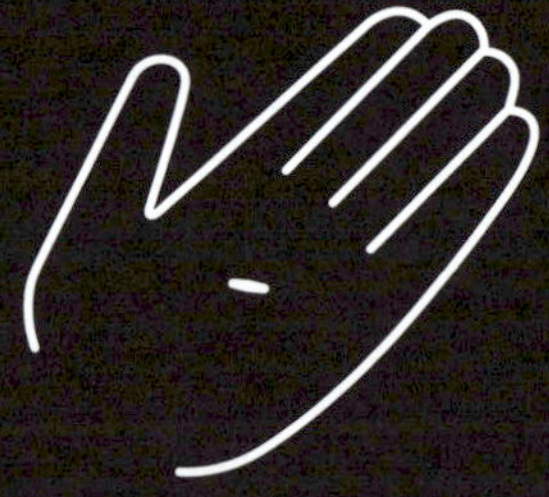

The experiment begins with a grain of rice.

Just one. Or a grain of salt. Or a single almond. Or some other atom of food.

It also begins with a friend. Or a partner, or a family member. Someone you might like to have a meal with.

Pick the grain of salt or the grain of rice or the single raisin or some other atom of food based on what you know of your friend. Perhaps they love rice, or eat oats for breakfast, or once worked in a vineyard picking grapes. Don't pick a salt cube for your friend if they have hypertension. Don't pick a milk chocolate chip if they are vegan. You get the picture. The food item should be associated with your friend, but it should also be something they might actually eat.

Take the item in your hand. Slow down a moment. It's so small it barely feels like anything. Barely any weight. But you can feel it. What does it feel like?

Mark the sensation.

→ The purpose of this experiment is to illuminate the ideas in this book. We are designing that experience together, and we all know that ideas are easier to understand when we try them than when we just read about them. It's an experience for you, and it will involve the design of an experience for your friend as well.

Making something for a friend, and making something for yourself: a strong aim. Is it strong enough to help you overcome the resistance to doing something maybe a little bit odd? If so, then we're probably aligned.

Now tear out the opposite page. (Or are you the kind of person who would never deface a book? Then you're free to re-create the frame on a separate piece of paper, but, also, we dare you to rip out the page.)

Go ahead and put the food item in the frame. Arrange it in a beautiful way. Be persnickety. Put it somewhere safe and we'll come back to it after chapter 3.

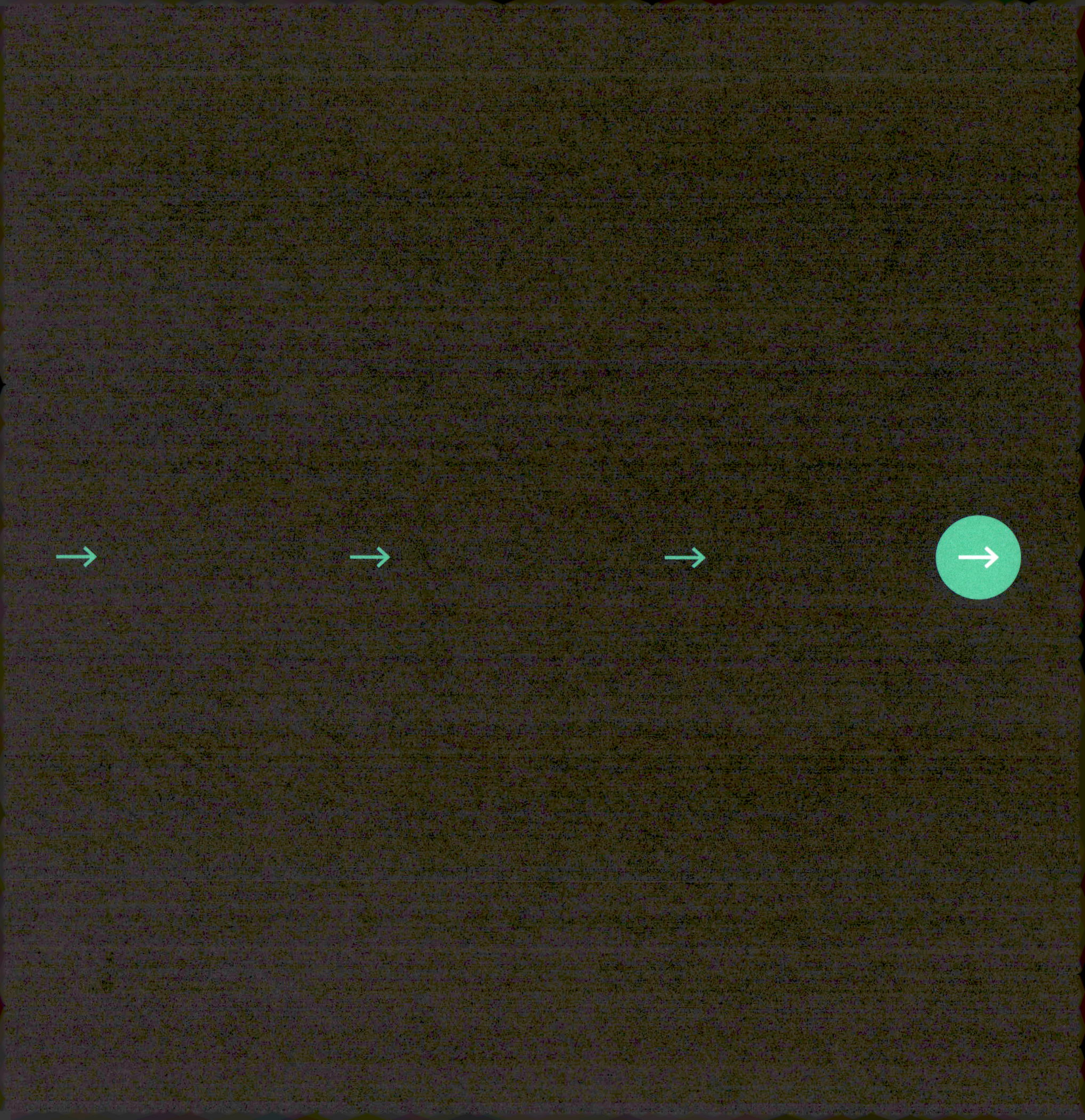

This page intentionally left blank!

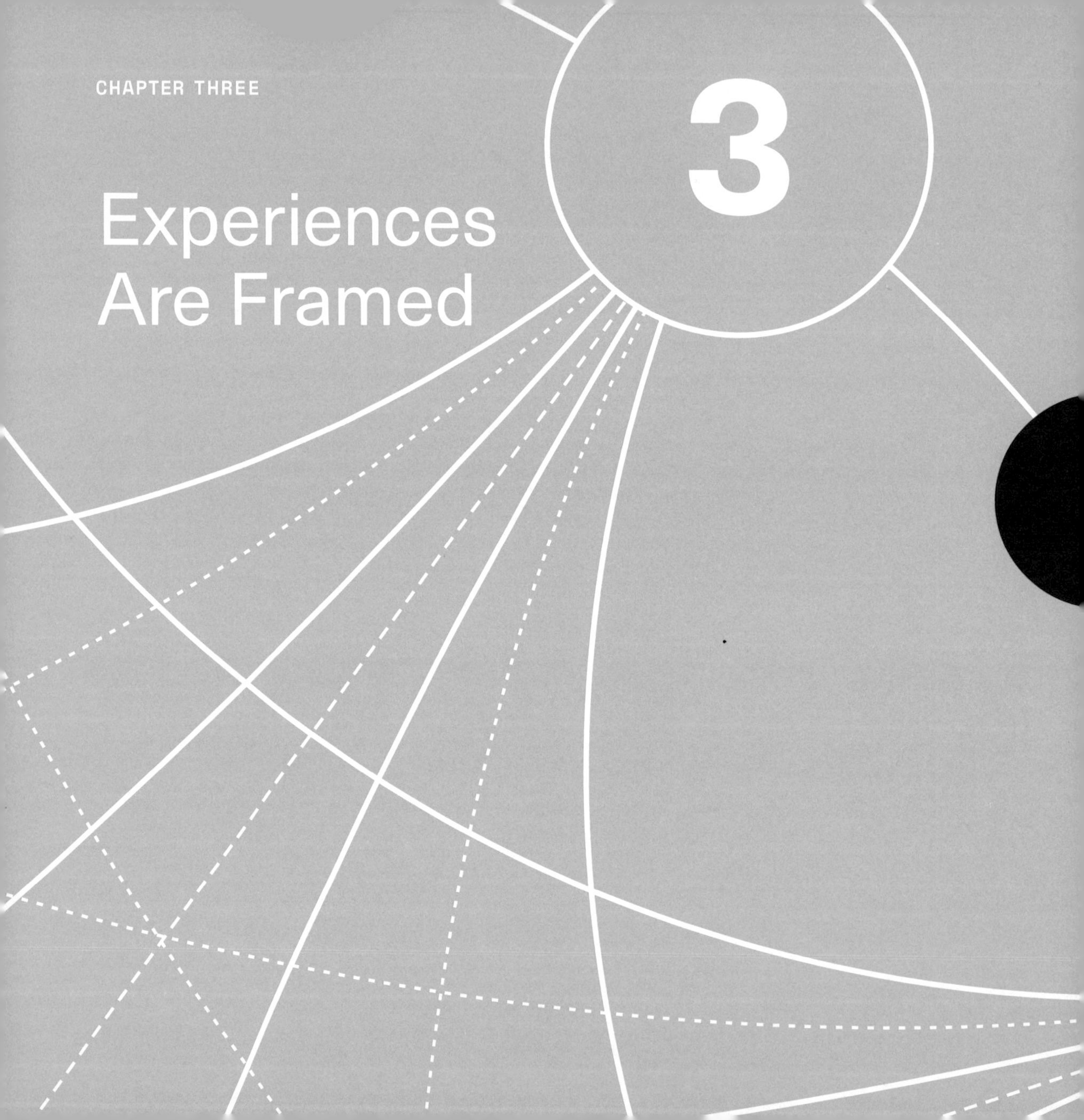

CHAPTER THREE

Experiences Are Framed

3

This book offers several frames. There's the page, the chapter, the book cover. These are navigated and maintained by your hands, which hold and press and turn and point, guiding your attention like a horse along a path.

Frames are the lines we draw around a thing so that we know what the thing is and what it is not. The frame around a photograph tells us where the photo ends. The frame around a door tells us where to walk. Empathy may be understood as stepping into the frame of another person. The frame around this book makes it clear what you should expect: lots of words, lots of ideas, something someone wrote hoping you would enjoy it. In the frames of the book, you expect to find nothing that will crawl off the page, nothing that you will have to talk back to, nothing that will spill onto the floor. The book will not change, and it can be opened at any time, existing like a player piano roll to produce a mental monologue. When you open the book, you become what the book wants you to be: a reader.

The experience designer considers the frame of the book before the object that is the book. For the traditional book designer, nothing outside these pages is relevant—your hands, the chair, the music playing in the room—these are not part of the design. But the book is a *porous* frame: it is small and time limited, and it takes work to keep the attention inside. Other stimuli continually invade the book: the room, the quality of light, that caffeine crash that just happened, that interesting thought about something else you've read. The experience of the book is shaped by the full experience you have while reading it. You are in two worlds: outside the frame of the book is your life; inside the frame of the book you are invited to look at things from an aesthetic, an analytical, or a contemplative perspective. Moving your attention across the frame means moving into an active relationship with a composed experience design.

Experience is continuous. Your senses take in the world continuously; you receive the whole of your visual field, the whole of your auditory field, the whole of your sensation. But attention is a limited window, capable of sensibly comprehending smaller groups of things based on the attentive need. We frame our attention: the face of the person in front of us, the television, the stage, the sunset, the annoying siren, the song in our head. When we do this, when we are deeply in the frame, other sensory information drops from our consciousness. Narrative and aesthetic experiences exist within frames. Some of them we build, some are accidental, and some are created by the designers of those experiences. The most classic frame is the wooden border around a painting. Inside: painting; outside: life. Inside: aesthetic or narrative possibility; outside: the mess of undifferentiated inputs. The frame changes your attention, setting the parameters for your experience. The frame structures consciousness, redefining the subject who engages with it.

In 1999 Daniel J. Simons and Christopher F. Chabris conducted the Selective Attention Test, in which they had test subjects watch a video of people in black shirts and people in white shirts passing basketballs around. Test subjects were asked to count the number of times the basketball is passed by the people wearing white. In the middle of the video, a person in a gorilla suit walks through the group and stares at the camera, beats his chest for a moment, then walks off. The vast majority of test subjects did a good job counting passes of the basketball; however, they failed to notice the gorilla. In fact, most insisted that there had been no gorilla until they watched the video again. Go find it online. (They discuss the experiment in their 2010 book, *The Invisible Gorilla*.) Your senses take everything in, but the frame of your attention is tight to the basketball players. So it is with all frames.

Frame	Structure of Attention	Subject*
Door Frame	A narrative of coming and going	A transitory individual, thinking about coming and going
Plate	Hunger, taste, the pace of the meal	Eater
Stage	Narrative, aesthetics, and actors	Audience
Bus	Comfort, practicalities of transit, danger	Rider
Museum	Aesthetics	Art appreciator/lover/hater
Church	Aesthetics, the sacred, community	A soul in a body
Bed	Sleep, amorous activity	Sleeper/lover/insomniac
Classroom (teacher)	The performance, student attentiveness	Performer/expert
Classroom (student)	The performance, insecurities about self	Learner
Pedestal (actual)	The aesthetics of the area above	Viewer/art appreciator
Golden Hour	Aesthetics of natural beauty	A body in nature/photographer
The sidewalk	Transit, obstacles, smells	A body in motion
Headphones	Sound	A mind focused on music
The workweek	Work, relaxation, work, rest	Worker
Bathroom	Relief, cleanliness	A mammal with parts to hide
And so on.		

*These are, of course, variable depending on the actual contents of the frame and the current nature of the subject, and that's the point. This process is and must be dynamic!

Let us consider the last example on the list. You walk into the men's bathroom, and you see a sink and two urinals on the wall.

The urinals, white, though wet in a slightly discomfiting way, are utilitarian objects, affixed to the tile wall and waiting. You do not hesitate. The room does not invite contemplation, not yet. Not until you are using the urinal. Then you are not an art appreciator, not a well-dressed man, not a great dancer. You are doing something private in public, and the design of the space is meant to allow discretion. Unless you are in an architectural mood, your engagement with the aesthetics of the room is largely utilitarian. Is it clean? Is it discreet? Does it hide your sounds? The subject position in the men's room is of a man going to the bathroom, regardless of who you really are in the world. This is distinct from the subject position of the women's room, or the gender-neutral restroom. The frame defines the subject, no matter how accurately the subject feels that definition is.

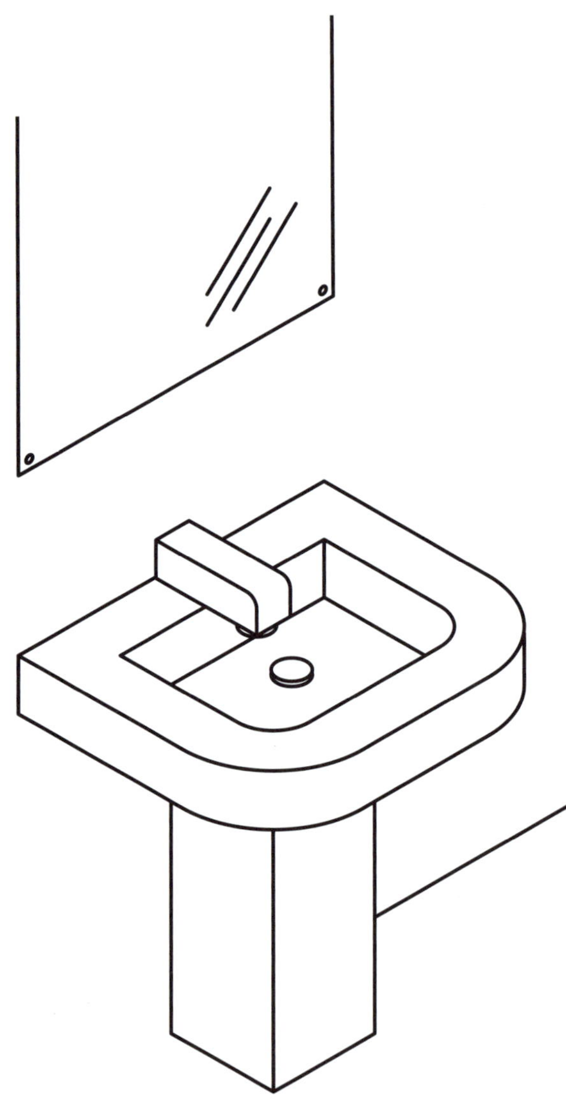

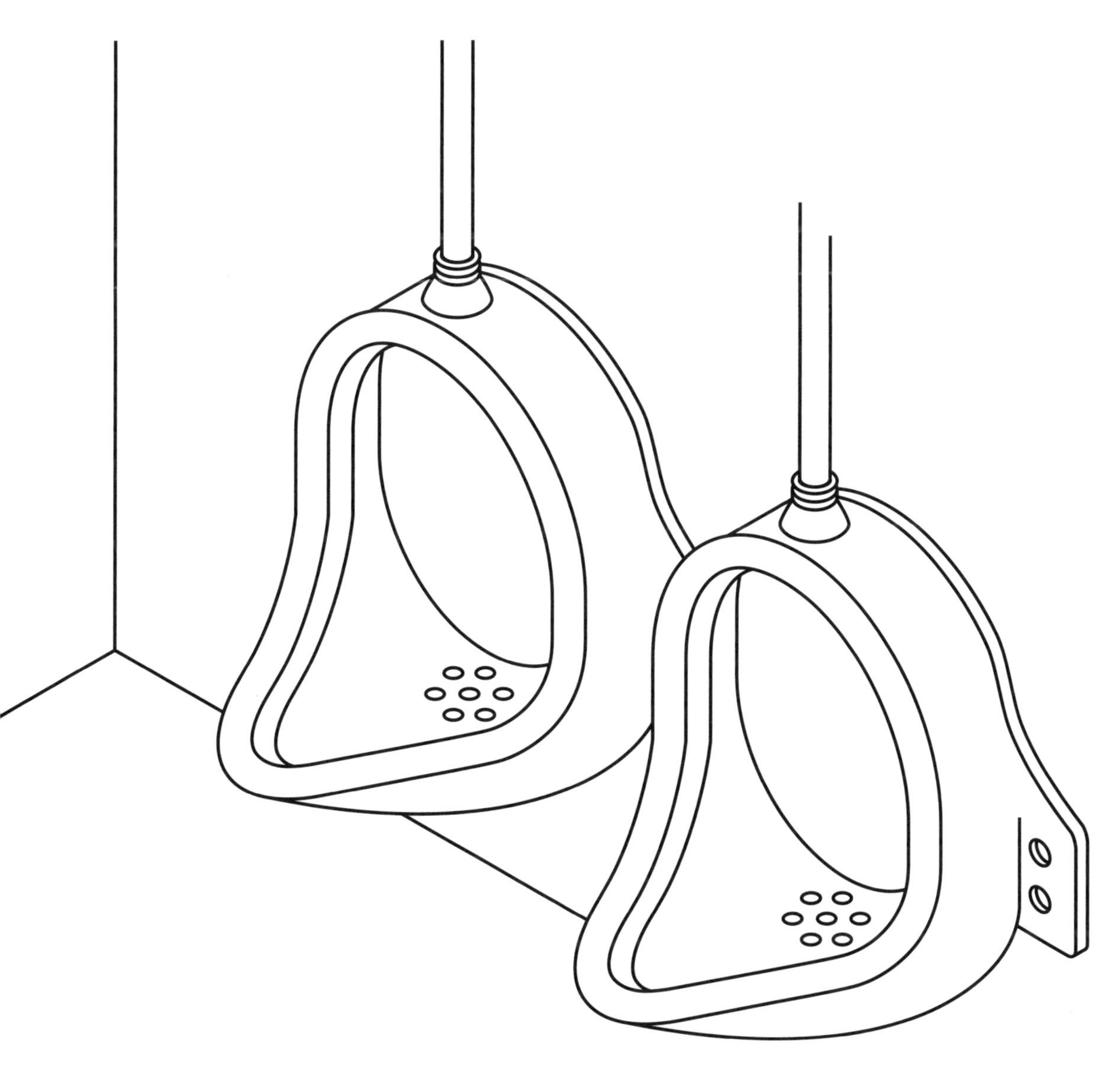

There are no pedestals in the bathroom because pedestals are for a different kind of attention.

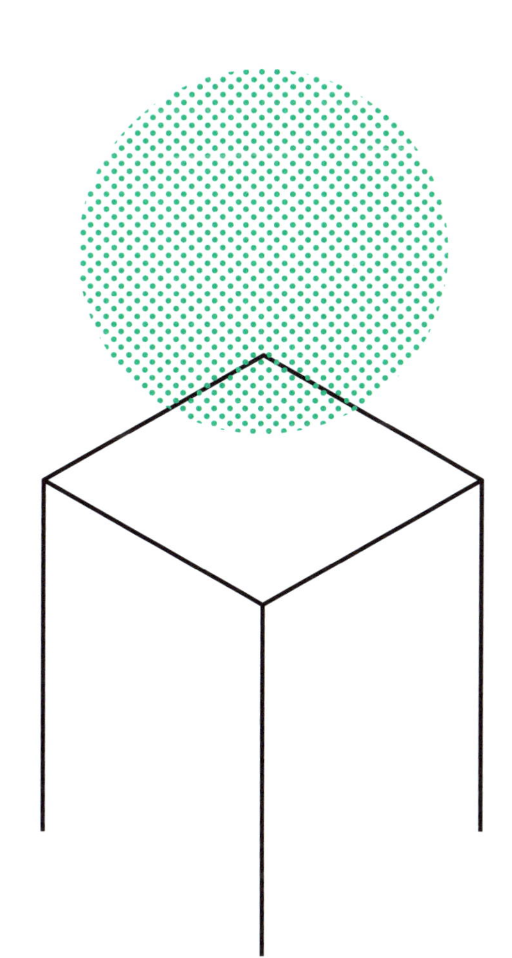

Then, of course, there is this:

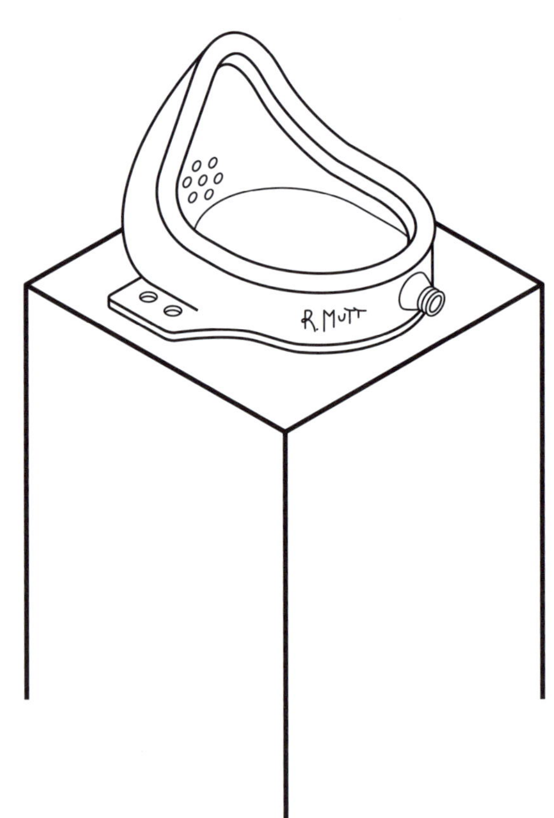

When the piece, *Fountain*, was first submitted to the Society for Independent Artists in 1917 (by Marcel Duchamp, using a pseudonym), the debate that ensued was: "Is it art?" The experience designer asks a different question: "What is the structure of attention generated by the frame?" *Art* is a particular structure of attention. An object on a pedestal in a gallery demands an "art" kind of attention because of the frame, whereas on the tiled wall in the men's room it has a "bathroom" attention. We look at *Fountain* as an aesthetic object because it is on a pedestal. Furthermore, it is in a museum, which is another frame. And it has a wall label describing it as art, which is yet another frame. The frames circumscribe the object physically and conceptually.

When you put the museum sticker on your shirt, a timer that frames the experience begins. You cannot wear that sticker forever. Have you ever walked home with a sticker on your shirt from a museum, or a wristband from a concert or a doctor's office still on? What an odd feeling: a strange, broken frame. Tearing it off and throwing it away closes the frame of the experience, allowing you to fully return to the rest of your life.

Frames can get quite large. The artists Christo and Jeanne-Claude put a frame around an entire island. Inside the frame the island was now a work of art.

Christo and Jeanne-Claude, *Surrounded Islands*, Biscayne Bay, Greater Miami, Florida, 1980–83.

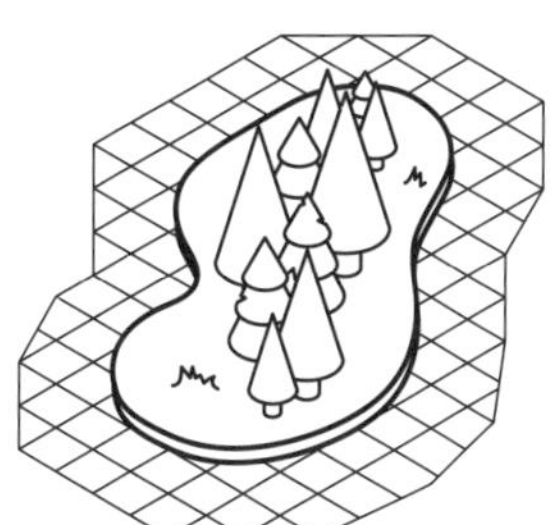

James Hannaham,
Planet, 2011.

James Hannaham

American, born Bronx, New York. 1968–

Planet 2011
Found object
Entire contents of the planet Earth
5,972,000,000,000,000,000,000 tons

Gift of the artist

Planet, one of Hannaham's first wall placard pieces, cleverly recontextualizes the world as a found object, thus subordinating planet Earth to a description on a relatively small card. In this way, the artist plays on the manner in which the text on a wall placard can dominate the experience of a work of art. Instead of encouraging us to interact viscerally or emotionally with the art, a placard may help us to understand or justify the work's existence or supposed meaning, often in order to figure out or even de-fang it. During this process, museum-goers may also informally assess an artwork's monetary value based on the fame of the artist, their judgment of his or her level of skill, the materials with which the work was fabricated, the length of time since its creation, and other factors.

In addition to complicating our relationship to our celestial home by re-framing it as an art object, *Planet* asks us to contemplate the accident of our existence as well. The world is indeed a found object for all who arrive here, one with which we are expected to interact successfully. The planet itself, this piece suggests, is a work of art we must strive to make sense of, without guidance from museum curators. Indirectly, Hannaham also asks us to consider our world a commodity produced by a homosexual African American man, which may cause spectators to question their relationship to such things as world history, private property, mass culture, sexuality, and race.

Conceptual frames can be a little easier to construct. James Hannaham's *Card Tricks* installation featured museum wall placards like ⟵ this one.

It's satire, of course, but not without experiential effect. The demand is clear: consider the entire contents of the planet Earth as one might consider a sculpture. It's an impossible task, and the wall label, in its effect, becomes an impossible intellectual task, a kind of a Zen art koan. The wall label itself is actually in a frame. Because the label is the art.

Sometimes the thing you're looking at is in the frame. Other times you, yourself, are inside the frame. This is what architecture does. *Interiority/Exteriority*, by Belina Costa (shown on the following spread), explores what it means, experientially, to be inside or outside based on how the situation is framed. Interiority begins with the frame of a tent, deepens with the frame of a walkway, continues to the deep enclosure of a basement bathroom. The first few frames are porous: the constructions allow much in from outside. The final frame is solid—the windowless basement room. We know this intuitively: when an experience has a solid frame, we are fully inside it, our attention is focused, and unrelated stimuli are less likely to pull us out of the frame. When an experience has a porous frame, we must actively choose how to enter it and how to stay in it. A movie theater is a more solid frame than a handheld device streaming the same film. Sunday Mass at the Vatican is solid, but Sunday Mass after making a pilgrimage along the Camino de Santiago for weeks is far more solid.

Consider, then, the two primary frames of the theater. First you have the building. It's notable that these are frequently monumental structures, often flashy and weird looking (even Shakespeare's theater, the Globe, was a funny-looking round building). When you step inside you are audience. You know what to do. You sit in your seat, your mind recalling what happened last time in the theater, the sounds, the time frame during which you

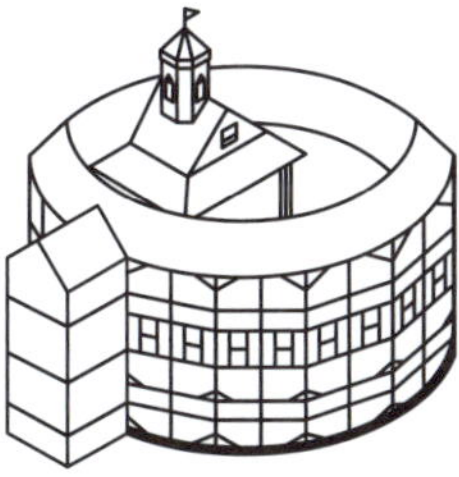

Belina Costa, *Interiority/ Exteriority*, 2015.

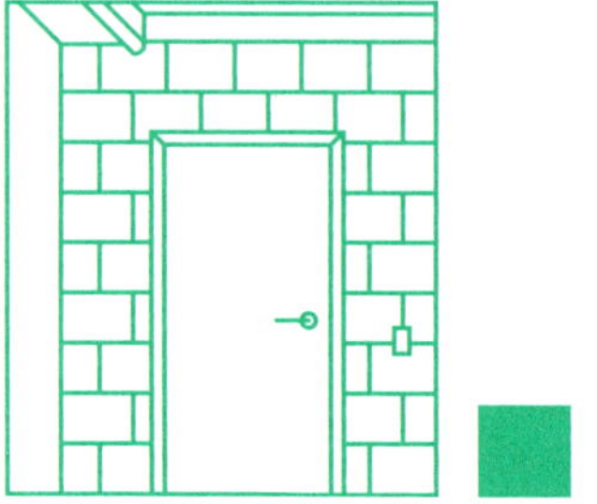

In this space I feel I can't breathe. I feel confined and isolated, bound and claustrophobic. It's an unpleasant, dark feeling with air. All is completely silent except for some low humming sound maybe from the plumbing. I feel defensive. I feel lifeless and mechanical.

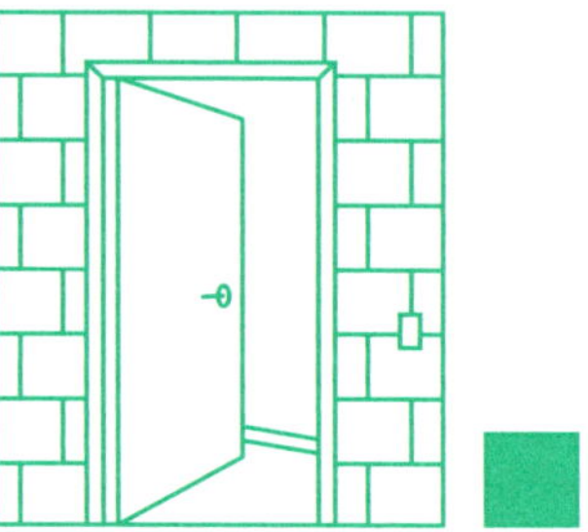

In being in this space with the door open, I feel a little better as if I can breathe. I don't feel the wind or a breeze. Not even artificial. Things are stale and I want to move about. It's very quiet. Light is in the direction of the opening.

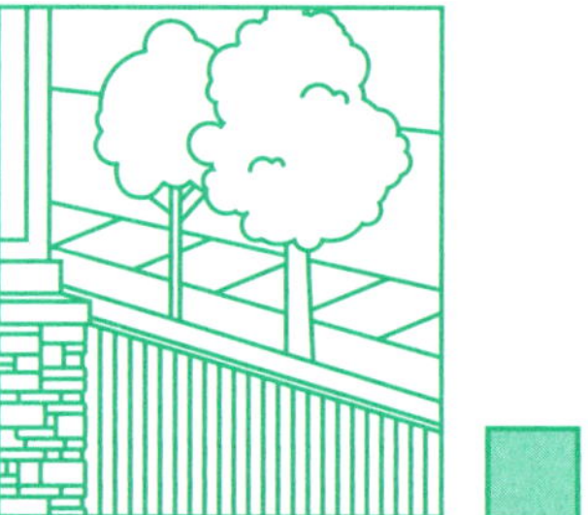

In being in this space I feel the natural world. It feels good to feel and hear the wind. The sun is warm and the sunlight is filtering through the wood. There's a light feeling and a dynamic natural flickering of lights and darks. I feel like relaxing and enjoying the smells.

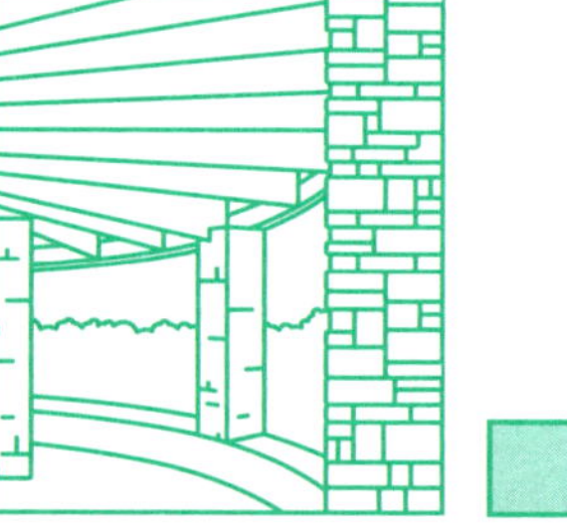

The shadows are dynamic here! I see the reflection in the metals and the roughness of the natural stone. It feels open but still like I'm in a particular space. I feel that nature is near. The sunlight randomly hits me. I like the structure but feel the "freeness" of the surroundings.

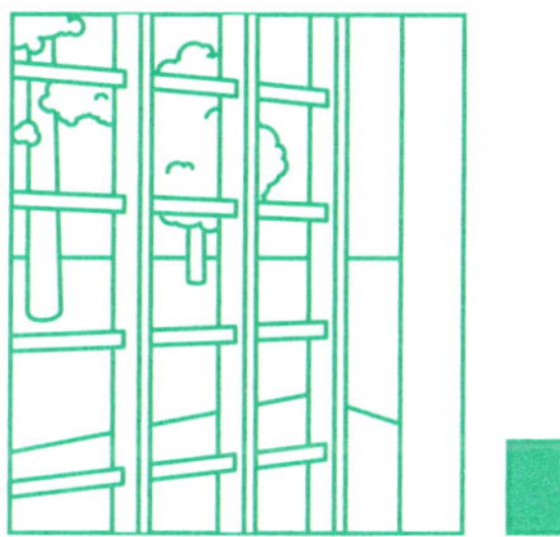

It feels good to see the trees. I can smell the grass and feel the very slight breeze. It is still dreary though and I feel things are stable. I start to feel the warmth.

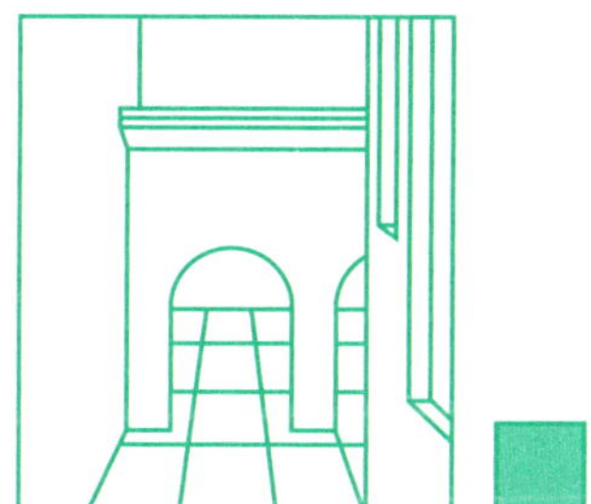

I feel like I am exiting and leaving a space even though there is no ceiling or roof above. I feel joy that the sun is out! I find myself looking for the sun. There is a complexity of forms and layers with the light. Inside and outside is blurred.

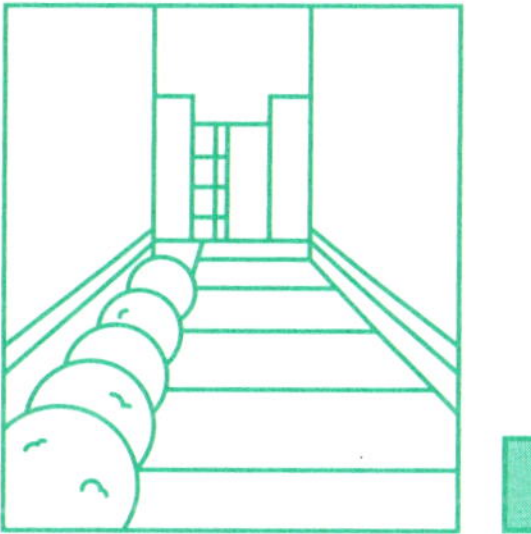

I feel protected but there is nothing above. I hear the wind and feel the wind. I want to run and touch the shrubs. Things are moving and shadows are cast between the buildings. I feel an expansion and a relief but still a bit confined. I am moving towards the light. Focal point.

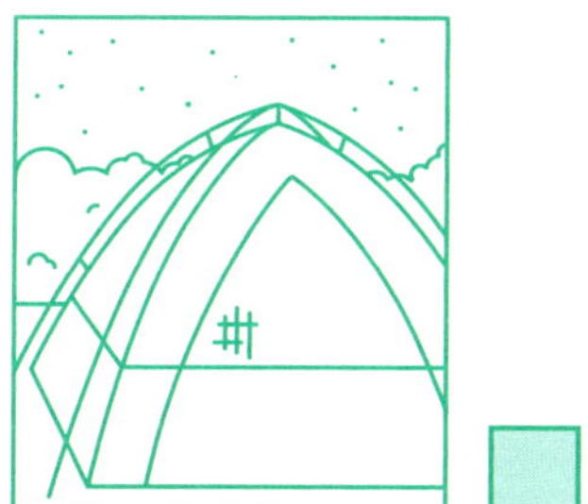

I feel a connection to nature here. Though I am in the tent, I can feel the lumpy ground beneath me. A breeze passes through the mesh screen. It is silent but this is a different silence. Peaceful. I smell trees and dirt. I can't stand but I don't feel constrained. The view is natural and spontaneous.

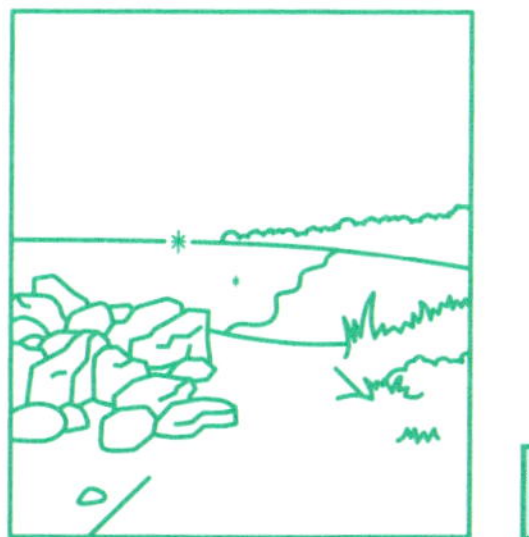

Being outside feels free. I feel happy and exhilarated that the sky is revealed. It is so vast, so perfect. The sounds of the waves are clear and the birds are present. I feel connected.

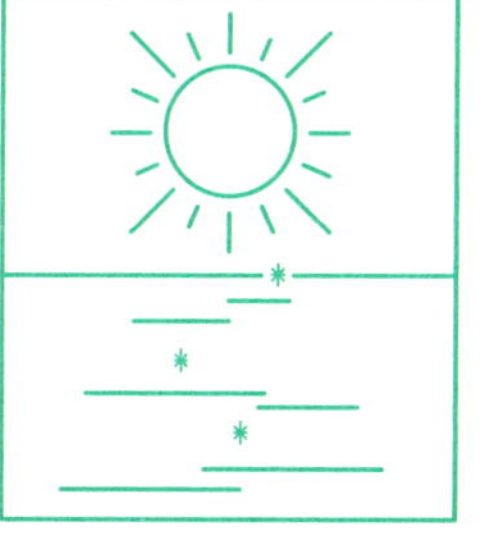

It feels awesome to see the horizon. The light is intense, endless and unlimited. I feel safe and glowing. The reflection on the ocean is amazing and the brightness is amplified. I feel a cool breeze. The natural motion is everywhere.

will have to restrain your other self, your non-audience self. Then you look forward to the stage, defined by the proscenium arch, which is what frames your view into the performance. Theater is frequently defined by its frames—it is *theater*, or it is *proscenium theater*. Inside that proscenium, fictions may occur. What happens there, even violence and murder, is not alarming; it is there for your contemplation. Reality, with all its danger and consequence, is outside the theater; abstraction is across the frame of the proscenium. This is an abstraction for you to contemplate, but not to touch. The experience on the stage retains the tactile qualities of a thought.

Immersive theater, however, is theater without the proscenium. The removal of the central frame muddies the waters, and the performance bleeds out of its proscenium frame into the rest of the building. One steps into the frame of the performance at the entry to the building (or the part of the building), and then the line between reality and performance becomes conceptual and textural. It is up to you now to cross this invisible frame, to open up to the work, to become what the world of the piece is asking you to be: participant, no longer audience. You may walk around the set, approach actors, occasionally open doors and explore. The experience gains the tactile qualities of a dream. If it is a good performance, you forget you are dreaming. In the middle of Third Rail Projects' immersive *Alice in Wonderland* dance performance, *Then She Fell* (2012), a dancer invites you to sit in a chair. She asks you questions and brushes your hair with a thick bristle brush. The tactility of the brush is an experience borrowed from reality, foreign to the theater. Sensations that belong in one frame are pulled into another, leaving the audience off-kilter and a little off guard: a good way to heighten the attention and break the audience out of habitual ways of seeing.

Still, however, there is the frame of the building. Some performance does away with this as well. There is a long history of getting out of the building and out of the notion of the circumscribed performance space. The Situationists did it, as did Vito Acconci when he followed strangers home, or Marina Abramović when she drove her minivan around in circles for hours.

Recently, however, we have seen narrative structures at a larger scale embedded into the geographic territories of ordinary life. *The Jejune Institute* begins with the audience member walking into a working office building in downtown San Francisco, riding up to the fifteenth floor, and asking the secretary for a particular office. The audience member is then sent down the hallway alone, past actual office workers who are actually at work and into an office where a video has just begun playing. It is the introduction: an invitation into a fantastical, cultic, semispiritualist world that exists in unknown space. This conceptual world is the frame of the artwork, and it exists in locations scattered throughout the city and online. The artwork is interwoven with the textures of reality, and the viewer must seek it out, struggle to distinguish it, and work to assemble its narratives. The vagueness breaks other structures: the temporal frames that generally structure aesthetic experiences are broken, as are the geographic frames, because the experience might pop up anywhere, and any time. A phone call or a text might suddenly arrive, and the conceptual leap will pull the audience back into the conceptual frame of the work. Like all frames, this one changes the audience member into a particular kind of viewer, one who looks at the ordinary structures of the quotidian as designed and full of compositional possibility. The joy of the work is the shape-shifting audience members undergo, pivoting from one subject mode to another, becoming a consciousness a little less rigidly attached to a known reality. The porous frame allows the qualities of reality to seep into the design and vice versa. Over time, both acquire the tactile qualities of a hallucination.

Created by Jeff Hull and documented in the 2013 film *The Institute*, directed by Spencer McCall.

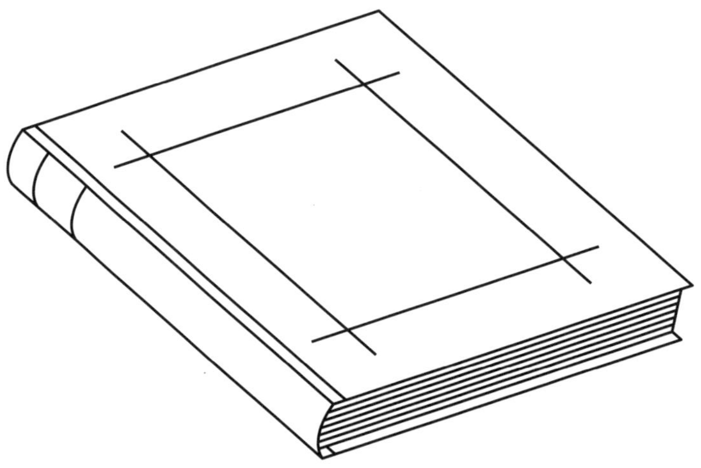

A porous frame

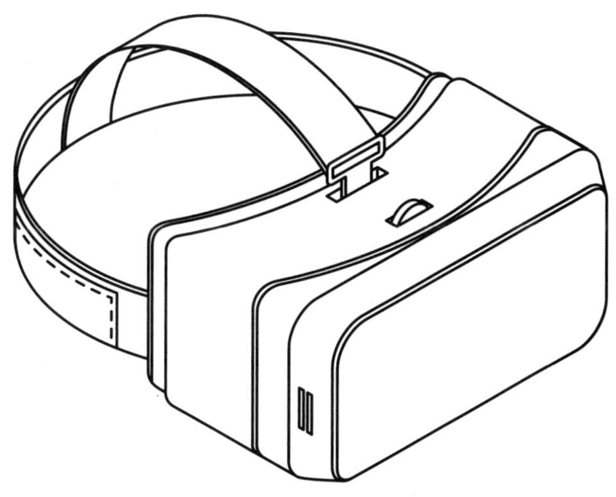

A thick frame

EXPERIMENT PART B

The Frame

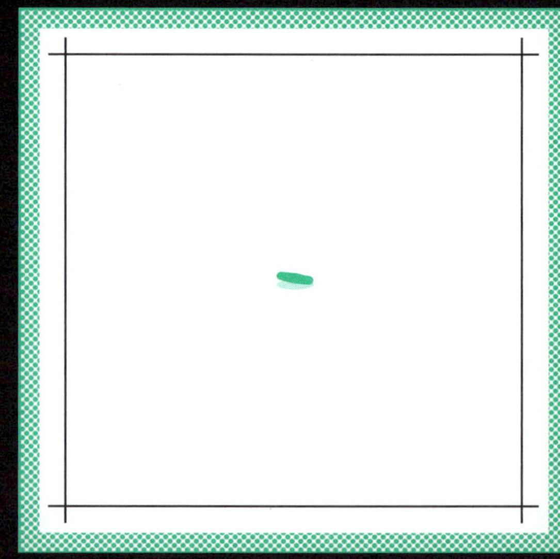

Let's go back to that piece of paper with the food item in the frame. The page is a little bit diagrammatic, a little bit symbolic. It's the frame of your friend's perspective. Write their name in the upper-left corner.

Inside the frame, objects are not objects; they are signifiers for your friend. Look at the grain of salt (or almond or rice or whatever) and meditate on what it tells you about your friend. How do they eat? How do they encounter beauty? When did you last eat with them?

→ We're turning this object into a symbol for your friend. What else can we have it say about them? This is internal work, but that's what thinking and reading are, anyway, right?

Now try putting some other objects into the frame: a coin or a key or a pen cap or something. Try at least three. Do they tell you anything about your friend? If they do, leave them in the frame. If they don't, remove them. The whole purpose of this frame is to allow the objects inside to become windows onto considering your friend. Yes, it takes some imagination, but that's what frames are for, guiding the imagination into a new understanding of what you behold.

Take a picture of the frame and the things in it. Make it look good. This will be the hero image of the experience.

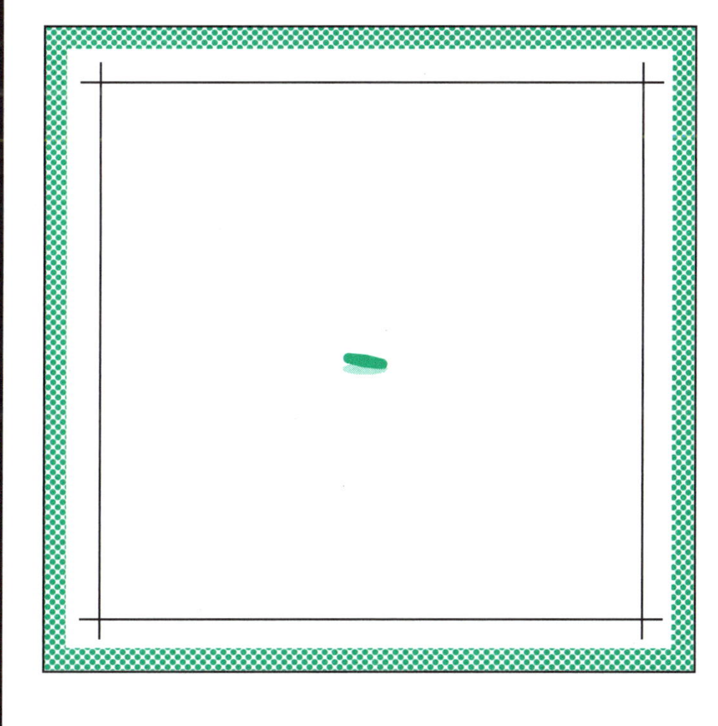
#ExpDesManifesto

CHAPTER FOUR

Powerful Experiences Engage the Whole Person

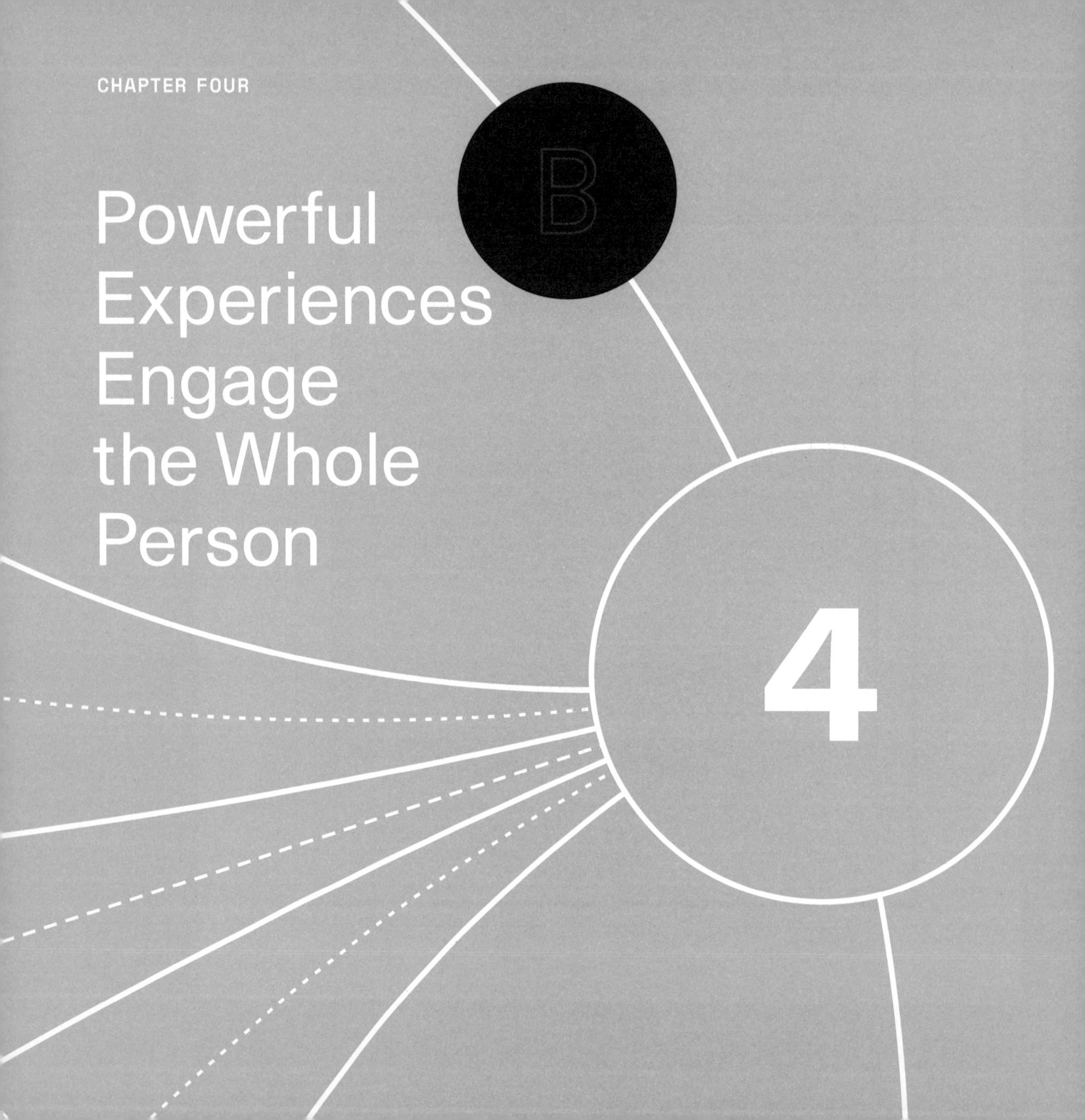

The terms *immersive* and *experiential* are often thrown around interchangeably. This is understandable; there is something exciting about new approaches to theater and technology that offer physical engagement where once we just sat motionless in our seats. Being physically surrounded by a design and having increased agency activates the senses and makes us feel a part of a world. The opportunities presented by physical immersion are profound: designers may engage senses other than sight and sound to communicate a story. They may choreograph audience bodies and build out the experience of being in a world through a depth of detail and a sense of discovery.

These are, indeed, experiential tools. But, as I've argued, no one type of design is any more inherently experiential than any other. In 1896 the film pioneer Louis Lumière projected a fifty-second-long film of a train arriving in a station on a seven-foot-wide screen in Paris. Audiences were astounded, and the world's interest was piqued. Apocryphal stories of viewers running in terror from the theater spread wildly, creating what might be considered film's founding myth.[1] Novelty is, indeed, powerful. We have, in some ways, come full circle; a theater audience watching a train arrive on a screen was as novel in 1896 as a theater audience getting on a train to watch an immersive murder mystery is today. But novelty is a trick that wears off quickly; it may generate powerful reactions, but once the new thing is integrated into your expectations for the frame of the experience, its magic fades. History is littered with forgotten immersive designs that sparked awe when they first appeared. It is just as unlikely that anyone will talk about immersive van Gogh installations or 3-D glasses in twenty years as they are to talk about Smell-O-Vision shows today.

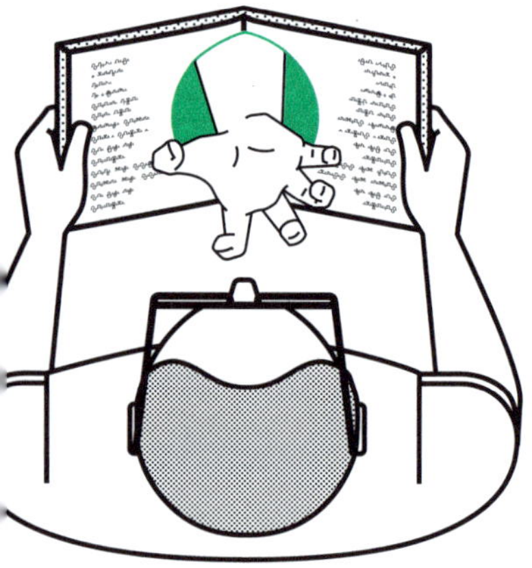

This is largely because immersive experiences tend to focus on novelty in physical immersion. Such immersion is a powerful tool to make us feel that we are in the frame of something new, that we may be someone different, and that we may behave in a new way. Physical immersion is not the only way to put someone in a different world, but it is the most reliable. We step into a new environment and our senses become heightened, enabling the *wow* reaction when the IMAX show begins, the titillation of discovery as we wander, unchecked, around the indoor forest of the immersive installation, and the terror of creeping shadows in the haunted house.

But we are not just bodies; we are minds and hearts as well. For an experience to have impact, it must be not only physically immersive but also psychologically immersive. For it to really matter, it must be ontologically immersive as well; that is, it must resonate with an audience's sense of meaning. Consider the immersion of a visit to the Vatican: it is immediately evident that the experience will be physically immersive. The Vatican is completely surrounded by the city of Rome and would seem to be just a complex of buildings within that city but for the frame of its independent nationhood, a fact that is affirmed upon your entry to the city as well as in the audio tours that walk you through the buildings. The assertion, however, creates a psychological threshold that makes you aware you have entered the frame of a new world. Once inside, your path of travel is largely linear, through tapestry-lined corridors, ornate courtyards, and period rooms that seem not to be so much transported from another time as fixed in that time, suggesting that you have stepped back in time as well. The tour designers well know that the Sistine Chapel is the main attraction, and so they put it at the end of the line, prefacing it with room after room of physically immersive experiences of Catholic history. After the Sistine Chapel, you are, of course, let out into an impressive series of gift shops and deposited, eventually, on the street with your souvenirs.

The experience is undoubtedly physically immersive. You are undeniably in the Vatican, and the deeper you go into the Vatican, the more you feel lost in its world. There is much to discover, much to learn. The immersion happens quickly, enveloping you in an aesthetic and narrative of grandeur that makes a point: this is a storied institution. If you care, if you are an art historian or a devotee of European history, or if you feel that these aesthetics and history are particularly important in your life, the experience becomes psychologically immersive. Things you were thinking about or studying, narratives in your life, questions you have had all light up as you pass from room to room, incorporating each impression into the existing narratives of your life. It is not just physically immersive, it is *interesting*, perhaps even relevant. It has an effect on what's on your mind.

If, however, the Vatican is a sacred place for you, the visit is ontologically immersive as well as physically and psychologically immersive. Perhaps you are a Catholic believer, eager to be moved by the paintings on the ceiling of the Sistine Chapel. The levels of immersion interweave and blend, and you might think you were going just to be interested and find yourself moved. Or perhaps you visit expecting to find meaning and discover yourself in a theme park of what you'd hoped would be meaningful, put off by the trinkets for sale in the unavoidable gift shops.

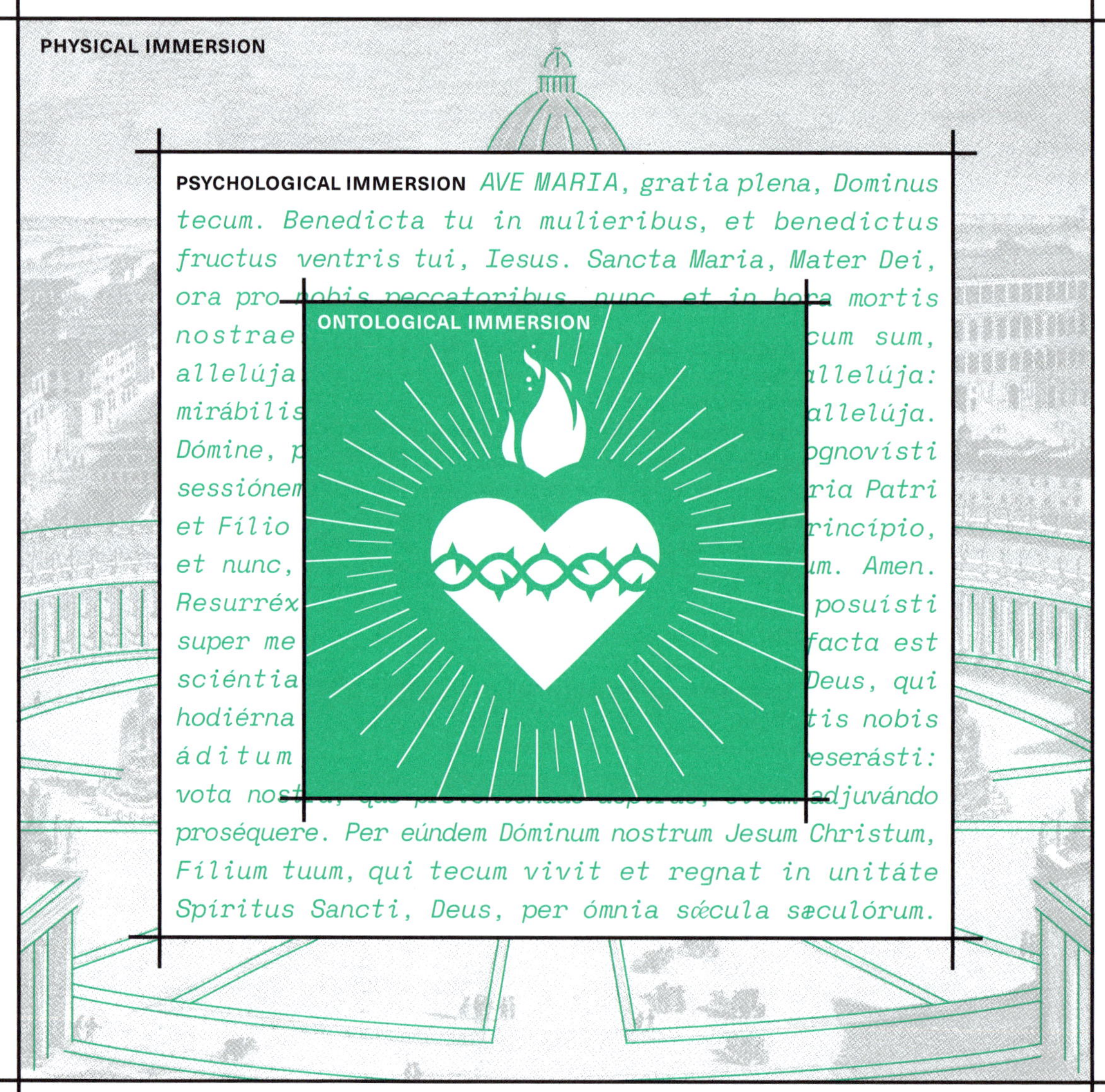
PHYSICAL IMMERSION
PSYCHOLOGICAL IMMERSION
AVE MARIA, gratia plena, Dominus tecum. Benedicta tu in mulieribus, et benedictus fructus ventris tui, Iesus. Sancta Maria, Mater Dei, ora pro
mortis
nostrae
cum sum,
allelúja
allelúja:
mirábilis
allelúja.
Dómine,
ognovísti
sessiónem
ria Patri
et Fílio
rincípio,
et nunc,
m. Amen.
Resurréx
posuísti
super me
facta est
sciéntia
Deus, qui
hodiérna
tis nobis
áditum
eserásti:
vota no
adjuvándo
proséquere. Per eúndem Dóminum nostrum Jesum Christum, Fílium tuum, qui tecum vivit et regnat in unitáte Spíritus Sancti, Deus, per ómnia sǽcula sæculórum.
ONTOLOGICAL IMMERSION

Three Levels of Immersion

Often, the levels of immersion are stacked—first comes physical, then psychological, then ontological, but this is by no means the only order in which immersion may happen.

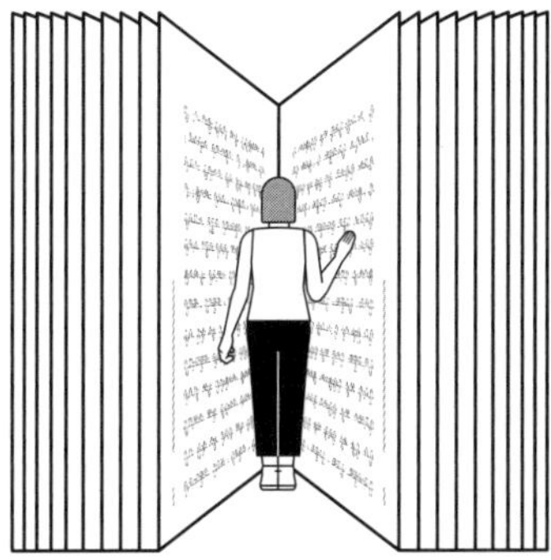

Physical Immersion

Being physically surrounded by something.[2]

You feel you are immersed when you are in an aesthetically defined frame. Everywhere you look, you see that you are inside. You may be physically immersed in architecture, in installation art, in a group of dancers, in a museum of icicles, in water. This is primarily visual and spatial but includes all the senses. You may be immersed in a smell, in a sound field, in a tactile dome.

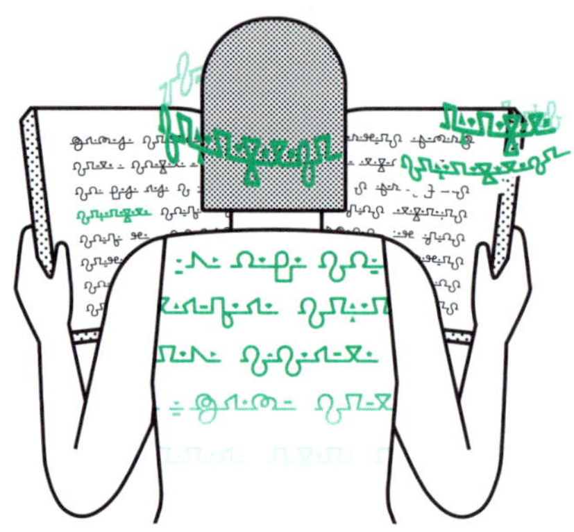

Psychological Immersion
Being psychologically engaged.

This is usually also a narrative engagement: you are really *into* the story. You are interested in what people are saying. You are following along as the plot develops. Also, the nature of the experience and the things that happen during the experience are connected to other things outside the frame. You have been thinking about a topic that is addressed in the experience. Or the experience involves stories you have been following. If you are really engaged, you are psychologically immersed. You may be psychologically immersed in the world of the experience, in a particular narrative thread, in some detail. Something needs to have caught your attention, something the experience designer crafted with your interest in mind. Then your attention must be maintained; if there is too much going on, or you find that following what's going on feels unimportant, you are likely to start thinking about something else, and the psychological immersion will wane.

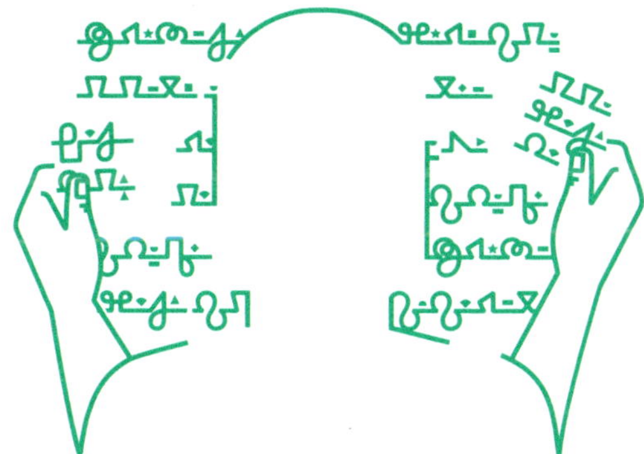

Ontological Immersion
Being meaningfully or spiritually engaged.

Ontologically immersive work *feels* important. It *is* important. It aligns with what matters in your life and it effects meaningful change. Successful rites of passage—such as coming-of-age ceremonies or weddings—are ontologically immersive. A twelve-step meeting—though it consists of just a circle of people sitting in chairs—can be ontologically immersive. An artist who journeys to the Utah desert to visit Nancy Holt's *Sun Tunnels* and other land art may find it ontologically immersive if, when there, she realizes what she wants to do as an artist. Ontologically immersive work is life-changing work. It is the work you remember, the work that gives you the fuel to go see all the other work that isn't ontologically immersive, just in case. Whereas physical and psychological immersion can keep you engaged for a short while, ontological immersion engages you long after the experience is over. To be ontologically immersive is not the goal of all experience design, but when it is the goal, it often becomes the fuel for the design process.

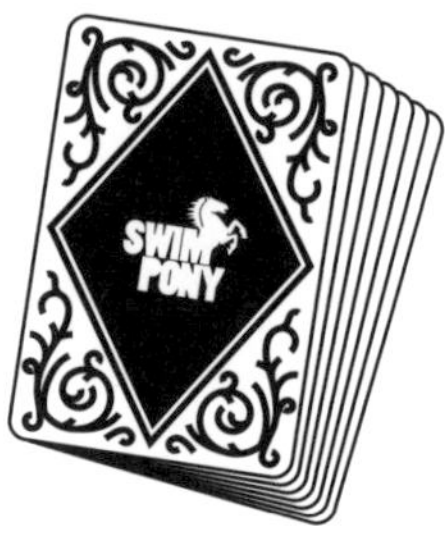

Adrienne Mackey and Swim Pony, cards from *The End*, 2017.

Philadelphia-based Swim Pony, a multidisciplinary experience design group directed by Adrienne Mackey, created a monthlong experience in May 2017 called *The End*. Week by week, the project worked with a combination of physical and psychological immersion to build toward ontological immersion. Using text messages, alternate reality game mechanics, and live performances, *The End* was a kind of memento mori, inviting participants to meditate on their own death; it began with the arrival, in the mail, of a notebook and a deck of cards, as well as an invitation that read, "Your presence is requested at The End."[3] Participants then entered into a monthlong text conversation with *The End*—a stand-in for mortality—which guided them each day through "quests" challenging them to consider death in different ways. Some days, participants wrote in their journals. Other days, they engaged with their communities. One prompt sent them to visit a doctor at a real doctor's office, who delivered them a (fake) terminal diagnosis. The final scene saw all the participants gather in a mansion inside a cemetery. It was a death party—both for the experience and for the participants. Here they connected with others who had been on the journey and reflected on how it changed their lives.[4]

Those who found *The End* meaningful were more likely to stick it out until the end. For them, it was ontologically immersive. It was ontologically immersive for Mackey, too; she created it, she said, because of her anxiety about death.[5] Physical and psychological immersion can be extraordinarily useful in laying the groundwork for ontological immersion. In this case, the playful beginning, with the text messages and the cards and the quests, used game mechanics and a sense of play to get the participant psychologically engaged before anything else. Play and game mechanics are great ways to build psychological immersion; simple motivational structures and rewards, as well as enjoyable narratives, engage the mind and keep us curious. The topic, however, was presented in such a way that to be fully involved meant really wrestling with an important topic in most people's lives: mortality. Thus the ontological engagement. Those who didn't find it meaningful probably didn't stick around for the full month of experiences. Physical immersion, in this case, came later—either at the immersive doctor's office or at the party in the cemetery.

The Swim Pony experience (as illustrated on the following spread) was interactive nearly all the way through. This is essential to work that aspires to be truly immersive, to truly involve the audience. A VR film you watch on a headset may surround you with imagery, but it is in some ways a less immersive experience than going to a movie theater, buying popcorn with too much butter, finding a seat next to a friend, and gasping at the same time when the killer leaps out of the closet. Without interaction we cannot connect our own lives to those in the experience design. Consider, for instance, a period room in a museum, with its original furniture and its roped-off walking area, keeping you out of arm's reach of the items. It does a good job keeping the objects from getting damaged, but how long would you spend in such a room? How long would it take until your interest flagged? Now consider instead another period room that offered a decent re-creation of the first, with newer renditions of the old furniture and facsimiles of the paintings on the wall, but you could touch anything, sit anywhere. Which would you visit and for how long? Which would you remember?

How you design the period room's immersion depends on the experiential intention you laid out in Phase Zero. If all you want is a 360-degree visual immersion and a sense of authenticity, perhaps the roped-off period room is sufficient. But what if your aim goes further, to show, say, what life was like in the Old West? Perhaps you would allow people to inhabit the room, read letters in the drawers, speak with historical reenactors. Or what if the period room is, say, a Japanese teahouse from the nineteenth century, and you wished to leave visitors changed by the philosophy behind the tea ceremony. Perhaps you might invite individuals trained in such tea ceremonies to host them there. Perhaps a ticket to the teahouse could be acquired only after studying the philosophy of a tea ceremony. Then the visitor might leave with a deck of cards in hand, their ongoing relationship to the philosophy of the tea ceremony played out in text message conversations with the host of the tea ceremony for the succeeding month.

Layers of Immersion in Swim Pony's *The End*

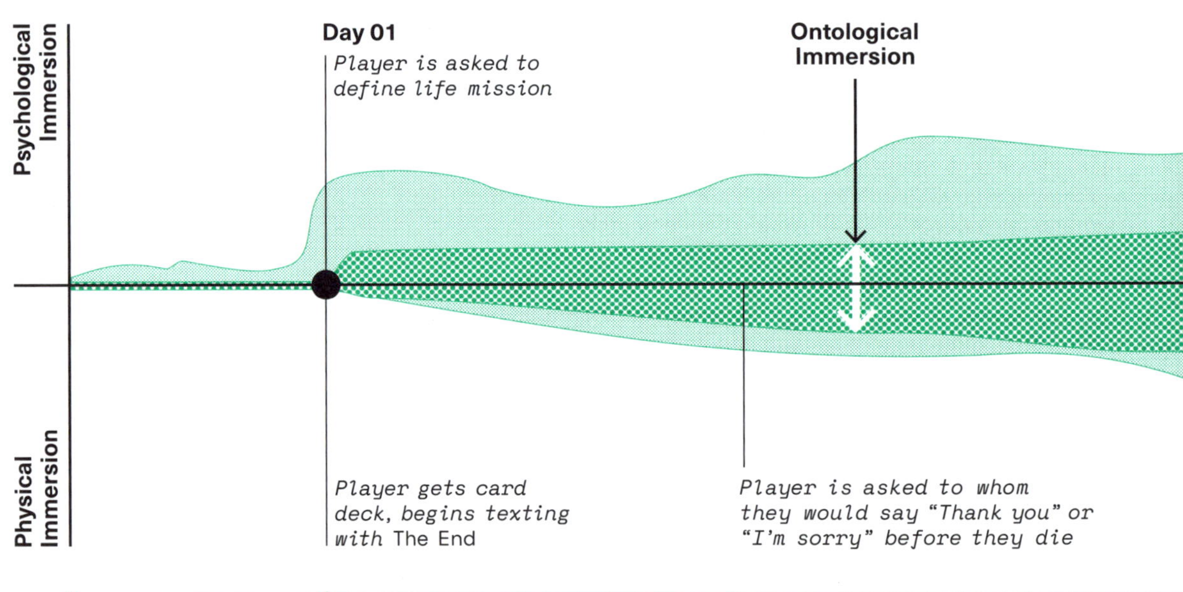

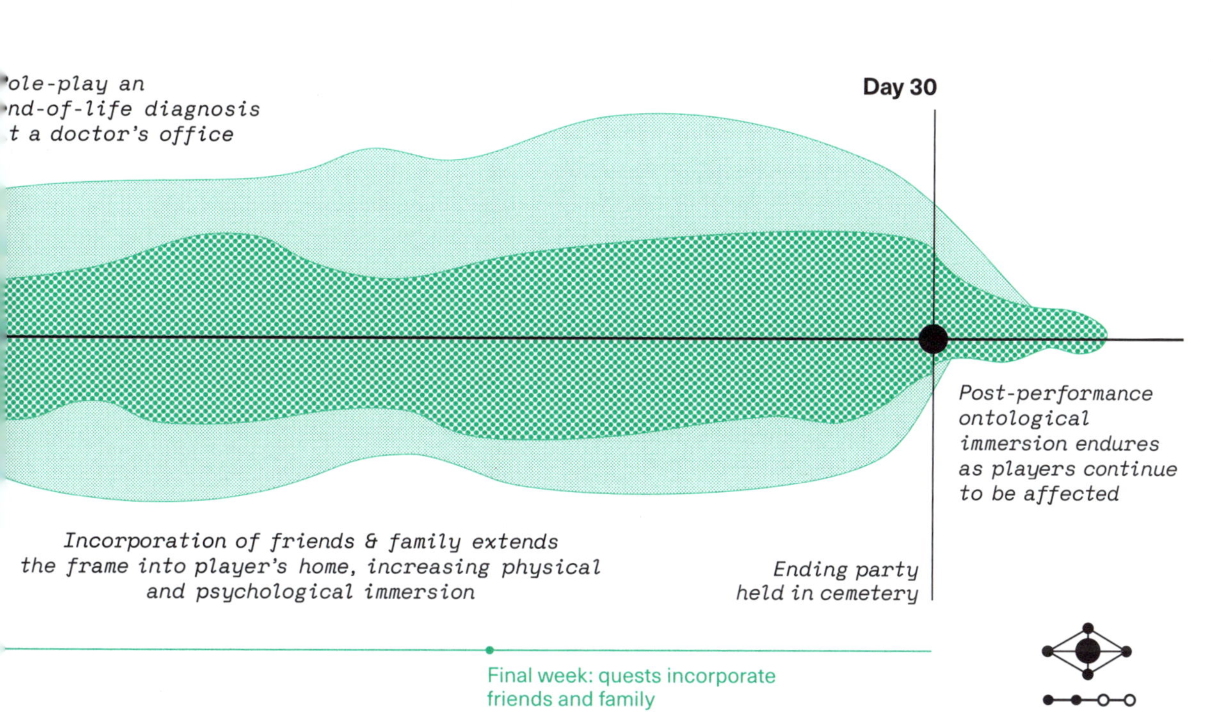
ole-play an
nd-of-life diagnosis
t a doctor's office
Day 30
Post-performance
ontological
immersion endures
as players continue
to be affected
Incorporation of friends & family extends
the frame into player's home, increasing physical
and psychological immersion
Ending party
held in cemetery
Final week: quests incorporate
friends and family

PHYSICAL

It is tempting, when designing interactions, to focus entirely on moving things along: having someone open the door, or get the story to the next stage, or give you the right answer. But it is the moments of interaction—or *touchpoints*, as the UX designers say—from which we assemble our memories of an experience. They should, therefore, be the most carefully considered design elements. Each interaction has its own experiential affordances, offering an individual the possibility of deeper immersion. During Phase Zero, a designer has the opportunity to identify not only how immersive they wish the experience to be, but how such immersion will build and end. Is there an arc to this immersion? When do I invite the audience to press the button, to contribute to the story, to confront a character representing their mortality? What key interactions will move an audience member along this arc? Are there different paths for audience members who might move through the experience with different levels of immersion?

PSYCHOLOGICAL

ONTOLOGICAL

This

I was

to be

at this **very**

Every year, millions of students walk into university classrooms ready to learn. These classes are taught by instructors who are experts in their fields, and they teach largely from books and existing material. The professors profess no secret knowledge, and many of them have published everything they know on the topic. Some even post their syllabi online and make readings and other media readily available. Why spend so much money to go to a temple of knowledge, such as MIT or Oxford, when all that knowledge is available in books and online for a fraction of the cost?

Because, of course, you wouldn't teach yourself electrical engineering on your own. That's just crazy. Institutions like MIT and Oxford are worlds where learning is the core moral value. The most powerful thing such an institution does is *exist*, offering students the opportunity to become immersed in the world and become part of a population in which they are identified as students for a number of years. Classes, then, are immersive experience designs within these worlds. They exist within physical and temporal frames and are structured through a variety of interactions with different experiential affordances. An art history class may have a lecture one day, a reading for homework, and an essay to follow that reading. The lecture, held in a communal setting in the classroom, is physically and psychologically immersive, but not very interactive. The subsequent reading and homework are interactive, each in a different way. The class may then have a field trip to a museum, followed by small group discussions over lunch. The physicality of getting to the museum is a kind of pilgrimage, elevating the importance of the sculptures the student will see once in the new environment. The casual lunch conversation, offering interactions between the students on the subject and building community, may develop a sense of belonging in the class, and of psychological immersion. The course may end with a term paper or an exam, demanding deep engagement with the material at the end of the semester, leaving students with a sense of individual accomplishment (or failure, alas). The course is a careful composition of different modes of immersion and interaction with different affordances. Too little interaction, and students may become bored. Too much, and it may be overwhelming. Too many field trips turn the pilgrimage into a commute, and too much time in the same room becomes detention. Put it all together in just the right way, however, and transformation is possible.

is what

meant

reading

moment.

(UNDERSTANDING)

(TEXT)

(PAGE)

CHAPTER FIVE

We Live in Many Worlds

5

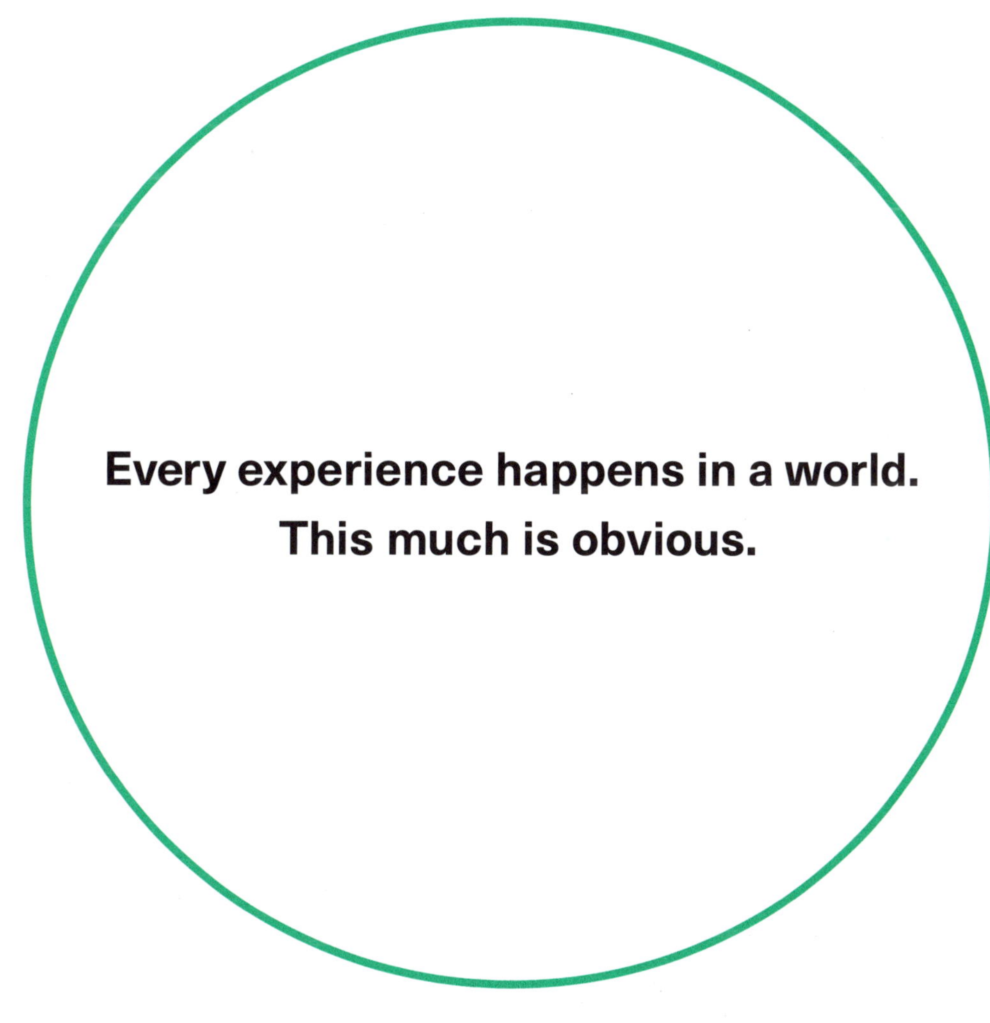
Every experience happens in a world.
This much is obvious.

That we inhabit many worlds is, perhaps, only slightly less obvious. It is evident in our language, not just in the movie trailer that begins with *In a world . . .* but when we talk about *the art world* or *the world of advertising*; when the overtired parent apologizes for the mess of toys, saying, with resignation, *Welcome to my world*; when a mind-blowing experience is not outside *the* world but out of *this* world; when the cancer patient receives her diagnosis and, at that moment, *her whole world has changed*. There are, of course, Disney World and World of Warcraft and WestWorld, which we can travel between. But there are also the world outside your window and your inner world. We move from one world to the next to the next, becoming a living part of each one as we do. Did the internet make the world smaller? Did the airplane? Are you saving the world with your work? Are you asking for a world of trouble? Are you planning on hopping on your ship to leave the religious persecutions of Olde England and start over in the New World?

This world-play points to the trouble with the idea of worlds: Is there one world or many? Strictly speaking, the world is everything. Experientially speaking, the world is the totality of one's context.

What matters, who we can be, what we should do, how we move around, what we look like, what is real, what is beautiful, how time works, who is in charge, what we want, whom we can expect to love, what we can expect to hate, which way is up, what happens when we fall, how we speak, how we think, all of it is determined, to a large extent, by which *world* we are in. No wonder we love imagining wildly different worlds. We read fantasy book series like *A Game of Thrones* or *Harry Potter*, and some sense of possibility lights up in us. We step into the refrigerator at Meow Wolf's immersive *House of Eternal Return*, participate in historic reenactments, or drift through the International Space Station while donning a VR headset. Heroes on their journeys begin at home, then leave home to visit another world—perhaps the underworld—in order to become someone different, or to become truly themselves. The underworld is fascinating, but it's also a distraction; the real story is who the characters become once they enter it.

These worlds are, without exception, *designed*. Occasionally, brilliant fantasists invent worlds wholesale, such as Middle Earth, Westeros, Narnia, or a Galaxy Far, Far Away. Burning Man, too, is such a world, as is Play Mountain or the Renaissance Fair. More often, the worlds we inhabit are collaboratively designed over time, possibly across generations. An architect may design a house, but the design of the home is a collaboration among the building and the town, the family members and their friends, all the media that enter the home, and everything the inhabitants carry across the threshold. The furniture designer who designs the bed and the industrial designer who designs the refrigerator and the fashion designer who came up with the idea of those

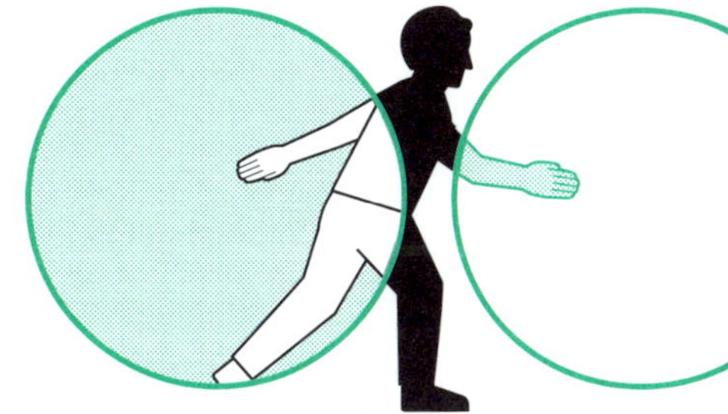

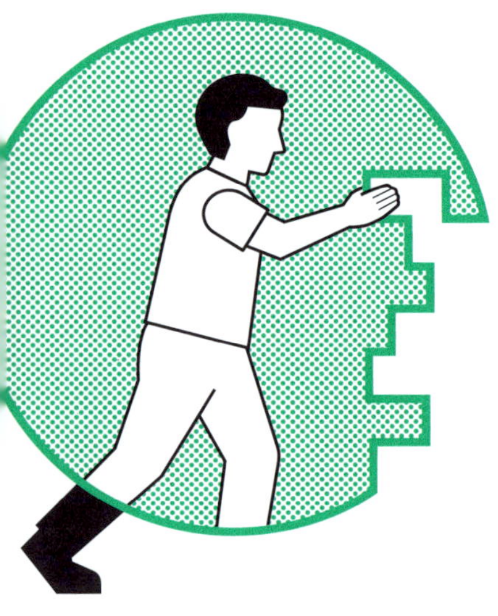

unusual slippers are collaborators in the design of that world—as are the baby who refuses to sleep through the night and the teenager who turns the living room into a gathering place for activists.

The world of the home is an ongoing, dynamic, collaborative, and occasionally intentional design process. The same can be said for a workplace, or a church, or a hospital. The same can even be said for a shop or a bus or a homeless shelter. These worlds are large frames that contain smaller frames within them. We move from one world to the next, supporting each world's structure by becoming what it needs us to be. Dad leaves home and on the street is a pedestrian, on the bus is a rider, at work is an assistant manager, at the shop a customer, at church a worshipper, at the drag bar a woman, at home, again, a dad.

The Elements of a World

Worlds emerge from the interrelation of four qualities:

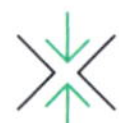 Place/Physics

 Aesthetics/Material Culture

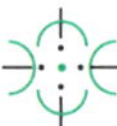 Population/Language

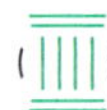 History/Myth

These categories, of course, overlap and tug at each other, and, if the world is to be a living world, they cannot be static. To effectively design a world, or an intervention in a world, is to make space for the participants to collaborate with you and to alter that world, a concept that we will continue to explore. This dynamism applies to each of the categories, even to the first one: *Place/Physics*.

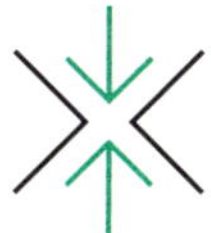

Place/Physics

> Our world is physical.
>
> —Ta-Nehesi Coates

The word *world* is most readily associated with *place*. One must travel to the underworld, to the off-world colonies, to SeaWorld. Another world is elsewhere, and even if one does not have to hop on a train or be carried over the rainbow, one must still *leave* this world and *enter* that one. We log *on* to World of Warcraft, we close our eyes and *enter* an inner world, the lights go down in the theater and we are *transported* to the world of the play. *Place* is the experiential counterpart to the more scientific *space*. Alejandro Iñárritu's *Carne y Arena*, an immersive VR experience of crossing the southern U.S. border, is built into a large performance space, but the participant, wearing the headset while walking across a floor covered in sand, is in the desert.[1] This desert is, of course, fictional, a cocreation of the audience and the artist, but so, too, is any world.

The key experiential marker of any world is its physics, which is to say, the way people and things move through space, effect change, and perceive. I am speaking, here, of the subjective understanding of a world's physics: how we experience it and learn to operate within it. Traditional systems of measurement emerged from such an understanding. A Roman mile was originally a thousand paces of the left foot.[2] An acre was the amount of farmland one farmer with one ox could plough in one day.[3] Such measures, of course, varied from place to place, and an acre of rocky land would, objectively speaking, be smaller than an acre of soft, easily workable land. The metric system, which came to dominance in the twentieth century, replaced such experiential measures with more objective measures and normalized the notion of space as unvarying and scientific.[4]

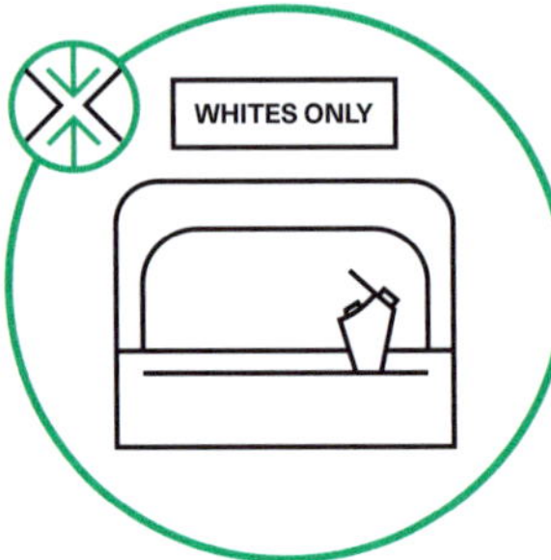

Physics: segregation.
Moral order: racist
caste structure.

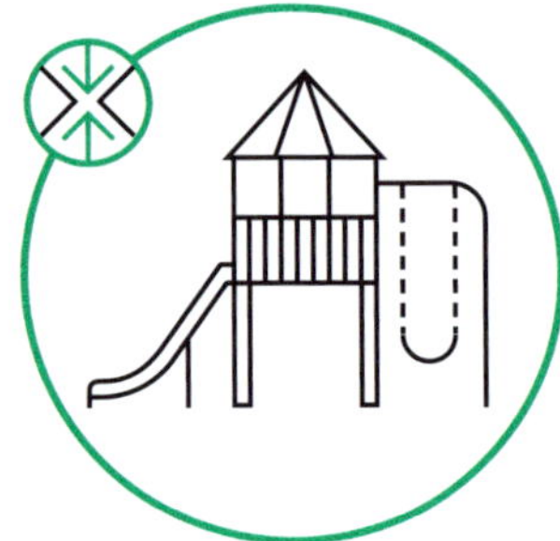

Physics: running,
sliding, climbing.
Moral order: play.

The physics, for instance, of *Harry Potter*'s Hogwarts includes flying broomsticks, pictures that move, and ghosts that pass through walls. The physics of *Star Wars* includes hyperspace and a spiritual "force" that connects all living things and can help you float rocks in the air and perceive the death of a loved one from a great distance. The physics of the Empire State Building includes jump-cut movement between floors in rapidly ascending elevators, whereas the physics of the tomb of a Sufi saint in Turkey includes *baraka*, which is a material form of blessing that will stick to all who come near it.

The Occupy Wall Street movement, which spread around the globe but began in Zuccotti Park in New York, was accused by outsiders of not having a clear agenda, not presenting a set of policy demands, and not offering a spokesperson with whom to negotiate.[5] But these critiques missed the point that the Occupy movement, being in many ways a critique of capitalism's agency

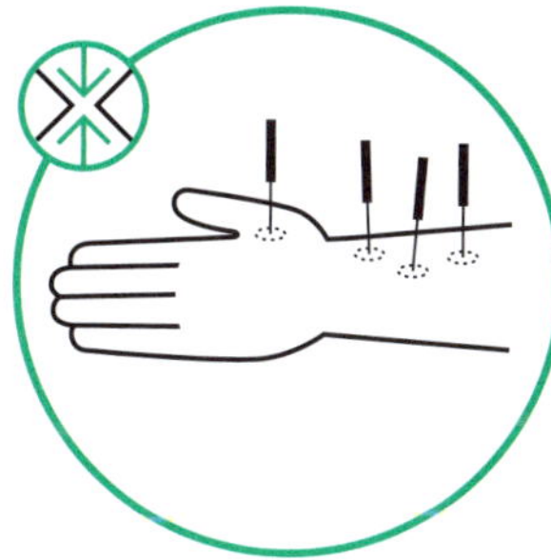

Physics: needle pricks/energy flows. Moral order: healing.

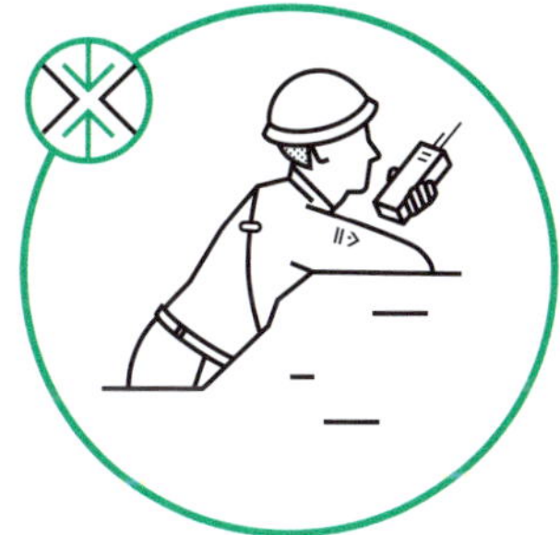

Physics: weaponry/ mortality. Moral order: victory/survival.

in building the modern world, was, in essence, a worldbuilding exercise. Both its title and its foundational activity—the occupation of a corporate park near Wall Street—are interventions in the physics of the world that protesters wished to change. Zuccotti Park, a neat, low-occupancy, "Privately Owned Public Space," functioned largely as a lunchtime outdoor patio for weekday workers.[6] People spent short periods of time in the space, and at the end of the workday they were not allowed back in. It was not a living space, or a gathering space for community, or a space in which to build structures. It was a space whose use was governed by the city and by the corporation that had built it. But when the park was occupied, all this changed; people moved in and stayed overnight and for a long time, temporary structures were erected, population density was massively increased, and the place was completely transformed from corporate park into protest center. Local regulations forbidding amplified sound inspired protesters to employ the "human

“A ‘miracle’ is the manifestation in this world of the laws of another world.”

G. I. Gurdjieff

microphone,” in which a speaker’s words would be loudly repeated by those near enough to hear so that those a bit farther away could hear as well.[7]

The laws of physics appear to be just that: laws, unbreakable but by magic. We no more expect to be allowed to spend the night in Zuccotti Park than we expect to flap our arms and lift off the ground. Magic is any activity that breaks the laws of physics of the world in which it is practiced. Lea Redmond’s *Seed Money* project, consisting of printed paper coins embedded with wildflower seeds that can then be planted, inserts small moments of magic into the physics of commerce.[8] Banksy’s art appears like magic on the walls of buildings in a city, as most people find it unimaginable to just put art on a building’s walls—how would you get away with it? But for street artists, it is a part of a world and, therefore, a matter of skill rather than magic. In 1955 Rosa Parks, an African American woman in the segregated South, refused to give up her seat so that a white passenger could sit when the bus driver told her to.[9] The physics of that world said Black people should relinquish their seats when white people wanted them. Her simple act, like that of the occupiers of Zuccotti Park, was accompanied by no policy demands, but it was an act of magic, breaking the physical (and societal) laws of that world and inviting others to doubt the legitimacy of such laws.

Inextricable from the notion of place is the moral structure that supports that place. The physics of Rosa Parks’s bus is a result of the racist moral structure of those who built the Jim Crow world. A mosque, which points the believer toward the holiest part of the Earth, and which is capped by the dome of heaven, wordlessly explains to its visitors the moral structure of the universe. The moral structure of a playground—that play is good above all else—is inherent to the ways children move through it: vertically, horizontally, at varying speeds, and continually engaged with the architecture. The physics of any world is built on the moral structure of that world, reflecting its values in such a way that an alteration to the physics—even one as small as putting seeds in money—will also be an alteration in the moral structure of that world.

"They sent the killer of Prince Jones back to his work, because he was **not a killer at all.** He was a force of nature, the **helpless agent** of our world's **physical laws.**"

———

Ta-Nehesi Coates

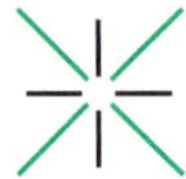

Aesthetics/Material Culture

A steampunk flying machine; the extravagant detailing of Louis XIV's Versailles; a Native American arrowhead poking out of a dry creek bed; a 1930s poster of Soviet workers, their hands jointly clasping a hammer and sickle, their gaze upward and optimistic. *Worlds are identified, reproduced, and evoked by how they look and feel, and by the objects they contain.* Oz is playful and coded with primary colors; Mars is relentlessly rocky and orange-brown; Count Dracula's castle is dark and moody. The aesthetics—especially the visual aesthetics—of a world are probably what comes to mind first when we think of worldbuilding.

But when it comes to worlds we actually inhabit, it may be the other senses that are most evocative. Consider the smell of home, the flavors of the food, the voices of family members. Can you recall the smell of the cleaning chemicals used in your high school? What about the sensation of the wind on the beach the first time you saw the ocean? These sensory identifiers get tagged to totemic objects serving as an index of the aesthetics and material culture of the world from which they emerge.

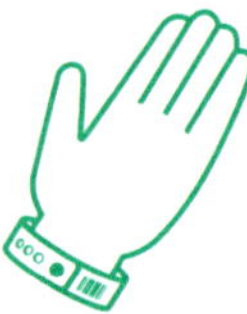

The hospital wristband evokes the plastic disposability, the general functionality, and the regimented nature of a hospital. The messy concert hand stamp, which takes some time to fade and is placed haphazardly on the skin, evokes the intense, physical nature of going to a club, the long, slow line to get in, and the sense of exclusivity. These objects, some carefully curated, others more emergent, serve as a style guide for the worlds they come from. A university ID badge suggests a world of smiling faces with controlled access to space. The badge, with its standardized photo and its ID number, implies a world not of personal expression but of standardized process. An Auschwitz tattoo—the monochromatic serial number on the arm of every victim—encapsulates the total dehumanization that was the engine of that world.

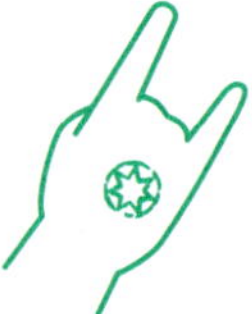

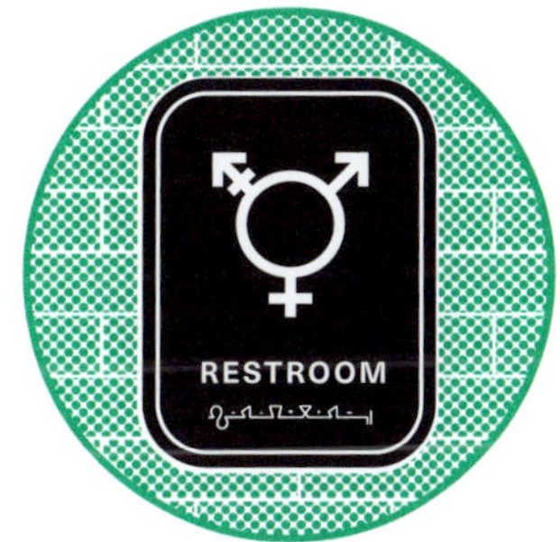

All-gender restroom signs began appearing in 2014, altering the way individuals could use public space.[10]

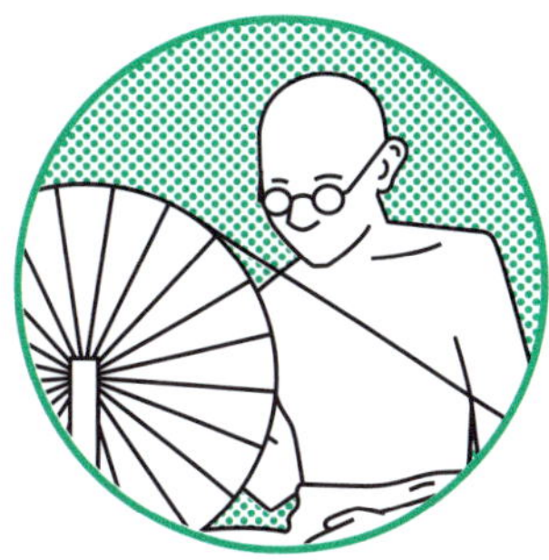

Gandhi donned traditional clothes and embraced the aesthetics of manual labor and traditional craft as key strategies in his worldbuilding-based approach for decolonizing the subcontinent.

When we create an object or image—either for a real world or for an invented world—we must ask what that creation says about the world. Does it illuminate the nature of the world? Does it alter the world in some way? Does it amplify a particular value system? Even small or seemingly whimsical designs, such as Lea Redmond's *Seed Money*, do this. Oftentimes it is the way in which these small projects change our understanding of the world that is the source of their delight.

You can, of course, find perfectly normal-looking apples in the hospital cafeteria and regular pencils on the International Space Station. But such objects do not communicate the nature of these worlds as thoroughly as, say, the light saber does for *Star Wars*, or the palm tree does for the tropical paradise. Finding those objects and defining those aesthetics are the full-time jobs of the bureaus of tourism and the travel writers. Tourists flock to New York to visit the Statue of Liberty and the lights of Broadway, to San Francisco for clam chowder in sourdough bowls by the docks, to Paris for the Eiffel Tower and baguettes. None of these is nearly as important to the people who inhabit those cities, but they offer the tourist a clear understanding of the world, along with an idea of how the tourists might experience life in such a world. It is a collaboration. Tourists post countless pictures online of themselves at these sites, usually taking care to leave the crowds of fellow tourists out of the shot. They post photos of the ornate balconies of New Orleans's French Quarter but omit the cheap motel they stayed in on the other side of town. They take photos of the ancient domed temples of Mumbai and do not mention the chai lattes they purchased at Starbucks.

As much as the worlds we visit are designed and curated, so are the worlds we live in, the ones that seem ordinary. Our public and private spaces are coated with text and images and architectural forms that tell us how to understand and relate to our world. Exit and

No Parking signs and striped crosswalks tell us how to move about and use public space. Shop windows tell us what to expect inside. The images on city buses tell us the personality of the city. Graffiti covering the side of a bridge tells us who is contesting the control of public space. Then, of course, there is packaging and advertising, the omnipresent onslaught of imagery and material culture competing to show us how to understand our world.

Every participant in a world is a collaborator in the production and re-production of the aesthetics and material culture of that world. Do you put on the uniform? Do you rebel and make every day into Casual Friday? Do you post beautiful photos of your dinner online? There is an ongoing, grand negotiation of the aesthetics and material culture of any world. It is the front line of worldbuilding.

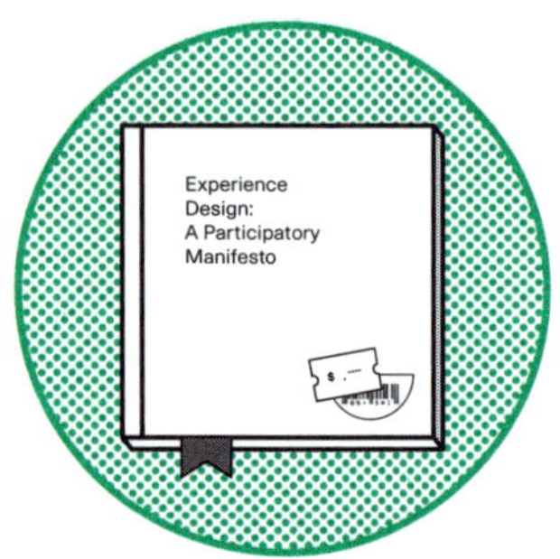

This text was written in a book rather than, say, as a long scroll nailed to the door of the Design Department or in a series of emails, because the book feels more authoritative. Look at the publisher's logo—doesn't it tell you that what's in here is at least respected by someone smart?

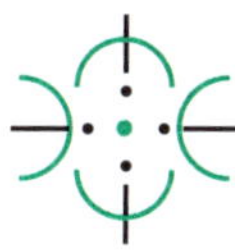

Population/Language

While individuals inhabit worlds, the limited number of roles those people may play defines the population of those worlds. When we ask who might be found in a particular world, we are asking not for the names of the individuals but for the types of individuals, the roles. In the world of a courtroom, one may be judge or juror, lawyer or audience, stenographer or bailiff. These roles define the functioning of the courtroom, and an individual may be a defendant one day and a lawyer the next. Roles that do not fit in the world are not accommodated. There is no place in a courtroom world for a clown or a lover, for a bartender or a preacher. In some other world, jurors may be bartenders or lovers or clowns, but in the courtroom they play the role of juror or they are asked to leave.

This role-playing permeates every aspect of human life, and it is nowhere more visible than in the games we play. We sort into teams, take on personae, select avatars, and are assigned capacities, permissions, and limitations. Are you a fourth-level mage? Are you a medic? A yellow pawn? A shoe? Part of the fun of taking on these roles is how we get to play at living a different life in a world with different populations.

Real-world roles can be far harder to step out of. Prerevolutionary Haiti, for instance, was a world rigidly divided into slave-owning *grands blancs* (big whites), non-slave-owning *petits blancs* (small whites), mixed-race people of color, free Blacks, and enslaved Blacks, the last making up the majority of the population.[11] This brutal caste system, extremely profitable for France and extremely violent toward the majority of the population, made Haiti its own particular world. From time to time, the French government attempted to legally limit the cruelty toward the slaves on the island through laws and decrees, but these had little effect because the problems of Haiti were a matter of the structure of that world's population rather than just a legal system.[12] To change the population structure of the world required a revolution: a kind of supernatural act necessary to alter the nature of a particular world—a kind of magic. It's no wonder that revolutionary leaders are often deified or considered to be prophets.

Population, experientially speaking, is nearly synonymous with *social rules*. This is an idea far broader than the laws or policies of a particular place. You may have an explicit policy that any person who enters your house takes off their shoes, but the different populations who inhabit your house will adhere to different social rules. A toddler may be allowed to be unruly and to jump on the couch, while a stranger may not be allowed in past the foyer. Your mother-in-law may be allowed, though perhaps under protest, to clean up after everyone, but your boss, invited over for dinner, would not be permitted to do so. Similarly, there are no laws requiring drivers to treat police officers with deference, but everyone knows they must, though some

Courtroom

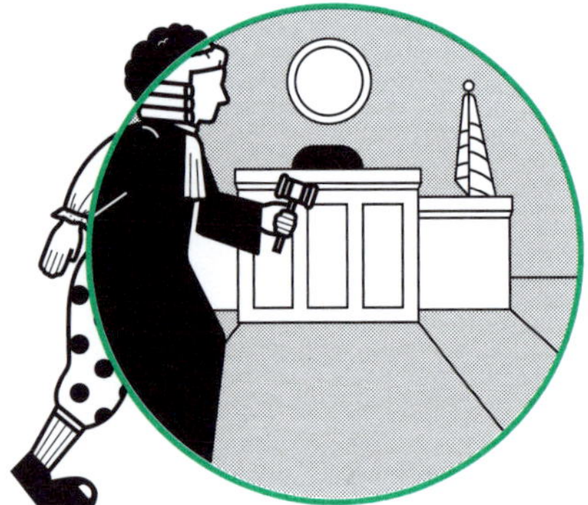

The Authority

Fighting Game

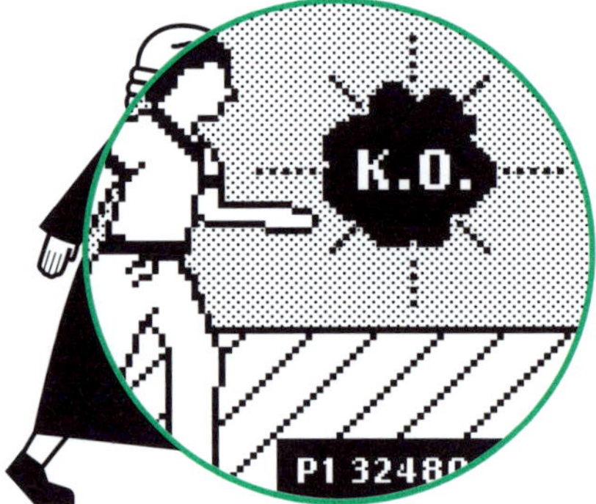

Warrior

subgroups of the population know that this applies far more intensely to them than to others.

Probably the most important tool for identifying and describing a population is *language*. Speakers of the invented language Esperanto, with its pan-European word structure and its globalist ethos, may be expected to adhere to the anti-nationalist philosophy that birthed it.[13] Dothraki—a language invented for use in the fictional world of *Game of Thrones*—expresses with guttural harshness the warlike nature of its speakers.[14] Natural languages, which have no identifiable author, are generally subtler and more complex, offering not only a means of communication but a tool for evaluating and reinforcing roles and relationships at every interaction. Who may address whom as *sir*, or *ma'am*? Who may demand that you *Step out of the car*? Why don't you ever ask a friend, *How may I help you*? In many languages, gendered nouns and

Esperanto

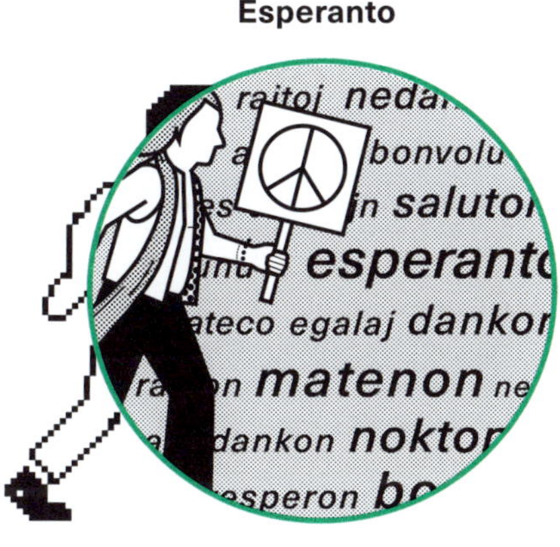

Anti-Nationalist Man

They

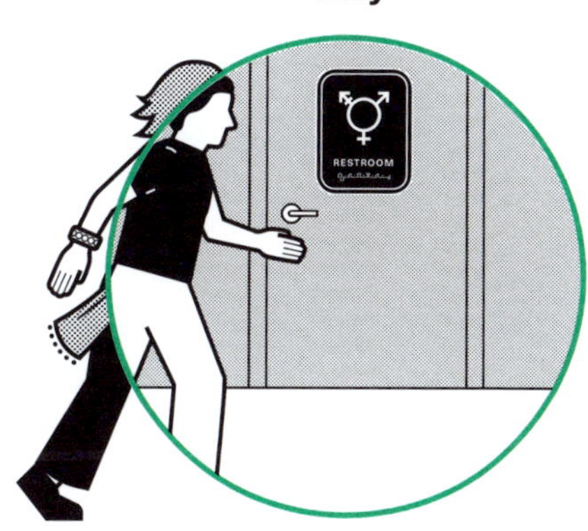

Nonbinary Individual

adjectives, as well as systems of formal and informal speech, define who is speaking and what permissions they have in their shared world. The social structure of the population is legible in nearly every verbal interaction. From the perspective of worldbuilding, this is the primary function of language.

Any one world, of course, may contain many different languages, whose use identifies one as native or immigrant, educated or parochial. Do you speak the Queen's English in London? Do you speak Puerto Rican Spanish in Spanish Harlem in New York? What access does this grant? How are you identified when people hear these languages? A named language, such as English, is no more a single language than, say, Americans are a single kind of people. Languages are sliced up and massaged and reworked to facilitate and maintain the population structures of their worlds. The language of a football fan is wildly different from the language of a boss, or of a lover, or of a parent, though the same individual may code-switch seamlessly between them. The fifteen-year-old boy who speaks Spanish with his parents, Spanglish with his friends, polite customer-service-ese at his weekend job, scientific jargon in his research internship, and archaic English in his prayers is moving fluidly among worlds and adeptly claiming roles within them.

"Wipe the language off everything and what do you have left? Some other planet."

James Hannaham

In 2015 *they* was declared the English word of the year.[15] This was not, of course, because the word was new, but because the growing use and acceptance of the word as a singular nongendered pronoun was considered to have become part of the language. The implications of such acceptance are vast—now, in the ordinary structure of the language, the population could be divided not just into a male/female binary, but into male/female/nonbinary. To be sure, plenty of people have long thought of themselves as nonbinary and have been accepted by specific communities, but the language for this had not previously crossed over into general use. Its incorporation into the larger language makes such a gender identity a part of the structure of the world, so that it begins to affect the physics and aesthetics of the world, altering bathroom use, appearing on student ID cards, inspiring fashion.

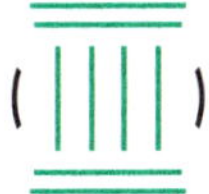

History/Myth

> A culture can be no stronger than its strongest myths.
>
> —James Carse

There can be no world without history, the telling and retelling of which is the relentless activity of any world. The motto, for instance, of Cornell University—"I would found an institution where any person can find instruction in any study," often along with its founding date, 1865—can be seen emblazoned on buildings and signs throughout the campus. Catholic cathedrals around the world are adorned with stained-glass windows graphically narrating the history of the religion in general and of the patron saint of the cathedral in particular. Havana, the Cuban capital, is decorated with countless images of its storied founders—Che Guevara and Fidel Castro—and has a temple-like museum in its center, housing the boat on which they sailed to Cuba. These are the origin stories, and every world has one, even if the origin story is "I saw the house and I knew it would be my home" or "the big bang." The truth of such stories—the metaphorical truth if not the actual truth—is essential to the structural soundness of the world. The story must be convincing, shared, and reaffirmed, and attacks on such stories often are taken as attacks on the values of the population. Enormous amounts of energy have been expended trying to reason that the Earth is only a few thousand years old, as some believe the Bible suggests, and that the founders of your country were preternaturally wise and good-looking, and that Cornell has always been a feminist institution, as evidenced by the use of "person" rather than "man" in its motto.

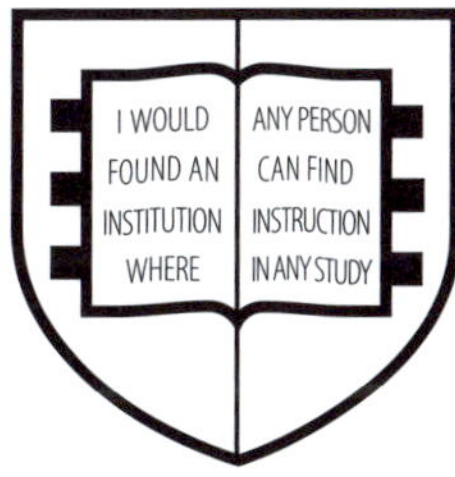

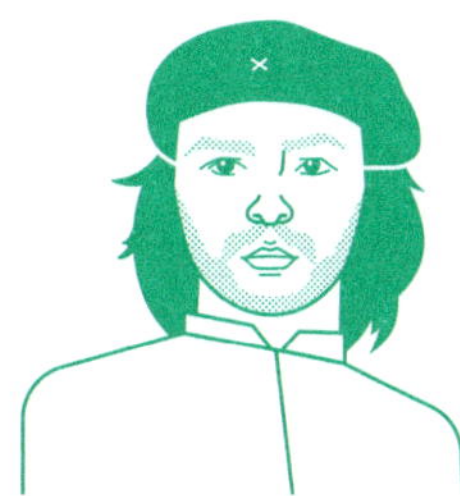

Origin stories are generally encoded in texts or oral tradition and serve to represent the basic structure of the world and of the people in it. When an individual discovers that the origin story they thought they knew was wrong, the world shifts for them, and who they are and may be is radically altered. A believer loses faith in creation and puts in its place the big bang, after which she may no longer be a child of God, may no longer be a sinner or saint, may no longer expect to go to heaven or hell. A Soviet apparatchik learns that the great leader, Stalin, was, in fact, a propagator of genocide, and the inner doorway to dissent appears.

The history of a world matters because it serves as the context for what is happening now. Any new story that takes place in that world may support or betray or repair the world's origin. The Jewish world, for example, begins with a great shattering of the oneness (*The Lord Is One* is a common refrain in Hebrew prayers) into countless shards, a history that tasks present-day Jews with doing good deeds to put the world back together again.[16] This history is evoked when the news spreads that a synagogue in, say, Pittsburgh is attacked, prompting the believer to send money, supporting not just the victims but the imperative of the origin story. The origin story of a world generally presents that world as having noble and idealistic beginnings that serve as a backdrop against which the recent history is deemed a failure or a success.

This page was originally created so that this circle could exist. This was the first circle ever to be drawn on this page, and it is a perfect circle.

We participate in worldbuilding any time we participate in the life of a world. The majority of our actions reinforce the structure of a world. We wear the clothes, use the language, engage in the activities that make a world a world. Creative or revolutionary worldbuilding is, for this reason, extraordinarily difficult but also potentially transformative for all participants in a world, for when a world changes, who anyone might be and what they may do must also change.

Worldbuilding, at every scale, has transformative power. Dante's *Inferno* offered medieval readers an imaginary moral world with which to evaluate themselves, just as, say, the world of Philip Pullman's novel *The Golden Compass* offers readers the opportunity to mentally project themselves into a life where they might always be accompanied by an animal who represents their soul, and with whom they can be in conversation. Games like Oregon Trail or Monopoly offer players the opportunity to see how they would fare as Western settlers or bare-knuckled capitalists. Fictions, like dreams, when powerful enough, give us the sense of having lived another life and offer models for ways of being that challenge the lives we take for granted in our home worlds. Fictional worldbuilding offers the experience designer the greatest control and the most room for speculation. In small communities, worlds may be radically rebuilt as well. Families, communes, religious organizations, art collectives, and others may successfully build small worlds, intentionally designing their clothing, their architecture, the social rules, the nature of their populations, and writing new histories and even magically reconsidering the physics of their world. Such small-scale communities are often seen to threaten the stability of the larger world built around them and may be viewed with suspicion. The endless stories of the evils of cults, conspiracy theories involving shady mob dealings or diabolical Jewish cabals, and even laws preserving the "purity" of a language act as moats around a world, resisting the challenges presented by other ways of being. The threat, in many ways, is real; to visit another world is to be a different person, and if one likes this other person, one may be tempted to make space for such a person in one's own world.

"I have a dream," says Martin Luther King Jr. in his most famous speech, "that my four little children will one day live in a nation where they will not be judged by the color of their skin."[17] This is worldbuilding at a large scale: an attempt to rebuild the social rules of a whole nation. It starts, however, with worldbuilding at the smallest scale: a dream, which is to say, a piece of fiction providing a model for how the greater world might be rebuilt. In small-scale worldbuilding, we may make huge changes to the world with the stroke of a pen. In large-scale worldbuilding, enormous energy must be expended by great numbers of people to make much smaller changes.

I can think of no one who understood the revolutionary power of worldbuilding so well as Mahatma Gandhi. His early life saw him moving between dramatically different worlds—from the village life of a merchant-caste family to Mumbai at the height of British colonial domination, to London, where he studied to become a lawyer, and then to South Africa, where the racial laws regulating the world were shockingly strict.[18] Through these moves he had the opportunity to observe the functioning of varied worlds, all united under the umbrella of British colonialism. The man he was able to be in London—a lawyer in Western dress affiliated with white English vegetarians and Theosophists—was very different from the merchant-caste Indian he had been in India, and very different again from the Indian he later was in South Africa, where he was not allowed to walk on public footpaths. In South Africa he led protests and campaigns of civil disobedience, and his successes, though mild by comparison to what he would later achieve, presented the Indian world with a model for a mode of resistance that could be imported into India.[19]

Colonialism can be understood as a legal, territorial structure of government in which one country wields political power over another, determining its laws and controlling its economy.[20] But its real power lies in its worldbuilding. Colonization inserts new classes of people into a territory and carries with it new sets of social rules, some of them mandated by law and many of them developed informally. It also carries language into new places, usually dividing and defining individuals on the basis of language, reserving access to economic and political power for the language of the colonizers. Colonists bring modes of dress, architecture, and aesthetics. They even alter the physics of the colonized land, restructuring who can move where, what means of transport are available to whom, and what the landscape looks and feels like. These add up to a redefinition of the population in such a way that the roles offered limit individual possibility and reinforce the stability of the colonial government. We tend to believe we are who the world says we are, and herein lies both the true power of colonial rule and the reason its effects may linger long after the colony is no longer officially a colony.

The British had, in one way or another, ruled India since 1858.[21] Before Gandhi, Indians and other colonized peoples had tried and failed to oust the British using violence.[22] Gandhi chose not to oppose the British militarily but to strike at the basis of its power—the worldbuilding. The core tenet of his political action was nonviolent noncooperation, an idea that was wildly disruptive to a colonial world.[23] Violence was fundamental to the physics of the British Empire; it was the primary means of social and governmental change. This fact was coupled with an imperative to cooperate with social rules to maintain power structures. The effectiveness of Gandhi's nonviolent measures was shocking to India and to the world, but from the point of view of worldbuilding, it made perfect sense. Gandhi gave up Western dress and donned the loincloth of the poor, an action that disrupted the aesthetic rules of how the population was structured—here was a man with power who dressed like those without power. Other actions challenged the physics of the world: his Salt March in 1930—a protest against the salt tax—saw him and nearly one hundred followers walk for twenty-five days and more than 240 miles to the sea to make salt for themselves. Such a trip would have ordinarily been taken by train or horse, and salt ordinarily produced in a British-run factory.[24] The salt they produced at the sea was, relative to the Anglo-Indian salt industry, economically insignificant.[25] But the march, along with all his other worldbuilding activities, presented the colonial world as unstable and susceptible to redefinition.

Possibly the most important event preceding the ousting of the British from India was the Amritsar Massacre, when a group of British soldiers opened fire on a walled garden in which peaceful protesters were trapped. Hundreds died, and with them died the image the British had of themselves as benevolent rulers. In the eyes of the Indians and in the eyes of the world,[26] the British, whose empire was built on the notion of bringing civilization to the world, were now merely oppressors and occupiers.[27] It was an event that tilted the world on its axis, and Gandhi, that most brilliant of worldbuilders, was able to take advantage of the tilt to build a new world entirely.

If colonization is a kind of worldbuilding, decolonization must also be understood as a kind of worldbuilding. One's homeland need not be occupied by a foreign government for one's world to be colonized. What one may look like, who one may be, how one may move, and how one understands one's history may all be colonized by the agendas of other worlds. Though decolonization may involve a change of government, it more readily involves changes of language, of history, of the structures of small communities, and of how one understands oneself.

Worldbuilding is an elixir for the imagination. A great deal of immersive theater and entertainment relies almost exclusively on worldbuilding for its allure. Successful worldbuilding compels us to travel, to switch careers, to buy cars, to vote for candidates, to convert to religions, to become activists, to read ten books in a series, to fall in love, to leave relationships, to seek, again and again, the self on offer in the vision of another, and, upon doing so, to come home and rebuild one's home world, or at least to try. Such worldbuilding is a design process with a broader scope than the solving of small problems. We may build aspirational worlds without the injustices of our default worlds: worlds where marginalized populations are centered, where disabilities do not hinder access and participation, where the problems inherent in social rules, in physics, in histories, are addressed. Or we may intervene in small ways, encouraging an ethic of sharing in public space installing a Little Free Library by the sidewalk or softening the urban environment by knitting sweaters onto signposts. Experientially speaking, worldbuilding may be a liberatory act at any scale. Redecorating one's home or playing a collaborative worldbuilding game like Dungeons and Dragons offers individuals a model of a different way of being. These things may lead to a new sense of self, a follow-on effect of worldbuilding, after which one might try to change one's own world, or to leave that world and find one better suited to one's new sense of self.

"We but
mirror
the
world."

Mahatma Gandhi

CHAPTER SIX

Narrative Is Everywhere

6

C

Narrative: The innate human activity of making significant connections among events, people, things, ideas, and so on. Narrative may be written, spoken, thought, embedded within objects, or hidden behind words. Narrative may be experienced as words, but also as colors, sounds, smells, sensations, intuitions, dream connections. A story may be confined to the pages of a book, but narrative follows wherever the attention leads, then continues in the subconscious.

Narrative is a "mass noun," like *water*. The allusion is apt; narrative is the water in which we swim, so ever-present that we cannot see it. This use of *narrative* is distinct from the ordinary noun, *a narrative*, synonymous with *a story*, just as the ordinary noun *a water* is synonymous with *a glass of water*. It is easy to comprehend a glass of water, but much harder to comprehend the omnipresence of water—in the clouds, in the air, in the cells of the body, to say nothing of the unimaginable depths of the oceans. So it is with narrative.

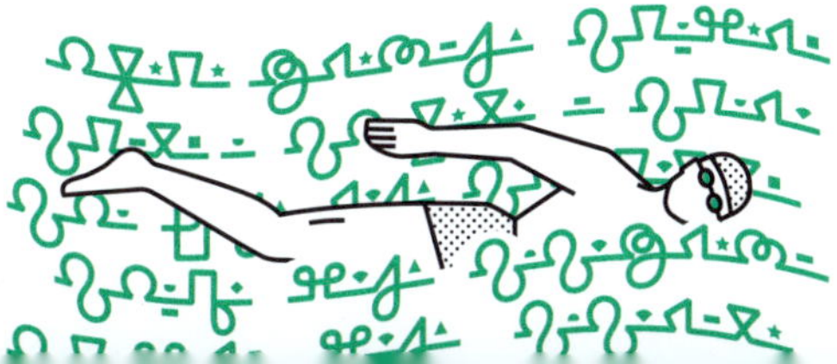

Story: A Discrete Instance of Narrative

In 2010 the hip-hop megastar Jay-Z released a book, *Decoded*, about his life and music. Anchored by a narrative about his life growing up in Brooklyn, dealing drugs, and discovering music, the book is a collage of prose, images, and annotated song lyrics. The reader is assumed to have encountered some of the music previously, but not to have fully understood it. A line like "I got 99 problems but a b*t¢h ain't one" is, on the surface, a derogatory statement about the women he isn't having problems with. But in that world, suggest the annotations, it was actually about

> a female dog, the K-9 cop coming to sniff the ride. When I was living my version of this story, we got away. The K-9 was late, and the cop let me go... it would have changed my life if that dog had been a few seconds faster.[1]

In reading the annotations, in reading the prose about the time and the place from which the text arose, an entirely different story emerges from the lyrics. Thus it is with all narrative. Every story is an interface between the story being told and the broader narrative it connects to within the lives of its audience. If you purchased the book, you probably had already heard of Jay-Z and had listened to some of his music, which means you already had a story of who he was and why that mattered to you. The book, then, was not a new story but an intervention in the story you already had about Jay-Z, and maybe in the story you had about yourself.

The object that is the book is static and discrete, completely contained within its covers and identical in every copy. The experience of the book is dynamic and connected and personal for each reader. Jay-Z's story of growing up must be compared to one's own. His images of home must be compared to one's own. The evolution of his values is measured against one's own. What choices has one made that resonate with his? How might one have responded in his circumstance? The two narratives intermesh, supporting or undermining or reinterpreting one another along the way. We say *I really connected with that story,* by which we mean that in the interaction between my own narrative and that of the book, an empathetic process took place. We see in the book an argument that the lyrics in his music must be understood as emergent from a time and a place, a narrative window onto a larger world. Formally, the story is the book. Experientially, the story is what is written within the book interfacing with the reader's own story, interfacing with whatever that reader had for breakfast, with the tone suggested by the book jacket, with the urgency of the news story that just played again on the radio about gentrification in Brooklyn, which the reader now realizes is where Jay-Z is from, though the Brooklyn he memorializes in his book is so wildly different from the one in the news story. Now the reader is tasked with assembling these disparate narratives into a single coherent one, which is, perhaps, a story of change, of legacy, of the dynamism of cities. This broader story is the more important story for the reader, the story within which Jay-Z's book is but one chapter. The experience designer may, in the end, write a book such as Jay-Z's, but their actual project is the one that happens in the audience's mind, the one that is assembled from a vast array of forms.

The book is a story, but also the purchase of the book is a story (*I got a great deal on this book . . .* or *It was expensive but worth it . . .* , and the like), as is the trip to the bookstore and on and on. *I went to the bookstore* tells a story, not just about what you did today, but about what kind of person you are, what you value, how much leisure time you have. This is done in collaboration with the branding of the bookstore. (Are we talking about an old-timey literati kind of place or maybe a more comics-focused fun shop?) Your name tells a story about your family history. Even the chirping of the birds tells a story about spring, perhaps, or the weather, or about how you have to wash the car. And so, when you step into the bookstore, looking for a book about the history of America, perhaps, or about God, both of which are very big stories, the bird and the branding of the shop and the drive will all be a part of the story in the book you read.

Our experience of narrative, like that of light, exists on a spectrum. That which we generally think of as stories—the books we read or the tales we tell, for instance—lives in the center of the spectrum, like visible light. At the larger and smaller ends are the stories so big or so small that we don't perceive them as stories. Big stories—such as identity, history, or God—are ongoing stories that evolve day by day. Tiny stories—such as a name, a gesture, a breath—charge the hours and minutes of our days with meaning. Big stories may involve the collaboration of large numbers of people. Small stories may happen in the blink of an eye, a brush of a hand against a knee, the placing of a morsel of food into a mouth. A good story shines brightly at its spot on the spectrum. A great narrative experience lights up spots all across the spectrum.

The experience designer builds narrative across the whole spectrum.

Stories at the "ultrastory" end of the spectrum can be particularly challenging to tell. What is the story of the universe? Of your country? Of your people? This last story has been the purview of hefty historical tomes, semester- or degree-long university courses,

The Human Story Spectrum

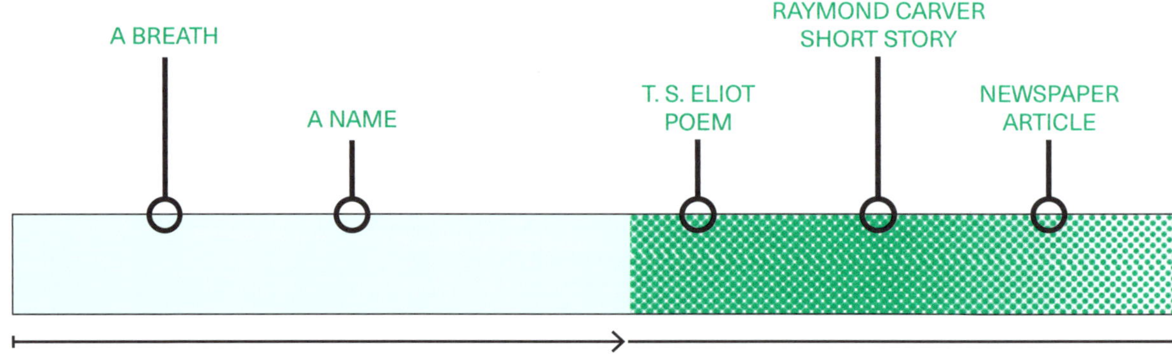

and history museums. Focused on artifacts, images, and text, history museums have traditionally taken an educational approach to telling the story of a people.

In 1999 the Jewish Museum of Berlin reopened with a new building addition. Daniel Libeskind, a Polish architect of Jewish extraction, had designed the primary focus of the new wing not so much to outline the events of Jewish history in Germany as to offer visitors an embodied experience of the story of Judaism in Germany.[2]

To enter, the visitor first passes into the frame of the "old" museum (which was once the Berlin Museum), with its installations and baroque architecture and museum aesthetic.[3] This is a place where a visitor is a person who will experience a history by observing artifacts, reading texts on walls, and wandering wherever their interest leads. The frame of this building is that of a museum, which is a form that relies on the content (the exhibitions) to tell the story.

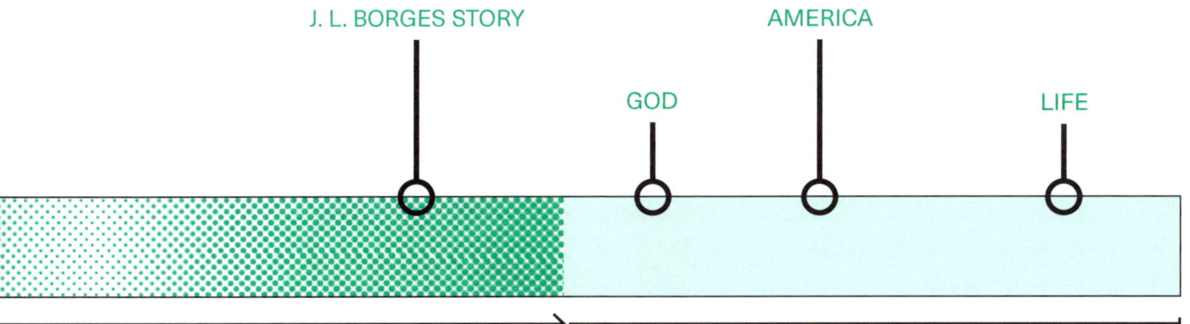

The form of a traditional museum does, of course, tell a particular story: that what is shown within it matters, is valuable, and has been expertly curated by people who have a deep knowledge of the material. Visitors take on the responsibility of assembling their own narratives from the various stories offered, turning the museum into a kind of choose-your-own-adventure book. The museum is a civic building, a part of the cultural infrastructure of its host city and thus a piece of the city's identity.

But to enter the Libeskind extension, one must descend a three-story staircase deep under the ground. Few frames are thicker than those that are entered by such a descent. It is a classic, archetypal way of inviting the audience into another world and another storytelling logic. We *descend* into sleep and then we wake *up*;[4] Alice discovers Wonderland after going *down* the rabbit hole; Orpheus travels to the underworld to retrieve Eurydice; great saints and beloved leaders may be visited in their underground crypts where, like Lenin in his glass coffin, they sometimes appear almost alive. Underground, the stories we take in are more metaphorical, less didactic. The descent invites visitors to expect a more metaphorical, participatory, transformative kind of storytelling, and at the bottom of the museum's stair, they are faced with three long, intersecting corridors. These are the three thematic axes of the German Jewish experience: the Axis of Exile, the Axis of Holocaust, and the Axis of Continuity. They are sparsely programmed with exhibits, as the story here is received through the act of walking each windowless corridor with its daunting vanishing point. As one walks, the dark, low ceiling feels heavy overhead and impels the visitor forward, instinctively searching for open space. Untempted by much else to look at, the masses of museumgoers, like the masses of the Jewish people, walk these metaphorical paths as they grow more crowded and uncomfortable, the axes of Exile and Holocaust both releasing their walkers into evocative atrium spaces—"voids"—suggesting with their hollow, unornamented forms the emotional quality of these histories. The final axis—the Axis of Continuity—leads, ultimately, out of the beautiful subterranean nightmare and back up into the light and views of the city and into the rotating and permanent exhibitions of the aboveground museum.

"I did something I believed in, which was to transform the entire structure into a discourse about German-Jewish history."

Daniel Libeskind

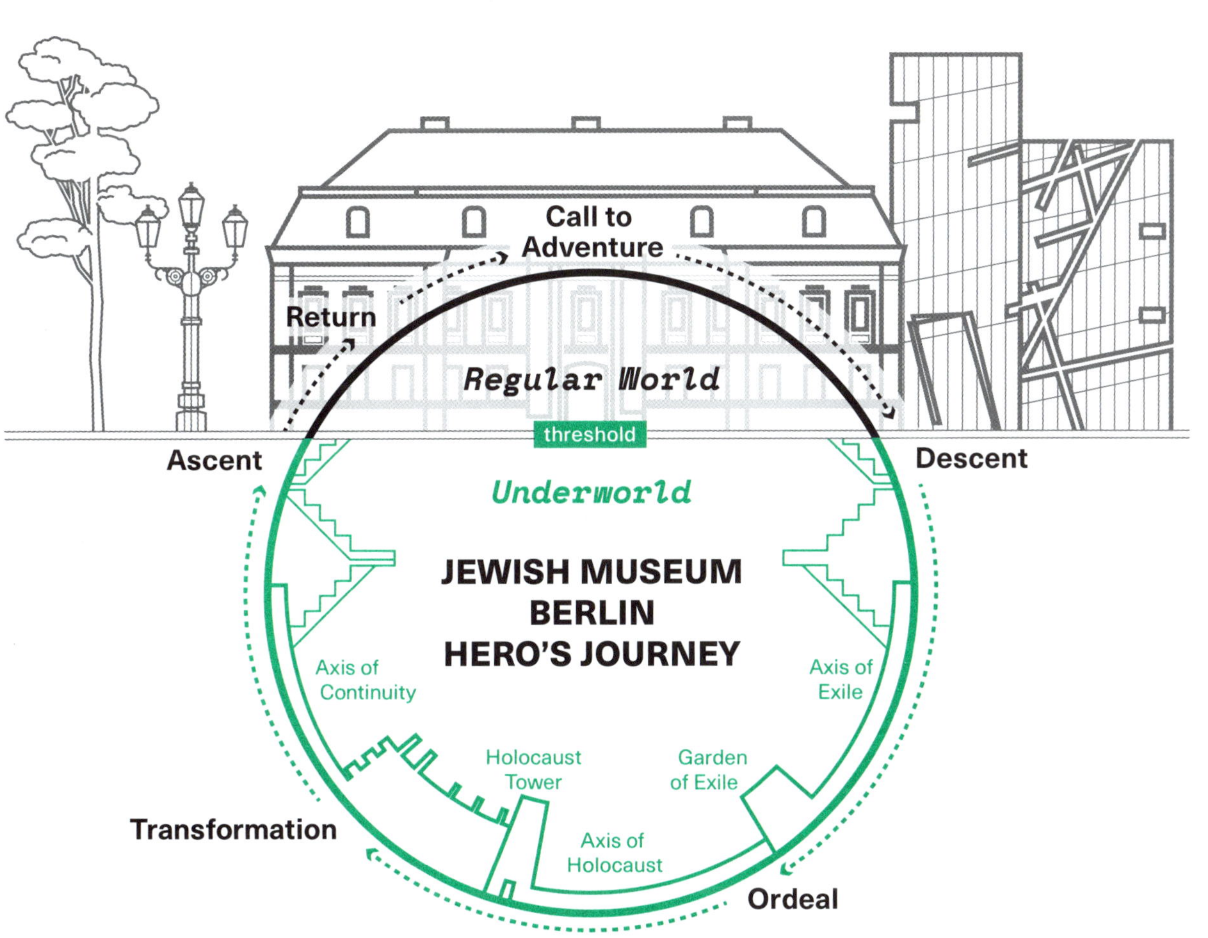

Call to
Adventure
Return
Regular World
threshold
Ascent
Descent
Underworld
JEWISH MUSEUM
BERLIN
HERO'S JOURNEY
Axis of
Continuity
Axis of
Exile
Holocaust
Tower
Garden
of Exile
Transformation
Axis of
Holocaust
Ordeal

A complex narrative structure! One moves from exhibition to evocation back to exhibition.

Joseph Campbell identified the astoundingly specific structure of the hero's journey in his 1949 book *The Hero with a Thousand Faces.*[5] The structure, derived from the study of myths across different cultures, can be found in Homer and in Spielberg, in religious pilgrimages and in tourism packages, in video games and in TED Talks. It is so powerful because it contains within it a road map to personal and communal transformation. Zoomed out, the narrative structure is simple: things were normal, then events of an entirely different quality happened, and the hero had to deal with them and was changed, then the hero came back to tell the tale. We use this narrative structure all the time when we talk about what we did today *(There I was, minding my own business, when who comes along but . . .)* or how we know what we know *(Before I took Professor Einstein's physics class, which was so much work, I thought humans were the most important thing in the universe. Now I know that . . .)* or why we feel sick *(I knew I shouldn't have done it, but it looked too good, so I took one little bite of that cake and immediately I felt . . .)* and so much else. These all contain the same general narrative movement that the Jewish Museum contains—passing from the frame of the ordinary world (where things are somewhat easy and predictable) to the frame of the extraordinary world (where the rules change, we face challenges, and we are altered by them), back to the frame of the ordinary world.

One need not, like a Hollywood scriptwriter, adhere strictly to the steps of the hero's journey. Each element has its own particular experiential qualities and may be the entire focus of the design. A political speech, when effective, is experienced as a call to adventure; solving a puzzle is a challenge to overcome; listening to experimental music is an encounter with the extraordinary world, where the known rules no longer apply. Each becomes a piece of a larger hero's journey when it interfaces with the narratives of our own lives, connecting disparate experiences with a coherent narrative through line.

One must never confuse the *written* story with the *experienced* story. Punchdrunk's UK/US/China production of *Sleep No More* is an adaptation of Shakespeare's *Macbeth*. But, while a standard production of the play is experienced as a linear narrative progression through five acts of royalty and betrayal, culminating in some seriously Shakespearean bloodletting, *Sleep No More* is an experience more of exploration than of plot development. In their adaptation, an audience member is masked and split from their group, entering the world at one of several different floors and then allowed to roam the world of the show freely. Most of the time is spent exploring the spaces and seeing what worlds they build, while occasional encounters with the performers lead to dance scenes that—if you know the characters and plot of the play well—tag into specific moments of the original play. If you don't, they are simply dance performances that may evoke more general narratives. An audience member is free to explore the space, looking for instances of performance—perhaps even the coveted one-on-ones—or to riffle through drawers seeing what stories may be discovered there. The experience is largely nonlinear, but the evening is phased, and by the end everyone is subtly shepherded into the final scene, the bloody conclusion reminiscent of the ending of the Shakespeare play.

Macbeth is, then, source material for the piece, but the story people walk away with is generally about their own experience. People talk about how they felt, what they discovered. Did they have a one-on-one? Did they get to eat the candy at the candy shop? Did they manage to follow a running character all the way from the graveyard to the room with all the pictures on the wall? In the end, theirs is an experience of discovering the world of the piece, of enjoying the anonymity of being masked, of being free to assemble their own adventure.

Happiness researchers (like Daniel Kahneman) have come to understand each moment of our lives as the intersection of the experiencing self and the remembering self, the former taking in a moment and the latter placing it within a narrative. We tend to design for one self or the other. What would it mean to design for both?

From an experiential perspective, of course, all narratives are interactive in some way. A newspaper story really comes to life when it sparks outrage or curiosity in its reader, who then does something with the story—shares it around, for instance, or goes out and votes differently. A ghost story progresses with the *oohs* and *aahs* of the children around the campfire. Even a Do Not Enter sign is an interactive narrative.

Sleep No More is an interactive narrative; it is formed in collaboration with the visitor and, because it is a thoroughly constructed world, the story you experience is different every time. Such interactivity engages the audience actively, opening the doorway to immersion and a more personal relationship with the piece. Designing an interactive narrative is an entirely different process from writing a short story, as the distance between what is experienced and what is written is much greater. At the same time, different approaches to interactivity have extremely distinct experiential affordances, so it is essential to understand the kind of experience you are trying to create before designing the approach to interactivity.

Interactive narratives can be broken down broadly into four types, each with its own design challenges and possibilities. These are:

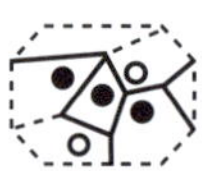

1. Worlds that are built through discovery of narrative

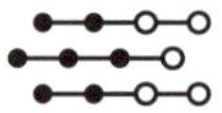

2. Linear plots that progress (or fail to) through audience participation

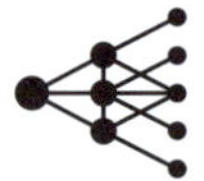

3. Plots that are assembled through audience choices as they move through branching narrative pathways

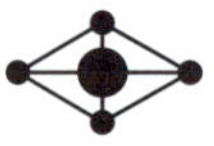

4. Narratives that emerge through audience interaction or collaborative improvisation

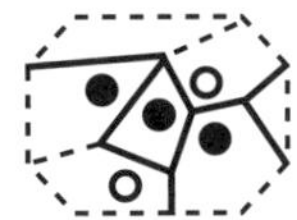

Sleep No More is, for the most part, the first kind of narrative. Disneyland largely works this way, as does Meow Wolf's *House of Eternal Return* and, for that matter, most art museums. As discussed in the previous chapter, a world is not neutral; it has an opinion about who can do what and be what, about what is good and what is bad. Such a narrative can be a narrative of being for an audience. At Disneyland, one may be playful and childish; at *Sleep No More*, one may be anonymous, moving about unnoticed like a ghost. Who can you be in your home? Your workplace? Your school? In this kind of narrative, the audience is the most important character in their own story, and the designer must design the opening of the story in such a way that it orients the audience, demonstrates to them who they are and can be. These are the rituals of orientation at a university, onboarding at a corporation, welcome at a cruise ship.

A great deal of tourism functions with this kind of narrative. Guidebooks and ratings websites and bureaus of tourism construct narratives of places with the promise that if you go there, you can be or do something entirely new. Paris is still the nineteenth-century City of Lights, San Francisco is all about sourdough and hippies, and "what happens in Vegas stays in Vegas." Tourism is a narrative collaboration between the place and the tourist, offering visitors a way of being in a world that is more or less fictional. When tourists show up in a city, armed with guidebooks and restaurant ratings and a sense of discovery, they are not unlike visitors to *Sleep No More*, armed with a general story of the place but eager to discover more for themselves.

Such narratives are not without structure. They have clear and important beginnings and endings, often phased through location or time within the experience. These are the closest a designer may come to nonlinear experiential narratives, and these are dependent on the collaboration of an audience, for whom assembling such a narrative is much of the fun.

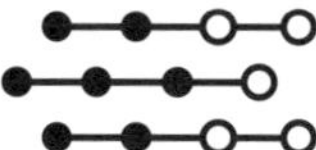

The second type of interactive narrative tends to offer the least freedom to its audience and the most design control to its authors, and it is also an ideal structure for personal and communal transformation. These are narratives that progress (or fail to) on a predetermined linear path with the participation of the audience. Jokes, magic tricks, wedding ceremonies, alternate reality games, treasure hunts, escape rooms, introductory college courses, arcade games, and most religious rituals work this way. These offer their audiences the opportunity to be a part of a narrative of becoming. Experiential aims for these may be varied, but they must be specific and well-crafted. An imperfectly told joke will fail to make the audience laugh. A flubbed magic trick will not induce wonder. A well-designed Philosophy 101 course will alter how a student sees the world. A great wedding ceremony will transform the couple not only in the eyes of the state but in the minds of the community as well.

The world's religions have long understood how such narratives may invite the believer to become a part of the stories that form the bases of those religions. *The Passover Haggadah* is a book that provides Jews with an interactive narrative meal in which they read through, eat through, sing through, and dialogue through the biblical story of Exodus, in which the ancient Jews escaped slavery in Egypt. When the event is successful, participants feel it is *their* story, that the metaphors of slavery and freedom are relevant to *their* lives. They have had an experience of the bitterness of exile when eating horseradish and speaking about the trials the biblical people suffered in the first person. Rituals such as this invite participants to enter bodily into a communal narrative. Here, the origin story of the Jewish world becomes the story of the participants, who are now the population of that world: a people and a heritage.

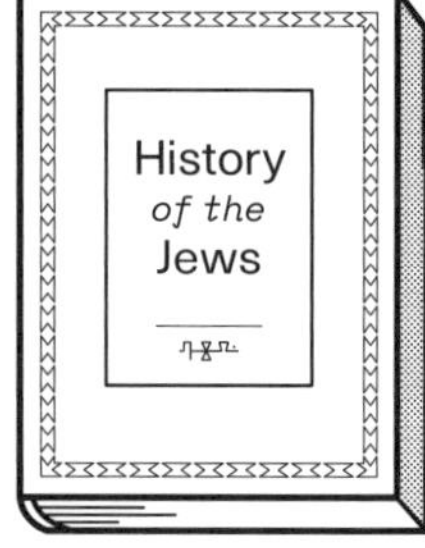

Many traditional pilgrimages, likewise, follow such a narrative structure. One walks in the footsteps of figures from religious stories, taking those stories into the body as much as into the mind. Probably the world's most important pilgrimage is the hajj, in which more than two million Muslims from around the world visit the holy sites of Mecca and Medina each year.[6] Pilgrims follow myriad paths to arrive in Mecca, but once they do, they travel a carefully prescribed route, wear clothing particular to the activity, and enact a choreography of devotion that places them kinesthetically into the stories of the Koran. The climactic moment of the pilgrimage is when pilgrims circumambulate the Kaaba, which is where Adam is supposed to have placed the tent given to him by God;[7] later they pray at Mount Ararat, where the Prophet Mohammed preached; and before returning to the Kaaba, they throw stones at towers representing the devil.[8] The journey is a metaphorical and literal walk through the key stories of Islam. It is prescribed and unalterable, and as such it invites the pilgrim to become part of a fixed, sacred narrative, and to be transformed by it.

Those who make the pilgrimage—which is one of the five pillars of Islamic faith—may have the honorific *Hajji* added to their names.[9] Name change is a common marker of the transformation offered by successful participation in such narratives: students who complete a prescribed course of study may append a BA or a PhD to their name, just as spouses may change their last names after the wedding, and politicians who take the oath of office are referred to as governor or president long after their elected term is complete. Many of these transformations are irreversible. A master's degree and a black belt remain part of the participant's identity even if their skills fade. A Shuar boy who successfully travels to the forest and demands power from the spirits who live there—the *arutam*—becomes a man in the eyes of the community and cannot be considered, thereafter, a child again.[10] These narratives are essential to worldbuilding; they affirm the value systems and histories of those worlds, often offering participants new roles within the world's population. These work best when the audience is completely given over to the narrative, their identity redefined by the story, aligning them with a new set of rights and responsibilities.

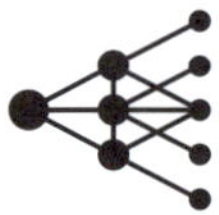

The third kind of interactive narrative is, perhaps, the one most commonly associated with the idea of interactive narrative. This is the choose-your-own-adventure structure, a favorite of book lovers and app games and early text-based computer games. In such narrative structures, the experience of choice is foregrounded, and audiences are repeatedly rewarded or punished for making right or wrong choices. There is much discovery here, as well as a sense of adventure—more finding your way through a maze than finding your way through a city. In its traditional form, such narratives may offer the illusion of a story with endless possibilities, delimited by the choices made by the reader. This illusion is painstakingly wrought, as a successfully developed story of this kind will necessitate the writing of many times more text than the reader ever encounters, even in several read- or play-throughs.

Meg Jayanth, author of the app *80 Days*, a decolonial branching narrative reinterpretation of the Jules Verne novel *Around the World in Eighty Days*, claims to have written over five hundred thousand words for her game, more than seven times as many words as in the original.

Choice architecture need not be wildly open, as in the case of Alejandro Zambra's 2014 novel *Multiple Choice* (*Facsímil* in the original Spanish), which, borrowing the form of the multiple-choice test, allows readers to choose from several options to advance the text as it develops, filling in blanks or editing the text as they go. This participatory structure remains largely linear, as does Julio Cortázar's 1963 novel *Hopscotch (Rayuela)*, which offers the reader multiple pathways through the text of the book, although once such a choice is made, the story path is set. Automated customer support numbers and SMS text interactions and chatbots usually work with branching narrative structures as well. *Here and There along the Echo*, a phone tree experience related to the video game *Kentucky Route Zero*, plays with the form, inviting people to press 3 for a list of the places people can't sleep or press 2 for help identifying something that's happening in the dark.

To see if it is still working, try calling (in the United States) +1 (270) 301-5797.

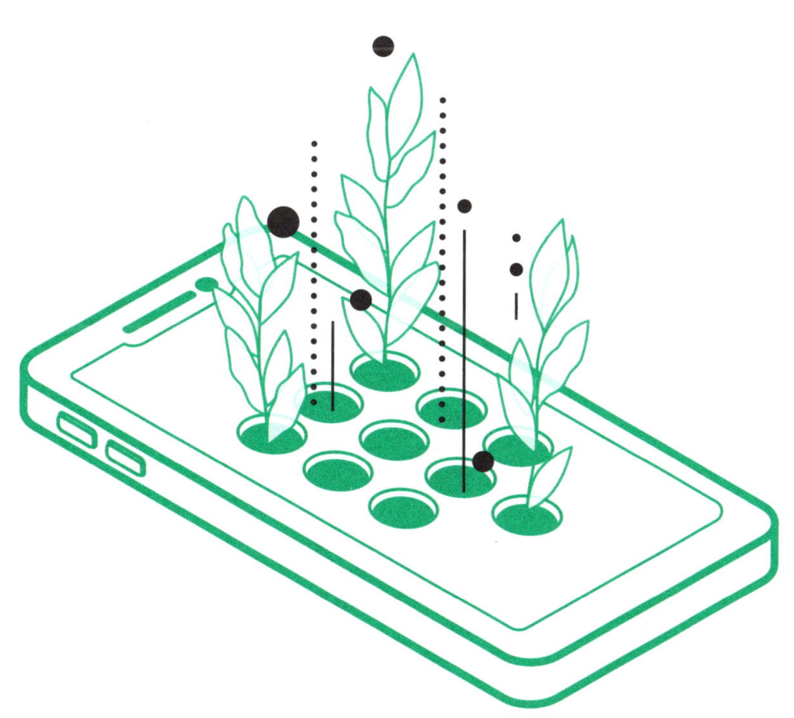

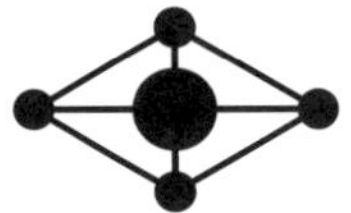

If writing choose-your-own-adventure narratives can be excessive and complex, necessitating the generation of far more narrative architecture than any one person will ever encounter, the fourth narrative form—narratives created in collaboration with an audience—might be the opposite. While a branching narrative is made to be experienced by many people, over and over again, a cocreated narrative happens only once, and only with those involved. In its purest form, this is the structure of a conversation: each participant listening to the others and presenting what they have to offer to move the conversation forward. It is improvisational, and it lives and dies depending on what each person offers and how well they listen. Participants must feel-in to one another, empathetically following and responding to what they receive from the others. This is not to say that such narratives are entirely unstructured; when one person says to another, "I'd love to talk to you about X," a structure is offered. Seductions, job interviews, and improv comedy are collaborative narrative structures that succeed or fail depending on the aptness of the underlying structure and the skill level of the participants.

This is the most interpersonal of the four types of interactive narrative. Such narratives may offer healing and insight. Psychotherapy, which is highly structured and requires years of training, is this kind of narrative, as are most forms of divination. Tarot cards, for instance, offer a symbolic and narrative system within which participants may develop a collaborative story about a person's life. The laying down of cards from a shuffled deck is a chance operation that forces the two participants to work together to make a narrative cohere. A successful reading can feel like prophesy, an unsuccessful one like quackery.

Medicine and healing may work this way as well. A simple interaction in which two people discuss one person's symptoms and together identify the problem and what to do to help is an improvisational, healing narrative. Before the collaboration, the ill person was a character in a story with an uncertain future and countless awful possibilities. The collaborative diagnosis completes the story, limiting the unknown and identifying a treatment or a path forward. The story itself is transubstantiated in the act of taking the medicine. When the story is well written, the experience can heal the patient, even if the pills they take are merely sugar. The placebo effect, that baffling phenomenon wherein a patient who takes fake medicine believing it is real will nevertheless be at least somewhat healed, is evidence of the transformative power of such narratives.

Narratives are so much more than entertainment; they are how we learn about the world, how we construct our sense of self, how we bridge the gap between ourselves and others. It is no wonder that so many feel compelled to tell their own life stories, to rewrite them and comprehend them. Jay-Z's *Decoded* is, in the end, a kind of memoir, written, as all memoirs are, in retrospect and reconsidering the people, events, and places of the past in the light of present understanding. When it came time to market the book, Jay-Z worked with the marketing firm Droga5 to physically place the entirety of the book in the locations where it happened. A plaque was installed on the Marcy Houses in Brooklyn, where Jay-Z lived. Texts appeared, also, on billboards and bus stops, wrapped around cars and on basketball backboards. There were texts on burger wrappers and in coat linings. One page was on Times Square, another at the bottom of a swimming pool.[11] This particular narrative of the place became, literally, part of the place, there to offer his fans an embodied treasure hunt to find the pieces and associate them with the nature of the place as it is today. The book then was able to interface with the countless narratives of those who lived in or visited these sites, whether or not they had read the book, a narrative intervention in their own sense of place, of home.

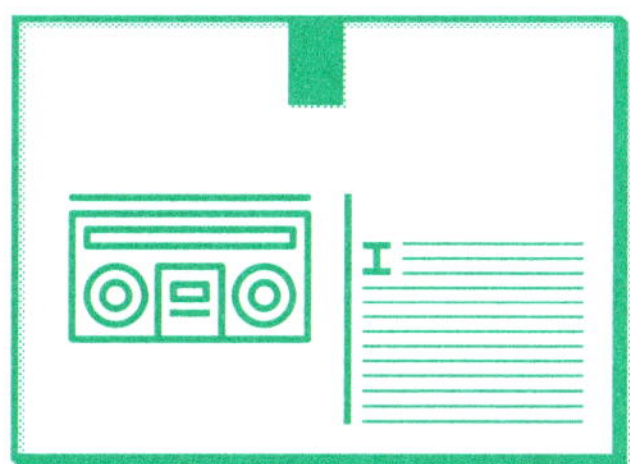

In Phase Zero of a design process, we ask what stories we are engaging with, not just because narrative is a powerful tool for affecting an audience but because it is everywhere. Just as there is no such thing as no temperature, there is no such thing as no narrative; it is a property of experience. Just because a story is about something, however, doesn't mean that the experience of that story will also be about that something. We must design with an empathetic understanding of the nexus of stories in the audience's world that rise to meet the story we have written. The experience designer must first decide what narrative experience they wish their audience to have, then consider the means of generating that experience. They may have to approach the writing in many different ways, combining narrative experiences at different ends of the spectrum. The visitor to the Jewish Museum, for instance, engages the story of Germany's Jews not only in the usual museum way—through the reading of educational texts and the contemplation of curated images, objects, and installations—but also through an embodied, metaphorical, dreamlike engagement with the themes that literally and figuratively underlie the stories communicated in the museum above.

So it is with our narratives; they layer one atop the other in unimaginable depth and complexity, one now rising to the surface, now sinking. Each narrative invokes another and is comprehended by another. The visible story affects the invisible story, and vice versa. From an experiential perspective, the creation of a narrative is always collaborative; we can no more hope to fully determine the narrative experience our audience walks away with than a parent can hope to fully determine the personality of their child. Designing effective experiential narratives does, however, mandate that the designer empathetically imagine the full life of the narrative, and with that comprehension, strive for a deeper, more holistic, possibly even a transformative experience of that narrative.

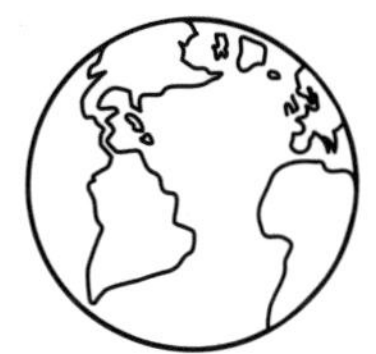

Story A:
The world

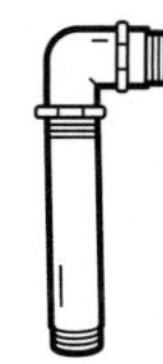

Story B:
This is not a pipe

EXPERIMENT PART C

The Invitation

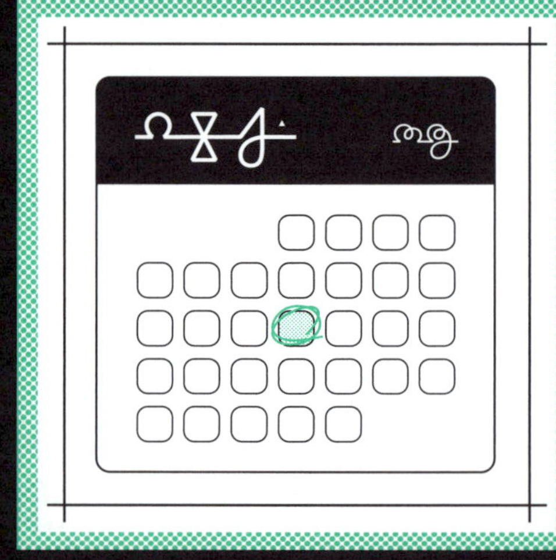

Now invite your friend for a meal. Could be dinner at your house, or a picnic, or something else. Specify time (sometime after you will have finished reading this book) and place. What is the intention of your time together? Is it just to hang out? Would you like to discuss something in particular? Will it be something more playful? Be clear, and then set some structure to support it. Ask them to wear something specific, or to bring that book they've been reading, or to bring their roller skates. Tell them what it's going to be about, or hint at it. Look to the hero image you've made for inspiration; maybe even use the image as a part of the design of the invitation.

→ While planning your invitation, consider how you will connect it to a narrative. Maybe the narrative is an ongoing story in your friendship. Maybe it is something fictional you've both encountered. Maybe the narrative is something you are making up. Your invitation should include something about this narrative. It may be: "Remember when we took that trip together last year and ended up in that one-stoplight town? . . ." Or it may be: "Once upon a time . . ." Or it may be: "So I'm reading that book you gave me about experience design, and . . ." Or it may be something else.

Before you send the invitation, recognize that you are creating the outer frame of the experience, not just an informational document.

The invitation is the beginning. It's a porous frame, and it extends in time from the moment the invitation is received until the end of the meal. How will the invitation alter things in the meantime? Make last-minute adjustments to take this into account.

CHAPTER SEVEN

Design for the Unknown

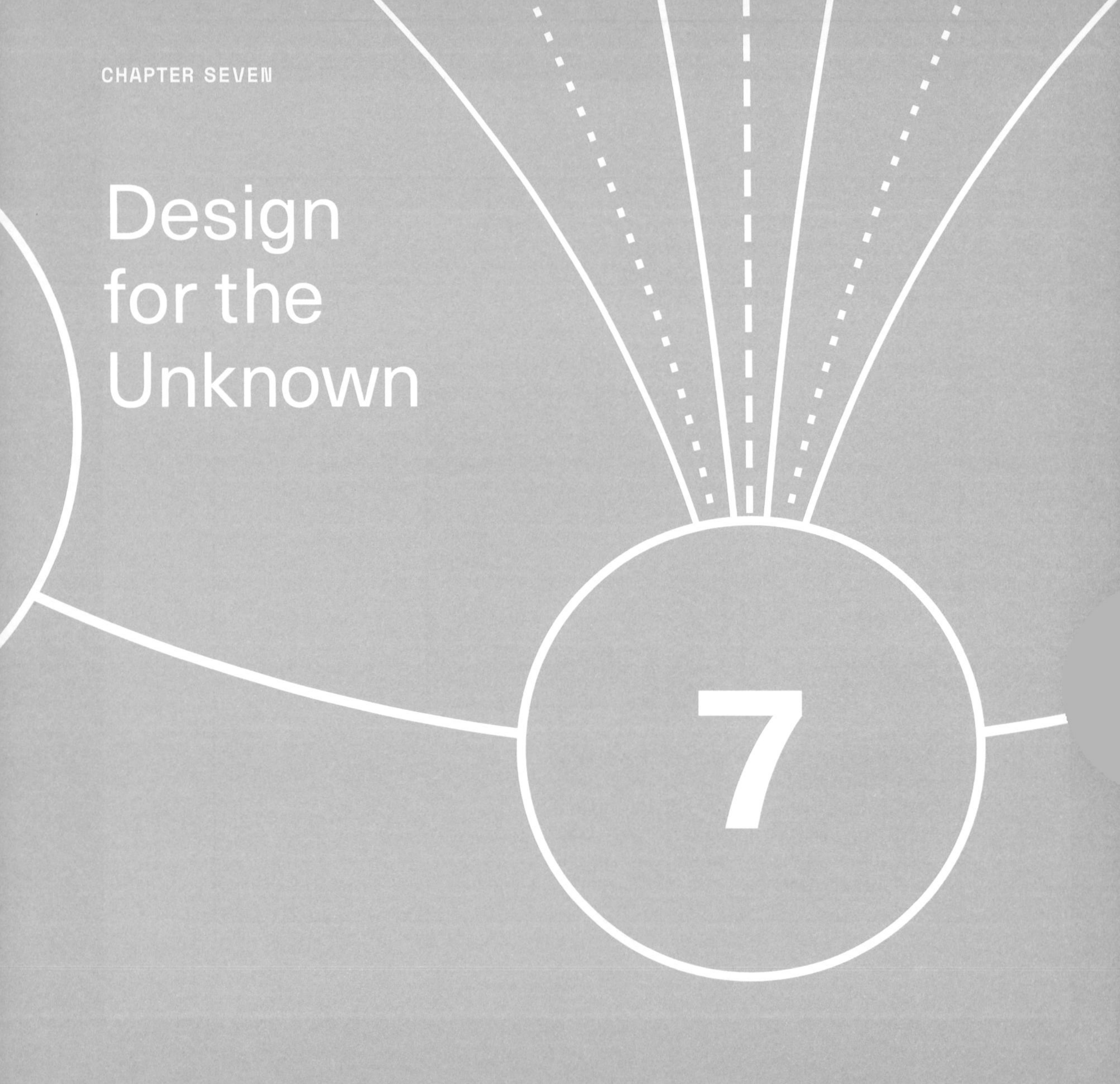

All experiences share one fundamental quality: they happen now, in the present moment. The present moment is an emergent moment; no matter how thoroughly designed an experience is, it cannot be fully known. For thing-based design, this is a bug, to be limited and controlled. For experience design, it is the feature that allows a lived moment to feel alive.

The defining quality of liveness is the unknown. You may dance the same waltz one hundred times, but if, each time, there is a sense that what is to come is even a little unknown, it will feel alive. It may be the new partner that brings the unknown, or the new pair of shoes, or your ongoing search for that state of flow. Do the same customer service job every day, with its scripted dialogue and predictable interactions, and you may find the unknown draining out of your life, even though each conversation you have is with someone you've never met.

For this sense of liveness to be truly felt, we must be open to it, curious about it, even hungry for it. In the unknown is learning, discovery, adventure, surprise, delight. One may find these things in nature, in study, and in meditation, but nothing compares to finding the unknown in other people. The unknown opens us to empathy, it keeps relationships vital, it generates culture. Even when an experience of the unknown is private, if it is meaningful, we will often hope to share it with someone we know, to unpack it together, to allow for the newness of it to affect them. We hide our gifts in wrapping paper before we hand them to our friends. We studiously avoid spoilers when we watch a movie with them. We become energized when we meet someone new, someone with, perhaps, an unusual way of dressing, a surprising set of opinions, a backstory waiting to be discovered.

How important is it for your experiences to be relational, even if just in the telling?

Try a thought experiment. A package arrives in the mail for you. You open it when no one is around and find, inside, a magical offer: you are invited to experience the most profoundly beautiful thing you have ever experienced. You will experience it alone. In your consciousness, it will last an hour, but when it is over you will be returned to the exact moment you left. Magic. The cost: whatever coins you can find around the house.

But you can never, in any way, tell anyone about the experience. You cannot write about it. You cannot share lessons you gathered from it. You cannot make art influenced by it. The same magic that stopped time for the experience makes it physically impossible for you to ever share it with others.

Would you do it?

The unknown and the relational are animating forces, a kind of divine spark. In 2021, in the depths of the COVID-19 pandemic, a nine-year-old Syrian refugee named Little Amal tried to walk into the town of Meteora in Greece. It was a town that had seen many refugees before her, and that, despite the ebbing crisis, still had strong feelings about such migrants. She, like others before her, was told she was not welcome. Like others, she had already walked a long, uncertain path from the Syrian border to this most picturesque of Greek towns. Unlike her predecessors, however, Little Amal was not human; she was the creation of UK-based Handspring: a 3.5-meter-tall wooden puppet, requiring up to four puppeteers to bring her to life. Though largely wood and fabric, Amal was, in many ways as alive as the puppeteers. Her itinerary was fixed, but what happened on her journey was not. In some places she was cheered on by supporters. She shook the pope's hand in the Vatican and was joined by a cadre of other puppets on the beach in France before being blocked by a police officer from crossing into England. When she did finally make it across, she was cheered by thousands who watched her kick a soccer ball in the Manchester United stadium. *The Walk* was an experience designed for the people Little Amal met along the way, for those who heard about her, for other refugees. It followed a set itinerary, but there was a liveness to *The Walk*, a relationality and uncertainty that were riveting to those who followed it. Her continuous encounters with the unknown helped Amal turn attention back to the plight of refugees in a way that another news story never could.[1]

To be live, to engage the relational and the unknown, is not the same as to be unstructured. Rather, the structures we design must protect relationality and make the unknown safe and rewarding. A night at *The Lightning Field* is very specifically designed, but that design prepares the visitor to take advantage of the unstructured time and the new relationships to be found there. A well-run brainstorming session employing strict timing and prescriptive rules *(no shooting down other people's ideas!)* may offer individuals the freedom to quickly find a flow state together. The tension between the need for rigorous, well-crafted design on the one hand, and the need for the relational and the unknown on the other hand, is the great challenge of experience design. Do you script every moment of every interaction? Should visitors ride on the train through scene after scene of the Small World you've created, or should they be free to wander about, to talk to the performers, maybe rebuild the exhibit in some manner of their choosing?

Throughout this book, notably when discussing worldbuilding and narratives, I have spoken both of experiences whose designs are the product of a single, clear intention, and those that happen over time as the result of the participation of larger numbers of people. These latter designs rely on relationality for their survival and their robustness. Possibly the largest collective experience design projects in the world are languages, each speaker playing a part in learning new words, engaging in new modes of communication, even occasionally inventing new expressions to see if they catch on. Did you start using the gender-neutral *they* in 2015, when it was declared the Word of the Year? What did *social distancing* mean to you back in 2018? What will you say the next time someone asks you what *experience design* means?

Much has been made of language's lack of specificity and the challenge of communicating exactly what one wishes to say. Despite the fact that native speakers of any language have more than forty thousand words at the ready, much is left to context, to interpretation, to relationality.[2] During the past two centuries, more than 450 documented languages have been invented by designers who were hoping to come up with a better or clearer or more humane approach to communication.[3] The overwhelming majority of these languages did not enter into common use by any communities. These failed for a variety of reasons, but the cases of Volapük and Esperanto are particularly instructive. In the 1880s, it seemed that the two languages, each invented by idealists who were hoping to create a universal language to bridge national divides, had promising futures. It was an exciting time, but by the end of the decade, Volapük speakers began to petition for changes to the language. They had quibbles with this or that word or bit of grammar. But the designer, who claimed to have received the idea of the language directly from God, refused. The community fractured, and many moved to Esperanto, whose adherents held annual congresses where participants would collectively add words to the language and allow it to evolve.[4] Today, Esperanto boasts more than two million speakers and learners, and the annual congresses are still held. Volapük, on the other hand, is largely forgotten.[5]

Esperanto survived because, like all living languages, it was allowed to evolve relationally to face the unknown. Such liveness is a powerful means of inviting people to deeply invest in an experience. If, as in the case of Volapük, it is not part of the design intention, it may end up destroying the whole endeavor. In 2016 San Francisco–based Nonchalance launched the Latitude Society, a project that may have been a victim of its own liveness. Part secret society, part alternate reality adventure, part collaborative worldbuilding exercise, the experience began with participants swiping an entry card and stepping off the street into a dark foyer in San Francisco's Mission District. After their eyes adjusted to the dimness, the only visible thing they found in the room was a fireplace containing not a fire but instead a wooden slide. The invitation was now clear: step in, and then spiral down the slide to the society's clubhouse, a series of intimate rooms and tunnels to walk and crawl and read through until the participants were sent out into the city streets to unravel the mystery of the society and to become a part of its community. The experience would continue for months after this, as community members were gathered into events and adventures, into a fictional world housed online, throughout the Bay Area, and in the clubhouse.

The society's most brilliant design, however, was its entry threshold. This is not the door between the streets of the Mission District and the dark foyer, but the way the entry card was offered. By design, members were to give such cards to people whom they respected or appreciated in some way, and, as they handed them the card, they were to describe how and why they respected the person. Jeff Hull, the project's creator, has said that, in any such design, "one must have a strong gate."[6] Despite the drama of the entry foyer, it was, in fact, this well-considered invitation that provided the strong gate, and that established the experience as a community-based design rooted in respect and relationality.

In spite of the work of many incredibly talented artists and designers, as well as a devoted audience, the Latitude Society

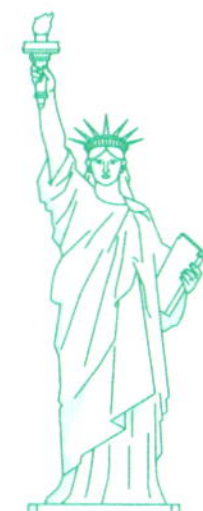
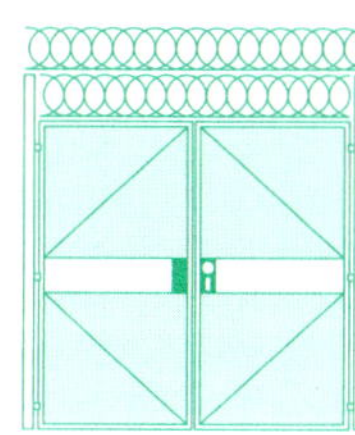
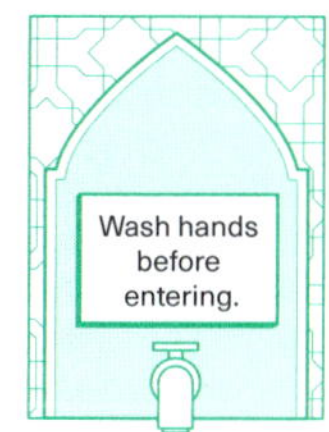

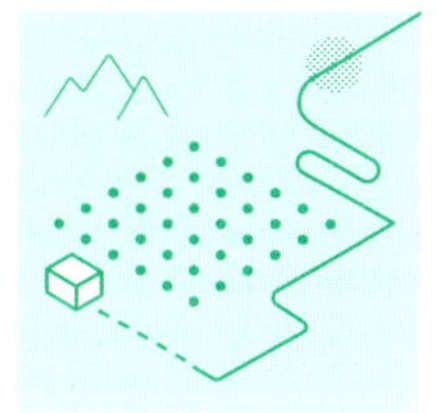
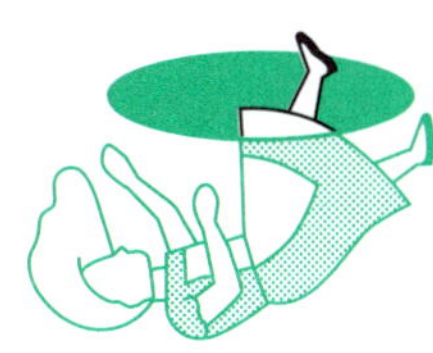

lasted less than a year. The project came to a halt in mid-2015 when Hull announced a monthly membership fee and paywall blocking certain community engagements. By this point, users had turned the Latitude Society into a living world, retelling its origin myth, evolving its language, expanding its community, and creating events.[7] Although a great deal of resources and design attention had been poured into the creation of the Latitude Society by its designers, its success was largely a result of the way the participants made it into a living world. The sudden announcement of the paywall restructured what was a communal project into a product, invalidating the relationality that was the source of its success. "This is not a religion," said Hull, "this is an entertainment." But participants saw it differently, and the project came crashing to a halt.[8]

Design is, in many ways, about the application and refinement of systems. The rule of thirds for image composition has been around for two hundred years.[9] Human-centered design has its double-diamond process of defining problems and finding solutions, guiding designers through divergent and convergent thinking. Game designers break their audiences down into user types employing systems such as Bartle's taxonomy of player types, which separates individuals into killers, socializers, achievers, and explorers and then encourages them to design accordingly. To avoid potentially fatal mistakes, emergency room workers use countless predesigned protocols to govern patient interactions.[10]

We build these systems because we need to build these systems. Our attention is inconstant, our blindness to our own biases pervasive, our ability to see the big picture in the forest of details unreliable. Systems make us more efficient and more consistent. A system can encode our best learnings into practice and allow for one individual to act on the basis of understandings of another. In *The Checklist Manifesto*, Atul Gawande suggests that checklists, the most basic of systems, can "defend anyone, even the experienced, against failure."[11]

Systems are the great force multiplier of our intelligence, but systems, fundamentally, are not alive; they lack presence. Systems may structure relationships and control for the unknown, but they cannot love the unknown. You can build a system to control for bias within an organization, but empathy is the work of the individual. You can repair the communication problems in a marriage using cognitive behavioral therapy techniques, but the creation of a meaningful bond demands a long, interpersonal search and openness to change. You can script a piece of interactive theater, but if the performer does not really listen after asking an audience member a question, that person will feel like they are a cog in a machine instead of a participant.

Designing for the relational and the unknown requires the designer not just to leave empty spaces in a design but to rely on the unknown and collaborate with it. Doing so demands patience, personal work, a willingness to break habit, courage, and careful crafting of one's own experience of making. To be able to embrace the unknown and the relational in design requires the same skills as doing so in life.

When the expected gives way to the unknown, we turn to each other. We are a social species, evolved to look to one another for support in the face of risk, and to share with each other whatever wonderful things we find. Artists such as John Cage liked to work with the way this fact sculpts our attention, crafting his compositions at the interface between the designed and chance. His 1952 piece *4′33″* looked like an ordinary composition but lacked any notes. At a performance of the piece, musicians would set up onstage and audience members would sit in their seats, and, at the start of the piece, no music would be played. This would continue for exactly four minutes and thirty-three seconds, during which time the ambient sounds in the concert hall would become evident; a cough or the scratching of a knee or a door closing somewhere would become the focus of attention, as would each audience member's unease about what to do or think. The composition was a frame, within which the unknown was elevated.[12] The discomfort audience members felt as they didn't know how to respond was relational. Someone might clear their throat uncomfortably, glancing at their neighbor to see if they were feeling a similar impatience. The piece, with its revelatory discomfort, completely transformed the experience of going to a concert; it was no longer an experience of listening to a piece of music but a framed encounter with the remarkable fact of humans in a space together, with their thoughts, their unpredictable noises, their uneasy attentiveness to each other, at least for four minutes and thirty-three seconds.

This page intentionally left blank.

This experience
intentionally
left unknown. . . .

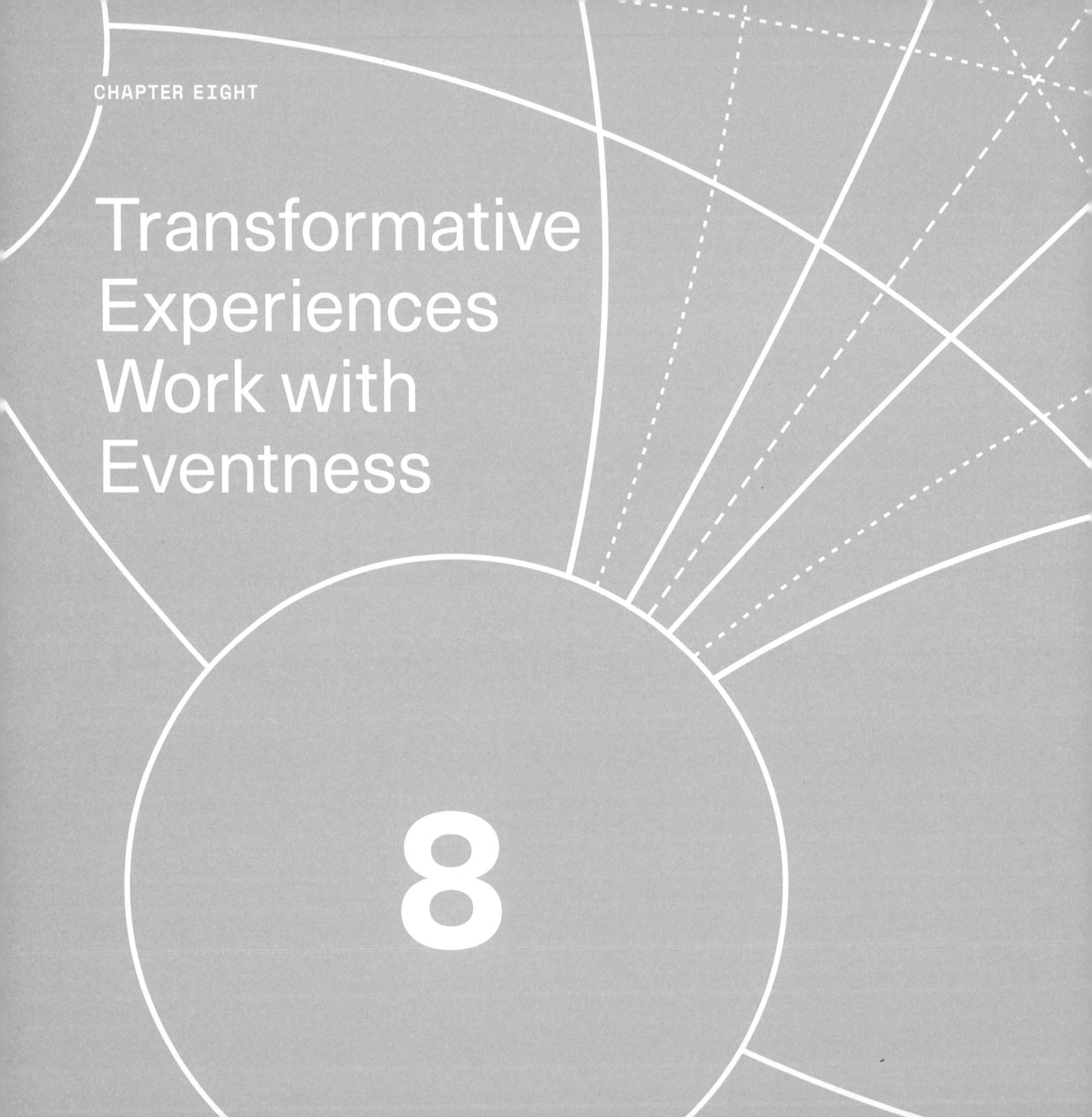

CHAPTER EIGHT

Transformative Experiences Work with Eventness

8

New Year's Eve. You are at a gathering with friends. You've eaten well, had a bit to drink, and are up past your bedtime, all of which charges your body with a bit of a buzz. Through the evening, the conversation has been about plans for the coming year, resolutions, who is going to lose weight or start meditating. The ball slowly drops. The countdown begins and everyone joins in vocally, chanting to mark the moment of the New Year exactly together, at which time champagne will be popped and kisses and hugs will be exchanged, a "Happy New Year!" resounding through the house. At 12:01 it is already over. You are in the New Year. Someone says, "I can't believe it's 202X already," and you laugh in agreement. Maybe this year can be better. Maybe you can enter it on a wave of optimism, your better luck complemented by your firmer resolve, your renewed sense of who you could be in this New Year.

The new page.

→

After you turn
this page, it
will never be
new again.

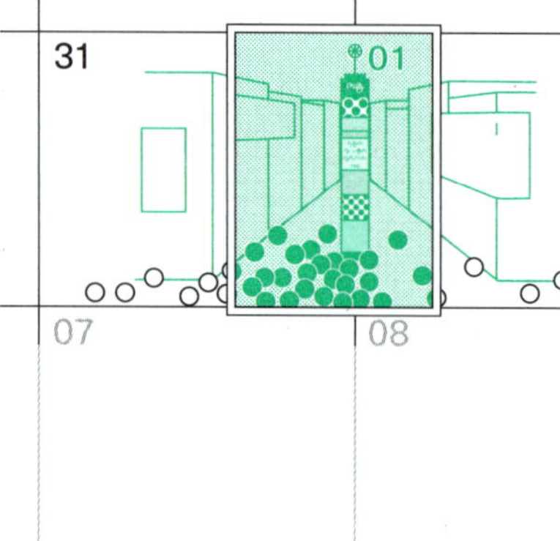

Or perhaps, if you are in Denmark, you leap off a chair into the New Year. Or if you are Japanese, you visit a temple to trade in your old lucky charms for new ones.[1] Or if you are Jewish, you cap a week of New Year's celebration with a day of fasting and atoning for your sins, to begin again with a clear conscience.

New Year's is an *event*. Celebrated, albeit differently and at different times of the year, by nearly everybody around the planet, it tends to be one of the most effective annual events because its main quality is that it transforms time itself. This was 2023, and now it is 2024. This was a tired year, full of bad news and personal failings, and now it is a clean slate, a new beginning. We travel to parties or public gatherings, or we transform our own homes for New Year's. Unlike a TV series, a New Year's can never be paused or repeated. Like a wedding, which does not legally require scores of watchers to make it effective, the next year will come whether we gather or not. But it is the communal nature of the event that makes it possible for this to be a new beginning, a time when we might become someone different. Everybody in your world knows that this event is a time of change. New Year's, when well designed, contains all the qualities of *eventness*.

Events matter because events are when change happens. Events are psychologically, physically, or ontologically immersive experiences that exist in particular times and places, are supported by architecture and aesthetics, and are generated in the space between us. Events happen within worlds, and they may at once maintain the integrity of those worlds and change anything in them, from their physics to their population to their social rules. Events have no pause button. Events are clearly delineated by physical, social, and temporal frames.

While the idea of eventness doesn't have a long history of application to design, the Russian philosopher Mikhail Bakhtin formulated the idea more abstractly, suggesting that an event is irreducible and unrepeatable, tied to the embodied place and context of the person experiencing it.[2]

An earthquake is an event. The moon landing was an event. The storming of the Bastille was an event. Crossing the Edmund Pettus Bridge in Selma in 1965 was an event. Your birthday is an event. Game night is an event. A birth or death in the family is an event. A Live Action Role Play (LARP) is an event. The first day of school is an event. Thanksgiving dinner is an event. A coming-of-age ceremony is an event. The Olympics is an event. Or each of these can be, if designed right.

Some of these events are planned, scheduled events, others are unplanned, but each, for those of whom it is full of *eventness*, is a time and place of change, clearly distinct from the time and place outside its frame. An earthquake is an event, but the long cleanup afterward, with its uncertain timeline and outcomes, its ebbs and flows of process, is the new status quo resulting from that event. The civil rights march across the Edmund Pettus Bridge was an event, but the ongoing struggle for civil rights was the rest of life that was altered by that event. A coming-of-age ceremony is an event, but the adulthood that follows the ceremony is the rest of life. Some events, like a LARP, do not necessarily change the life of the participant permanently, but they do allow the world and the participant to live a different life for a time. Thanksgiving dinner may be such an event, allowing participants to be, for an evening, thankful and embedded in community. Unplanned events tend to benefit from surprise and urgency, but well-designed events share this sense of emergence, of newness.

The life of an individual or a community may be broken up into ordinary time and extraordinary time, or what the philosopher Mircea Eliade calls the sacred and the profane.[3] During extraordinary time, new foundations are laid, the structures of self and community are changed, and time flows differently. During ordinary time, people and communities build on and respond to what was established in extraordinary time. Events happen in extraordinary time; the rest of life is ordinary time. An event cannot last forever, and ordinariness must be punctuated by events. Drawing the proper frame around the event is essential; the lecture that goes on for too long becomes an endurance test. Ordinary time and extraordinary time complement each other, and we need both for psychological and communal survival.

The structure of the hero's journey encodes this relationship between ordinary time and extraordinary time at its core. Although

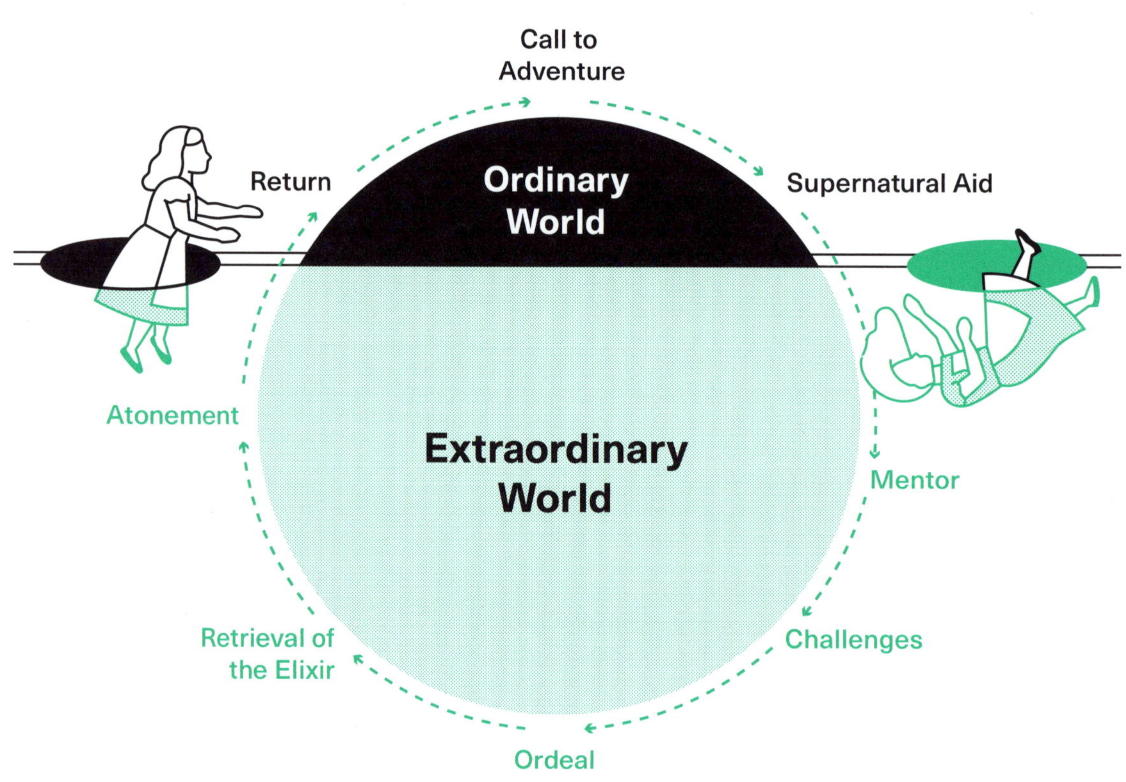
Call to
Adventure
Return
Ordinary
World
Supernatural Aid
Atonement
Extraordinary
World
Mentor
Retrieval of
the Elixir
Challenges
Ordeal

the inciting event—Alice going down the rabbit hole, say, or Lucy crossing through the wardrobe into Narnia—is the most memorable part of the beginning, these stories usually start by establishing the ordinary world. Alice is sitting by the river, watching her sister reading a dull book, and Lucy and her siblings have been sent to a country house to avoid the bombing raids of World War II. The contrast between the ordinary world and the extraordinary world is essential, as it explains how the hero understands and is challenged by the extraordinary world. At the end of her journey, the hero returns home transformed, having passed from the ordinary world to the extraordinary world and back, ready now to transform the community from which she came.

"Large sudden events did that; they changed the way time passed. Not technically, maybe, but as a measure of how he and Bobbi were to each other, and were to themselves."

James S. R. Corey, *Persepolis Rising*

Five Aspects of Eventness

The transformative power of an event for an individual or a community depends on its *eventness*, which has five aspects.

Structuring of Time

Before anything else, an event must be appropriately structured within a time frame. For regular events, these are planned and culturally standardized. A meeting is thirty minutes to two hours. A religious service is one to three hours. A party is two to three hours. An American wedding, with its related events, takes place over a weekend. A retreat is two to ten days. Anything more or less than what is expected will stretch or shrink the event and eventually break it or turn it into something new. An audience's attention is structured around expected norms of event times, as is their capacity to inhabit a different way of being. If the party lasts twenty minutes, it's hard to switch out of your everyday mindset and actually have fun, and if the party lasts all week, it might be a bender.

Time within the event must be well structured for participants to be able to become fully part of the event. Well-defined entry and exit thresholds can bring participants fully into the experience, and a considered staging of activities must account for the way participant states build on one another. This does not mean that an event must be scheduled down to the minute, or even that all elements of an event must occur in exactly the same order for everyone. A conference, for instance, may be a composition of free-roaming time to visit booths and scheduled panels with evolving themes, bracketed by opening and closing talks that bring everyone together. An immersive theater piece may begin with a time of exploration during which each audience member follows their own path as they learn about the world, then move on a schedule through narrative moments. The conference will be punctuated by lunch and dinner breaks, the immersive theater show, perhaps, by musical interludes or moments of spectacle.

Events usually have a focus moment. This is the wedding vow, the New Year's Eve ball drop, the toss of the graduation cap. The structure of an event curates our experience of time, and these focus moments, which tend to be brief, will often see time stretching out. The ten seconds before midnight on New Year's Eve may be experienced as far longer than the hour preceding it. Research has shown that we remember shorter experiences more than we do longer ones, which explains why these focus moments tend to be such a small part of the whole event, and why events are so memorable, though they make up a tiny proportion of the time of our lives.[4]

Specification of Place

Either participants must leave the place of their ordinary lives or the place of their ordinary lives must be reframed. It is perfectly possible to pray, or study history, or dance at home, but for such activities to be events, we must head out to the temple, or the classroom, or the dance hall. A solar eclipse in your hometown changes the place where you live, at least temporarily. A port building unexpectedly exploding in Beirut completely transforms the world of the city. On Halloween, jack-o'-lanterns and other decorations convert a residential street into a landscape for the hunting of tasty treasures by costumed young people.

Many places are purposely built for specific events. This is a revival tent or a county fair or, in the case of Burning Man, an entire temporary city. We must clearly cross a physical and temporal threshold into the frame of the event. The greater the sense that the place is both specific to the event and extraordinary, the greater the *eventness*.

Event: Whirling at Jerrahi (Whirling) Dervish Lodge

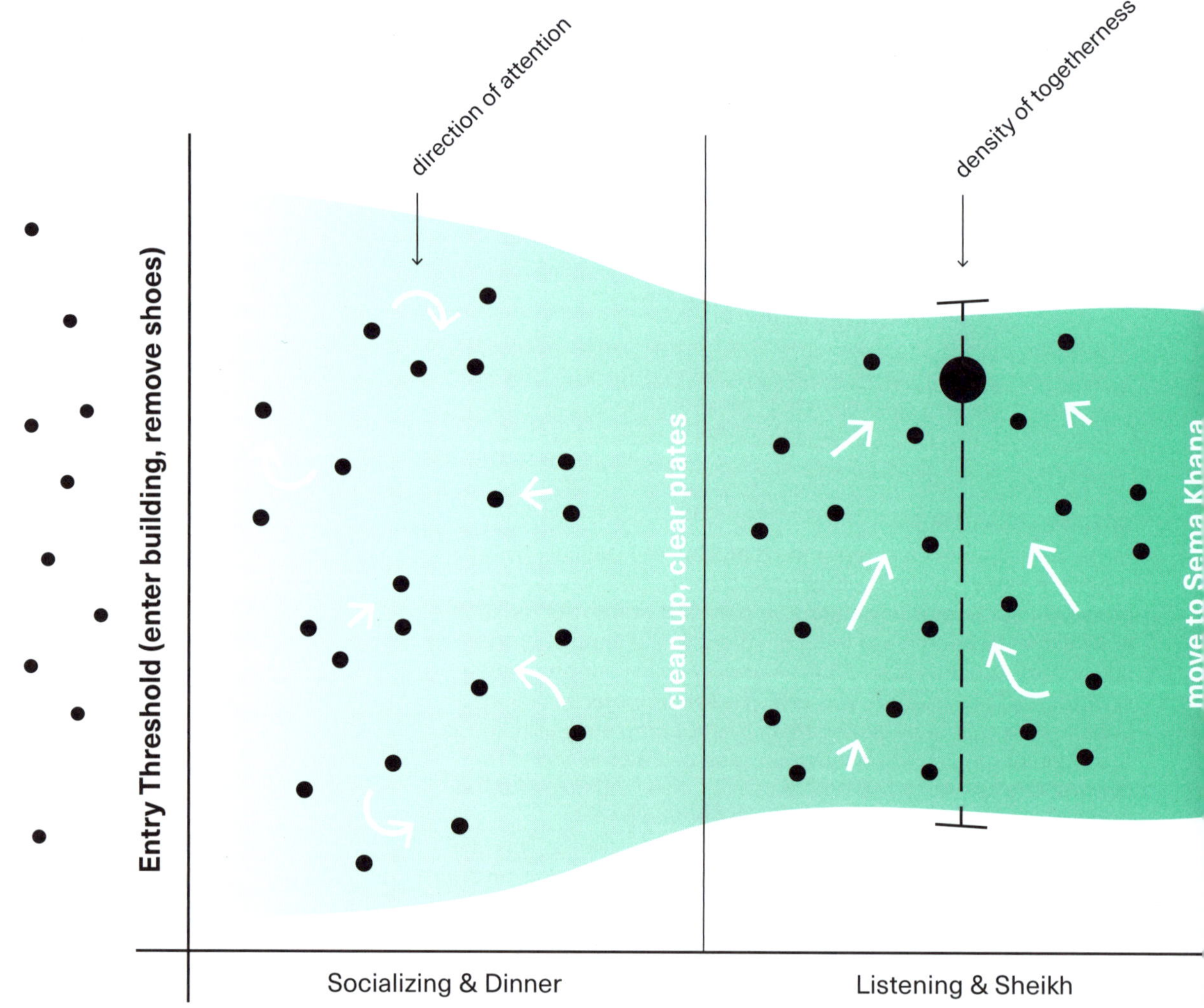

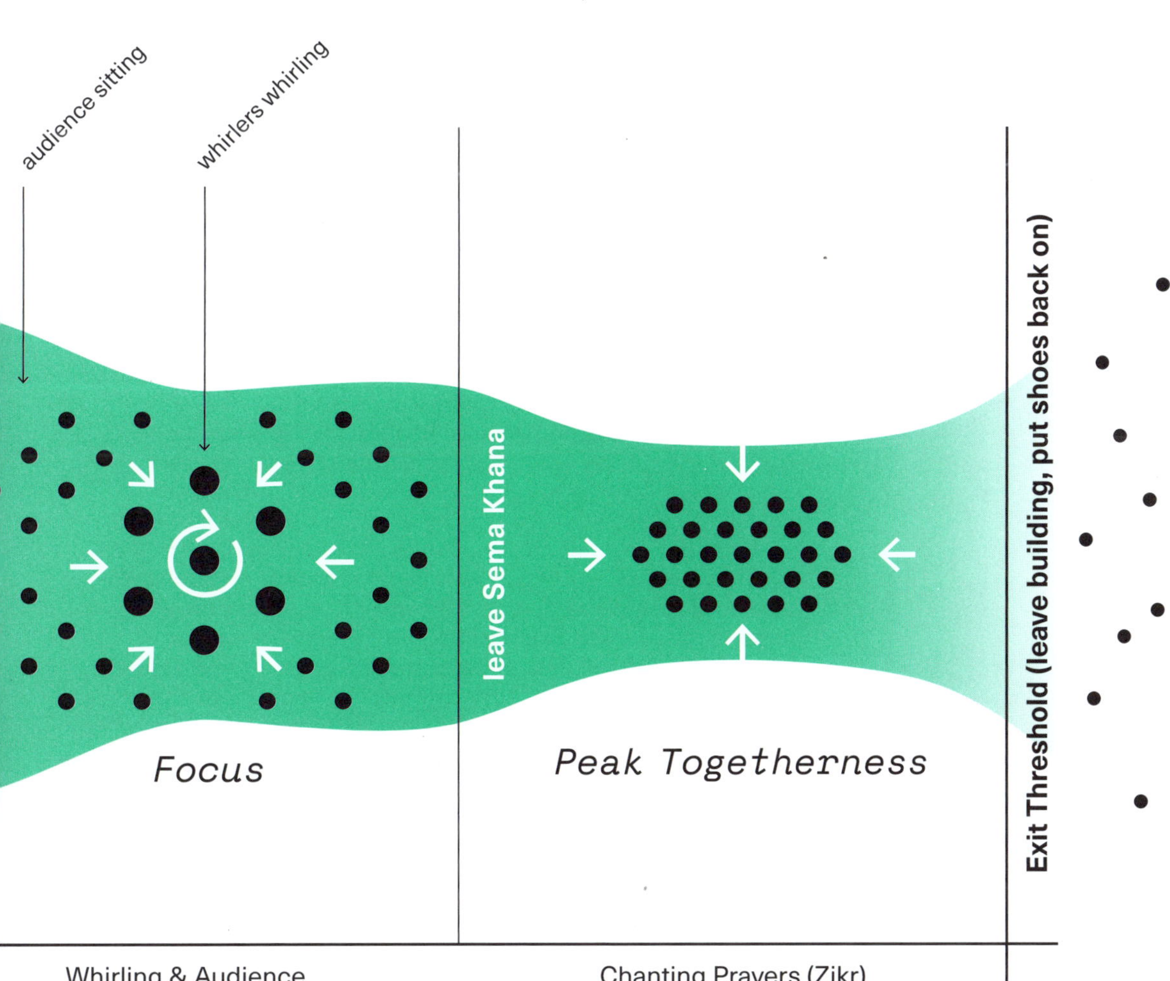
audience sitting
whirlers whirling
leave Sema Khana
Exit Threshold (leave building, put shoes back on)
Focus
Peak Togetherness
Whirling & Audience
Chanting Prayers (Zikr)

Physical Engagement

Every event has its own type of physical engagement, but it is both the appropriateness of the physicality and the clarity with which it differentiates the event from everyday life that make it eventful. We dance at celebrations and stand quietly at funerals. We sit attentively at lectures and walk until our legs get tired at a march. The entry and exit thresholds of events are denoted by physical engagements. You wash your hands before entering the mosque. You stand for the national anthem before the beginning of the football game. You remove your coat and embrace the host at the dinner party. The place determines much of the physical engagement. You drive through the desert to get to Burning Man, pull just the right book off the bookshelf to enter the secret speakeasy, run magically through the wall to get the train to Hogwarts.

Or, if you wish to choose a different branch of the narrative, you take a knee.

The temporal choreography of an event frequently corresponds to a physical choreography. Going to a punk music show may begin with standing and waiting, lead to listening when the band starts playing, climax with the physical intensity of bodies thrown against each other in the mosh pit, and end with exhausted postshow hanging out. An evening of worship at a Jerrahi Dervish lodge begins with relaxed socialization, followed by dinner, which is followed by conversation with the sheikh. After this, the dervishes ascend the stairs to the Sema Khana, where the whirlers perform the whirling dance of devotion. Then, after a break, all engage in a zikr, a chanting prayer session in which all devotees chant as one in a crescendo and decrescendo of breath and sound. The diagram of this physicality moves from relaxation to collective eating, to attentiveness, to synchronized choreography. The attention of dervishes on such an evening is increasingly more aligned, beginning with small socialization groups and ending with an experience of the whole group as a single body. This progression is, itself, a diagram of what it would be to attain oneness with the divine.

Maintenance or Transformation of a World

The primary function of many events, as well as nearly all holidays, is the maintenance of a world. A Jew who fasts for Yom Kippur, a Muslim who circles the Kaaba in Mecca, or a Catholic who takes communion on Easter may all find the practice personally transformative, but participation in the practice also serves to reaffirm the structure of the believer's world, connecting the present moment with the world's origins. The eventfulness of a holiday may be measured by how important people feel it is in the maintenance of their world. In most worlds, New Year's is pretty important, as it structures the year. Graduation day valorizes the activity of study, demonstrating to all in the community that it is transformative. But can you say, offhand, when Arbor Day is? Holidays that no longer do the job of transformation or maintenance tend to fade into the shadows of our calendars, offering at best an extra day off from work or a deal at a used car lot. Like graduations, coming-of-age ceremonies—such as a bat mitzvah or a Shuar boy's journey to encounter the spirits who live in the rainforest—are transformative for the individual but also serve to reaffirm, for all present, the structure of the world in which they happen.

On Election Day, voters feel that they are both maintaining and transforming a world, and get-out-the-vote drives generally emphasize both activities. We all have to vote to maintain a functioning democracy, they say, and they also say that if you wish to see things change, you need to vote. The fact that active voters are not dissuaded by the statistical insignificance of their single vote speaks to the role that both maintenance and transformation play in the event.

Unexpected or unscheduled events are more likely to be transformative—a death or a birth in a family, for instance, or a family member's being arrested. Nobel Prize winners and their families speak of how everything changed for them when they received the "Magic Phone Call."[5] The call changes the world—for the family, for the artistic or scientific communities of which they are a part—even though the financial benefits don't accrue until much later. The call also maintains the world for the Nobel Institute and those connected to it.

Event	World	Entry Threshold
New Year's Eve at Times Square	New York City	Arrival at Times Square
Thanksgiving	U. S. secular culture	Gathering at dinner location
9/11 (2001) for those not physically present at the event	United States / Western world	Hearing the news
Amritsar Massacre (1911) for those not physically present at the event	India/British Empire	Soldiers surrounding the protest
University Class onsite	University	Walking into the room
University Class online	University	Clicking the link
Bar mitzvah	Jewish community	Entering the synagogue
Surprise birthday party	Friends and family	Shouting "Surprise!"
Hockey game	Fans of the teams	National Anthem
Graduation	The university community	The first long speech
Voting (in person)	The country	Walking into the voting location

Physicality	Focus	Transformation / Affirmation
Standing in the freezing cold with a huge crowd	Ball drop	New Year (transformation)
Comfort of a warm meal in company	Meal	A community rooted in gratitude (affirmation)
TV/Phone Calls	Towers falling	Fear/patriotism/war footing (transformation)
Reading about violence in newspapers; experienced as a story	Massacre	British Empire is perceived, internally/externally, as oppressors (transformation)
Attentiveness, walking, sitting, taking notes, interacting	Lesson	Learning (transformation)
Sitting, clicking	Lesson	Learning (transformation)
Sitting, singing, listening	The young person's first time leading the congregation	Adulthood in the eyes of the community (transformation)
Shouting "Surprise," talking, eating, playing games	Hearing "Surprise!" and also blowing out the candles	Growing one year older (transformation)
Sitting, standing, eating, cheering	The game-winning shot	Community (affirmation)
Sitting, walking, listening	Receiving a diploma	Becoming a graduate, getting initials added to name; validation of the academic mission (transformation, affirmation)
Waiting, walking, filling out a form	Inserting your ballot into the machine	Selecting new leaders; validating the democratic project (transformation, affirmation)

Participation in Communal Narrative

All New Year's celebrations invite participants to join in telling the grand communal narrative of time and, specifically, of the year having suddenly changed. A typical secular European or American New Year's also involves groups of people telling the story of what the past year was and what we imagine the next year will be. A Chinese New Year's celebration includes in that telling an orientation of all participants within the narratives of the Chinese Zodiac. When the Nobel Prize call is made, it connects to a narrative of scientific (or social action or literary) development for the individual and the community of which they are a part. The call elevates their work over that of other competitors, affecting each community's understanding of itself. The event later becomes a turning point in the longer narrative of that field or of that community.

Communal narratives and histories are largely assembled from events, and these are events in which the participants feel that they are witnessing or engaged in a larger narrative. At a wedding, at a protest rally, at the opening night of a new show, the narratives of what the primary participants—the couple, the speakers, the performers—are involved in intersect with the narratives of the witnesses. This point of intersection is when the psychological and ontological immersion happens. You can feel it. If all the wedding guests care about the couple's union, the eventfulness is tangible. If what the speaker at the rally says feels tired or off point, if it does not give witnesses to the sense that what is being said will change things, you can feel the eventfulness draining from the room.

The coronavirus pandemic, which officially began in March 2020, revealed in previously unimaginable ways what eventness is, why we need it, and what we will do to find it.

The beginning of the pandemic was full of eventness, as the ordinary suddenly became extraordinary. Travel stopped, schools and shops and workplaces closed, homes became the focal points of all activity, and people began to wear gloves outside and wash their groceries before putting them away. Many became ill and many died, though not nearly so many as would die over the following years. The world was transformed; each person's individual narrative collided with the collective experience of the pandemic. Homes became schools and workplaces and quarantine zones. Social distancing and a fear of miasmic air and toxic environments restructured our physical engagement with our environment.

All this change had, at first, an eventful quality, heightening attentiveness to communal relationships and reordering the personal and professional lives of individuals. But events that go on for too long can no longer be events. Experientially, the event ended, but the world was changed; places of public gathering were closed, private gatherings were discouraged, and the social activity that was not shut down was moved largely online. Those who did not get sick learned how to live with the pandemic, which is to say that the pandemic was no longer an event, no longer extraordinary. Not only did the event of the pandemic come to an end, experientially speaking, but the ongoing health crisis sucked the eventness out of much of the rest of life as well. Classes, funerals, conferences, religious services, performances, exercise, Thanksgiving dinner, graduation ceremonies, political activity, and more were moved online, obliterating the specification of place and flattening the robust physical engagement of these events down to clicking and posing, perhaps to changing a virtual background.

The financial and health effects of the pandemic hit many people very hard, but the social isolation and lack of eventness hit far more still, with devastating effects. Mental health challenges rolled across the population; starting in May 2020, teen suicide attempts in the United States jumped to a staggering 50 percent above prepandemic levels.[6] Despite the conveniences and cost savings of online education, which U.S. higher education was aggressively innovating, college enrollment plummeted in fall of both 2020 and 2021.[7] The Tokyo 2020 Summer Olympics (held in 2021), which saw athletes competing against a backdrop of empty seats, was the least-watched Olympics in history, even though more viewers, arguably, were at home near their televisions. Drained of eventfulness, these activities were drained of their meaning.[8]

In the midst of all this, George Floyd, an unarmed African American man, was slowly choked to death by a police officer, Derek Chauvin, as onlookers watched and filmed. The killing was not unique; the history of police violence against unarmed African Americans goes back centuries. In recent decades, however, these killings have increasingly been captured in cellphone videos and disseminated on the internet, bringing the names of victims such as Eric Garner and Tamir Rice into the public consciousness. But George Floyd's death, witnessed by millions around the world, sparked protests that not only defied bans on public gathering and participants' own fear of contagion, but became, when taken together, the largest worldwide protest in history.[9] In a time when other modes of collective response had been drained of their eventness, the mass protest transformed the public square back into a site of gathering. It saw participants risk contagion and counterprotestor violence to become part of a population and mark an inflection point in the history of civil rights.

We may have powerful experiences on our own, but they lack much of the power of eventness if they do not connect us to others. Events are vital to the existence of both the individual and the collective. In their role in both affirming and transforming individuals and communities, they keep worlds from falling apart. A community with no events in time just becomes theoretical. A life with no events may not easily change without great personal effort. Events within small communities—a family, say, or a friend group—need not be large. Going out to the movies or taking a trip together can be an event. For large communities, events must be larger, especially if they are to be transformative. The effectiveness of an event, however, is a matter not so much of the size, of the level of spectacle, or even of the number of participants, but of how effectively the elements of eventness are composed to align the experience of the individual with the needs of the community.

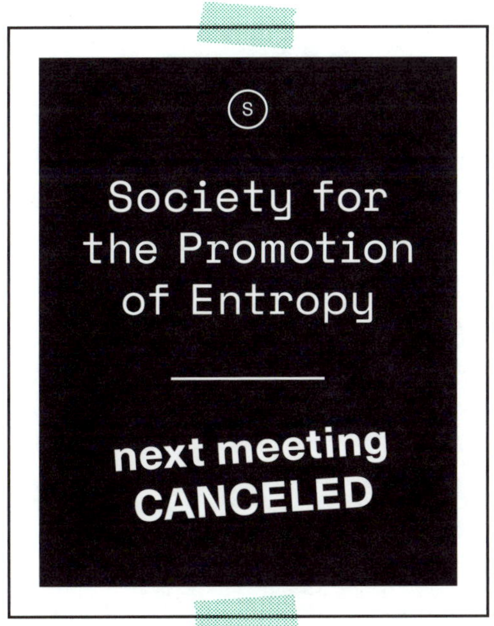

CHAPTER NINE

Use Diagrams

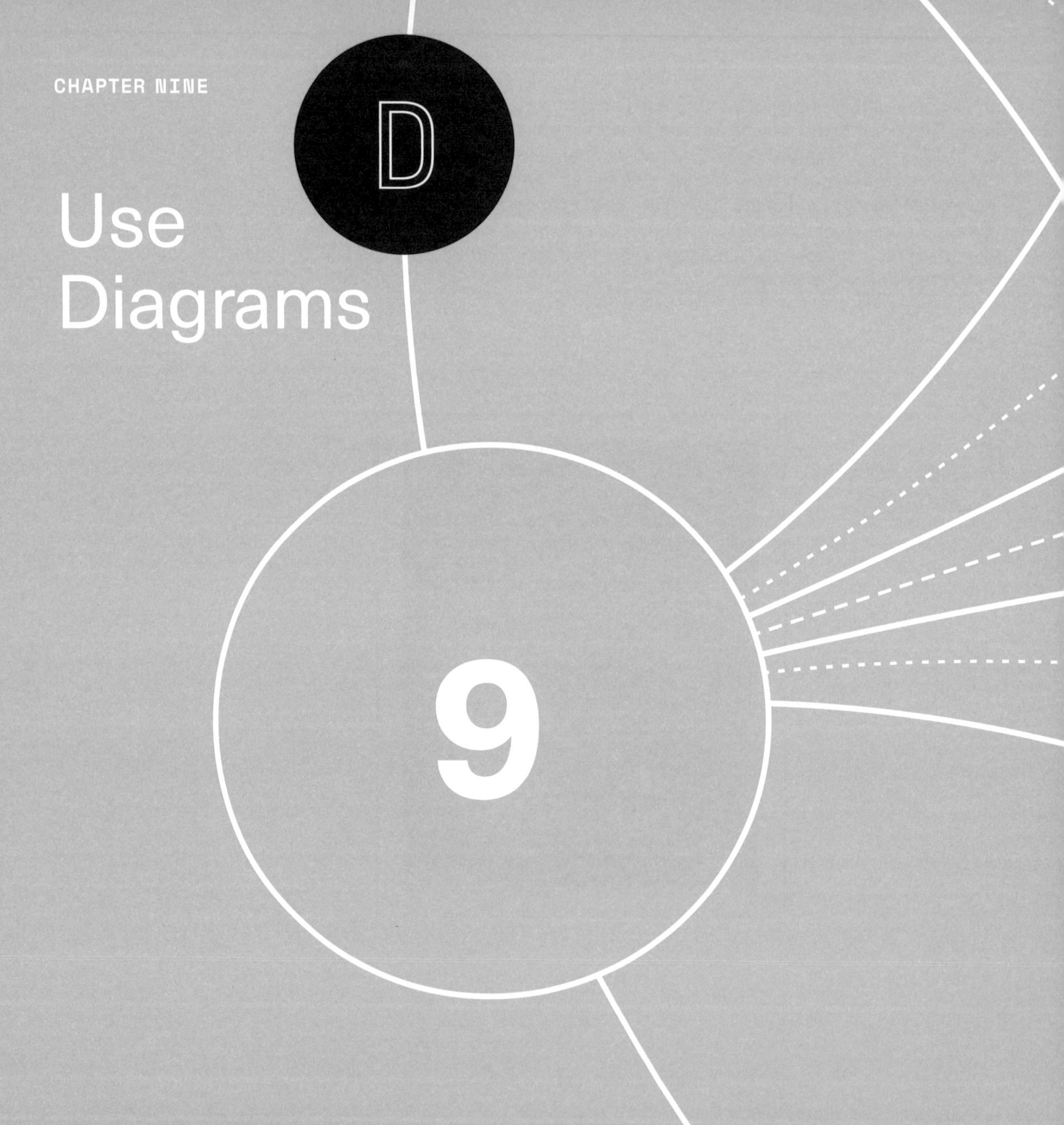

If we are to shift our aim from designing things to designing experiences, old forms of notation will no longer be sufficient. Scripts, floor plans, recipes, schedules: these are all object-oriented notational systems, and they are essential in the development of the objects used in the design of an experience. But to design the experience itself, we must use *diagrams*.

Just as the nature of a built world determines who one may be and what one may do, so the nature of a compositional system determines what a design may be and what experience it may create. If you compose a film using scriptwriting software, your film will be focused on the combination of dialogue and stage direction. If you compose that film shot-by-shot using a storyboard notebook, your film will be focused on the imagery. Designing a building based on floor plans will prioritize entrances and exits and square footages, while designing a building based on watercolor perspectives will emphasize views and finishes and affective qualities.

A traditional musical score drives the musicians note by note from opening to closing, maintaining specific tempos and timing performances exactly. The limited language of a traditional score allows for an incredible range of possibilities, but it doesn't, for instance, tend to encourage performers to improvise, interpret, or take breaks of unspecified lengths on their own.

Consider, by contrast, this score by Travis Weller. ⟶

While the score does specify some notes, it is focused largely on structuring how the musicians will relate to one another and how they will improvise. Weller's aim was to generate not so much a particular melody but a particular creative experience for the performers. Hence the unusual form.

Travis Weller, *Long Distance Duo*, 2017.

Long Distance Duo

for Abe and Dare
from Leanne and Travis

Duration: 8-10 min

I. Apart ~ ad libitum

II. Together ~ harmonics

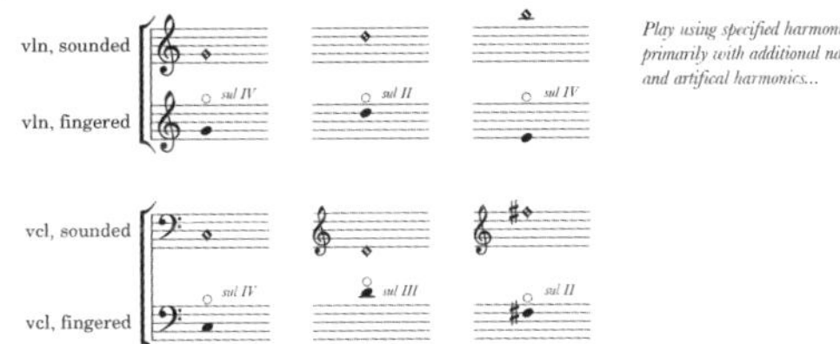

Play using specified harmonics primarily with additional natural and artifical harmonics...

III. Apart

IV. Together ~ rhythmic

With a general tonal guide from previous section (III) begin to play with a unified tempo, but a contrasting meter. Simple progressions of three-six pitches. Always changing and shifting in relation to one another...

V. Apart

VI. Together ~ unison

Very steady. Blend into a single sound. Just loud enough for ideal resonance. Cellist may use natural harmonic if desired.

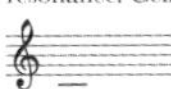

VII. Apart ~ subito

VIII. Together ~ quietly, meditative

Long tones. Very quietly. Slow development and shifting timbre. Vary bow placement *pont-norm-tasto*.

IX. Apart

X. Together ~ melding

Quasi-ad libitum. Using harmonic pitch material from previous section (II) move between contrasting speeds of tremolo, gradually coming together for the end of the piece.

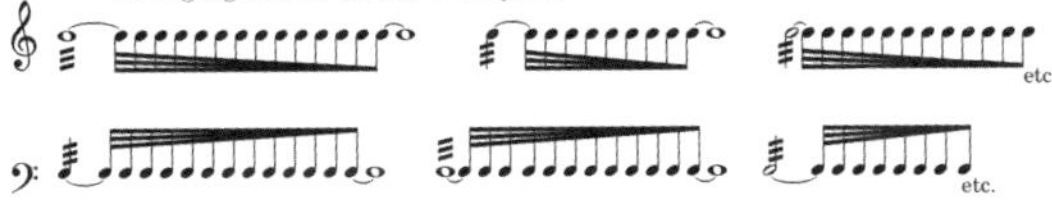

The landscape architect Lawrence Halprin, in his 1969 book on the diagramming of performances, *The RSVP Cycles*, uses *scores* roughly as we are using *diagrams*. "There are many different kinds of scores," he says.

> The most significant discovery we have made in modern scoring is the influence of the scoring device itself on the resulting product. We have begun to realize that, to a considerable extent, the technique of scoring controls what happens.... In classic musical scoring for example, notes and time intervals are established, as are pitch and time. Even the quality is established (by words) and the performers' positions are absolutely fixed in space on stage.... Except for some limited passages where improvisation is called for, traditional music leaves little latitude except "interpretation" to the performer.[1]

The primary difference between Halprin's rather expansive use of "scores" and the diagrams I am discussing here is that scores are largely diagrams that structure how things will be done, whereas diagrams may do this, or they may encode ideas, relationships, and approaches to design.

We engage with diagrams (what Halprin calls "scores") everywhere, whether we are assembling an Ikea cabinet, using Google Maps to find our way home, or checking the weather.

A diagram is a mode of graphic communication that encodes ideas and priorities and structures relationships among people and things, qualities, and events, and has the potential to be dynamic and exploratory. Diagrams, importantly, structure how we understand designs, both as makers and as users. Making a map using Google Maps will prioritize roadways, giving secondary priority to other forms of transportation, and then to businesses. This is useful for a shopping trip or for finding the quickest way from A to B, but not so useful in describing the emotional tenor of a neighborhood. A stock market chart reduces the labor of millions of individuals to a single measure: greater or lesser perceived value. A family tree describes

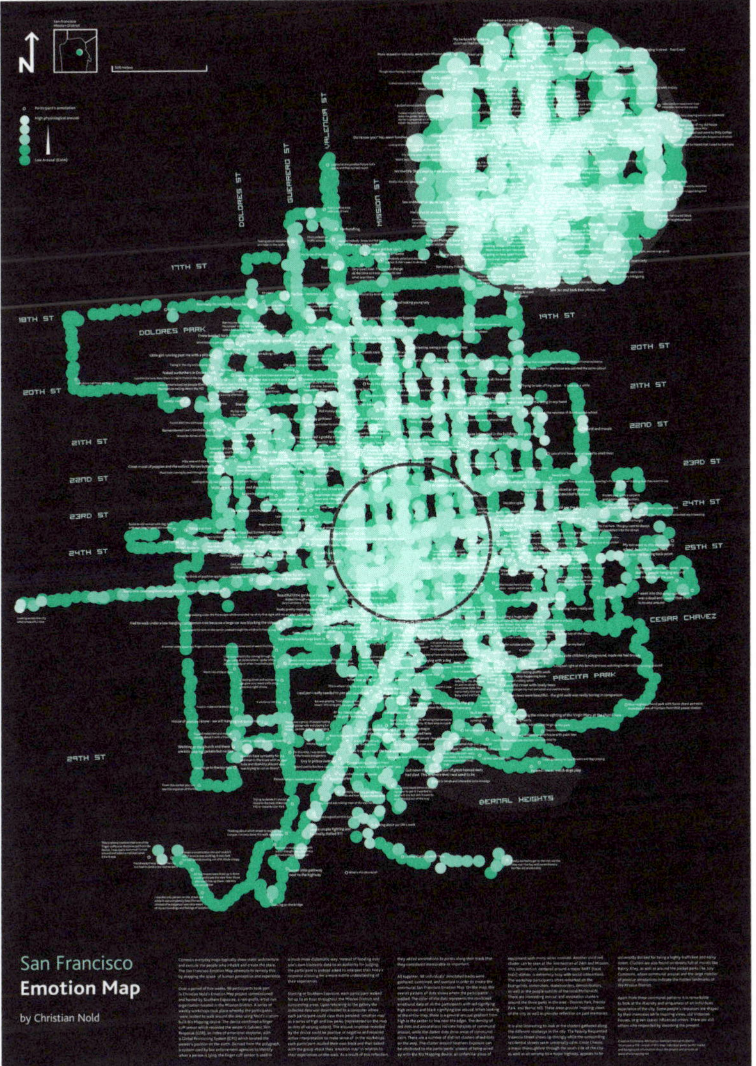

Christian Nold's *San Francisco Emotion Map* (2007) was generated on the basis of participants' emotions and reactions. Any time participants felt something they geotagged a note and marked the intensity of the emotion.

a family in purely genealogical terms, presenting whose genes—rather than whose worldviews, whose ideas, whose habits, whose stories—were passed to whom.

These reductions are necessary efficiencies, maybe even the point of diagrams. They filter out an understanding from the chaos. Many of them, however, have formed a canon of representation, limiting the possibilities of those with other priorities. This canon—this collection of diagrams used by makers and audiences—is the engine of thing-focused design, predetermining the parameters of a design and answering questions before they are asked. Known diagrams lead to known forms and can be resistant to experiential thinking. An ordinary architectural plan does not include acoustics or the search for just the right food for the dining room, just as a standard lesson plan, so focused on the timing of the material being delivered, does not notate the flow of comprehension in the minds of the students. These experiential design elements may be in the intentions of the architects or teachers, but the notational systems they use for their work do not support such intentions, and they are thus rarely communicated.

Much of design is about translating concept into form using graphic notation—that is, *diagrams*. As I have argued, human experiences are complex, interconnected, and rarely limited to the traditional frames of traditional forms. Most traditional notational systems cannot cover all the elements of an experience. To properly design for experience, then, the diagram must be part of the design process, as that diagram will determine the experiential scope of the project.

Symbols, Graphs, Maps

> "The diagram is a possibility of fact—
> it is not the fact itself."
>
> — Gilles Deleuze

The diagrams useful to the experience design process may be divided into three overlapping categories: symbols, graphs, and maps. While we are interested in how these diagrams communicate, we are more interested in diagrams as process-oriented tools for making. There are many wonderful examples of diagrams as interpretation of existing data—data visualization—but that is not our focus here.

Symbols

Diagrams begin with symbols, which we may understand here as the basic unit of graphic communication. Symbols work because those using them and those looking at them agree on what they mean. The representation may or may not formally resemble what is represented. In other words, the symbol of the cross looks like an actual crucifix, while the symbol of the Star of David is more of a geometric abstraction. Their shapes may represent relationships or forms, but this is not necessary. A house in Monopoly looks like a house, but a dot on a metro map looks nothing like the station it represents. Symbols on maps are often explained in keys.

Words and letters are generally considered a separate category from symbols. They do, however, function much as the symbols on the following spread do. They are graphic images that communicate meanings that are agreed on by members of a community. The letter C in English sounds quite different from the letter C in Turkish

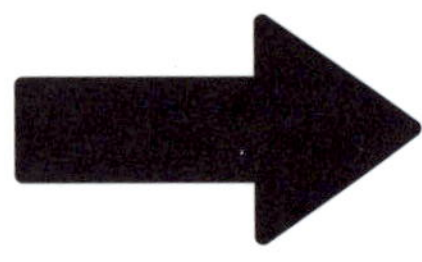

This Way: arrows are so common we forget they are symbols.

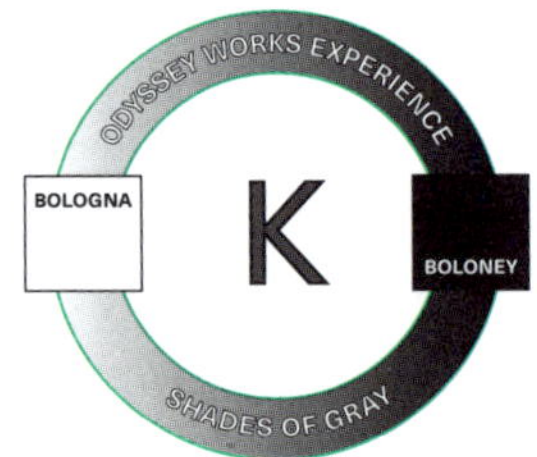

Odyssey Works's Bologna / Baloney symbol: the experiential aim of Odyssey Works' 2011 performance was to balance classical symmetry with more contemporary experimentation.

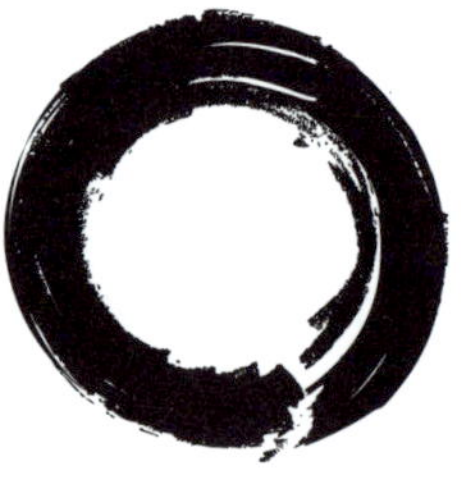

Ensō (Zen circle): enlightenment, as demonstrated by a single brushstroke.

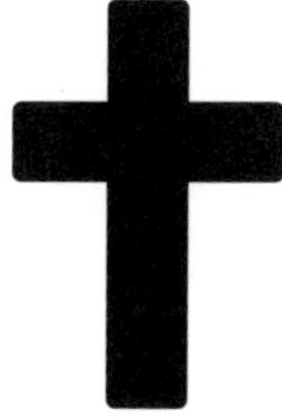

Cross: broadly speaking, Christianity or Jesus.

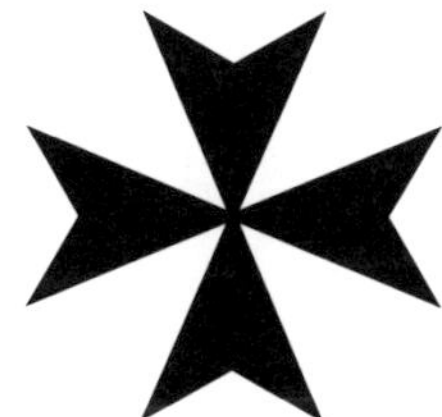

Maltese cross: specific crosses specify different aspects of Christian heritage; the Maltese cross is associated with the Knights Hospitaller, a medieval Catholic military religious order.

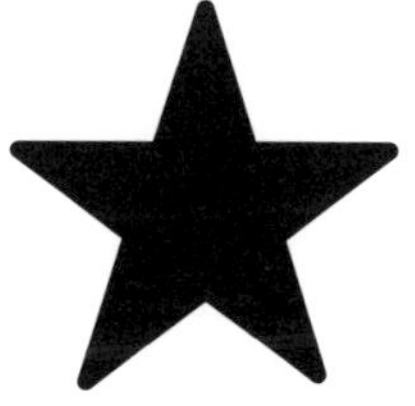

Five-pointed star: various references. A magical talisman for some; an attractive ornament for others. For the ancient Greeks, the star communicated the Platonic notion of the ideal world and the real world.

The linguists refer to this as "the arbitrariness of the sign." To go down that rabbit hole, begin with Ferdinand de Saussure and set aside some time.

(which is more like a J). We have a tendency to convince ourselves that words and symbols are structurally connected to what they represent—that is, that the word *dog* somehow contains the nature of a dog, or that the octagonal shape of the stop sign somehow embodies the meaning of stopping. These meanings are just things we agree on, but the fact that we feel this way about them speaks to the power of symbols to crystallize meaning in themselves. A cross may evoke powerful emotions in a Christian believer, and the Cornell University crest may do the same for wistful alums.

The power of the symbol is that it offers a shorthand for an idea and, when effectively employed, evokes that idea any time it is encountered. Symbols are imbued with a specific meaning in the key of the diagram ("a star represents a city"), outside the diagram by explanation ("the pyramid with the eye in it on the dollar bill represents . . ."), or because we are already aware of its standard use (mathematical symbols, for instance, or variations on the image of the crucifix). Arrows, for instance, are so common that it is hard to consider them not innate to directionality; it's hard to think of them as derived from something used for hunting. If we use such a symbol—so widely accepted—we can then vary and play with it to fit our needs. The arrow can go both ways or go in circles. Boxes are symbols, as are lines, even dots. This symbolic language is so common that we forget it is symbolic, and its commonality makes it quite useful for communication. Other symbols may be more complex or esoteric, encoding within them ideas that either need explanation or are for only a small community to understand.

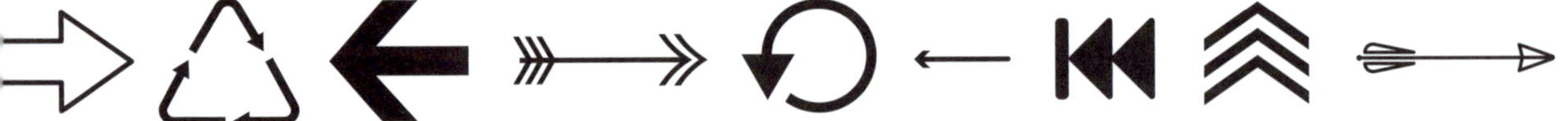

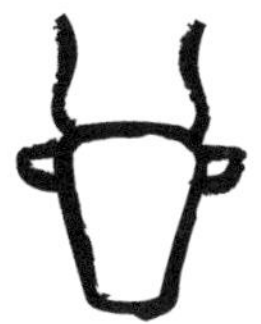
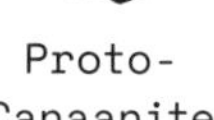
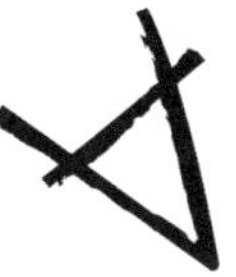
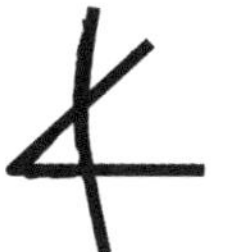
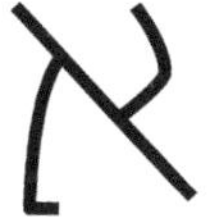
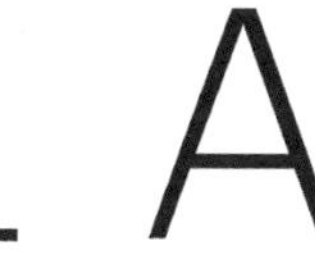

A: The evolution of letterforms (aka glyphs) over time is a great example of how symbols may look like what they symbolize but do not need to.

To select a symbol for your diagram is to select a purpose. That which you are trying to explore will be contained within a symbol. Often, it is best to start simple and ask: What am I trying to do here? Draw a circle, or a rectangle, and begin to work and rework it. What does it represent? What could it become? That circle may be, for instance, a single idea in a book about experience design. It represents a principle. It has parameters. Maybe it is big because it is important. Maybe it has a thin line around it because it is more or less influenced by other principles. Circles are wonderful because we generally accept them to indicate things, generically and variably (as opposed to, say, rainbows or smiley faces).

Then, perhaps, we add a line, another symbol most people know to indicate boundaries or connections. One circle connects to another circle by a line, and now they are in relationship. This thing is connected to this other thing. Now we can begin to play with the line, with the connection, with the amount that one line is influenced by another. We add color and then the symbolism becomes obscure. This one color may represent anything, so a key is needed. The diagram begins to evolve. But how to structure it?

The circles used in this book's table of contents indicate the different chapters, and they are bigger or smaller based on whether the chapter has more or fewer words. This reads easily, despite the fact that there is nothing round or circular about a chapter.

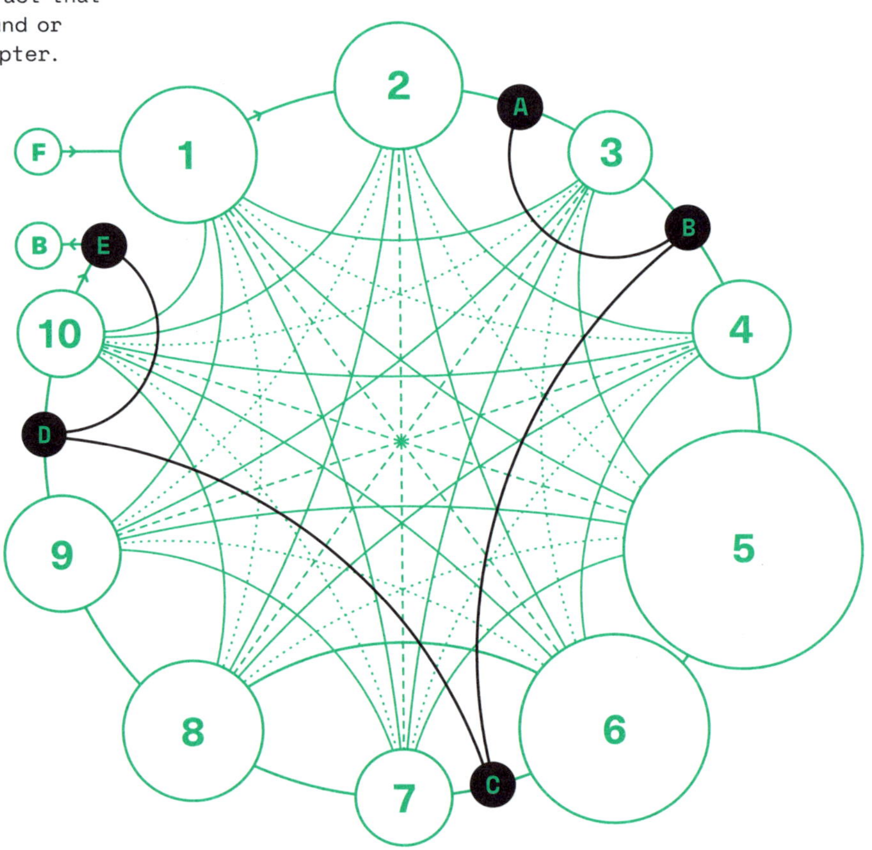

Graphs
Graphs are grids. Graphs are charts. Graphs are most of what we think of as diagrams or data visualizations. On a graph, where something is located tells you something. Probably the best-known of these is the Cartesian grid with its x and y axes. Here, x often represents time, with its inexorable rightward flow, while y represents some value that changes over time, like the value of your stock climbing triumphally higher and higher or carbon emissions, doing the same, terrifyingly.

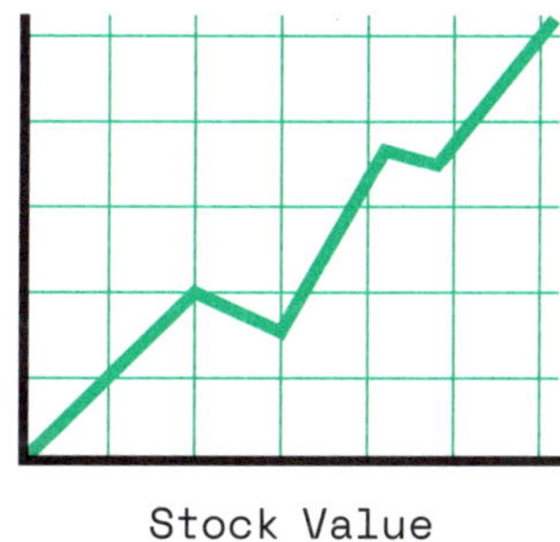

Stock Value

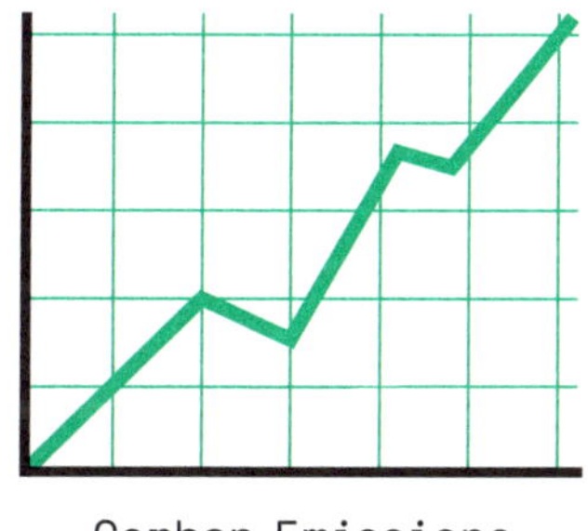

Carbon Emissions

Or x and y may be related parameters.

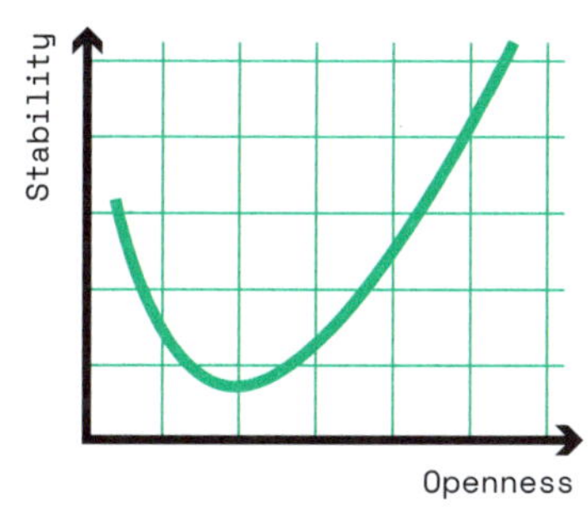

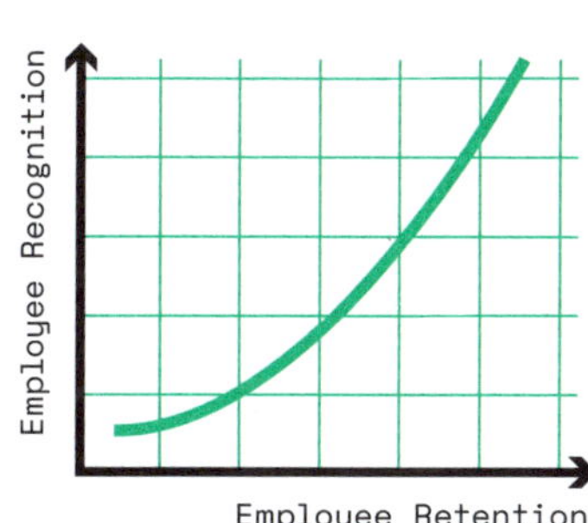

Graphs may be circular or spiral or even three-dimensional.

The spiral form of the graph of the Odyssey Works' performance *Pilgrimage* was chosen to allow for a rhythm of repeating themes happening at increasing intervals. It was also used to suggest a porous frame, so that the performance would fold back into regular life rather than abruptly end.

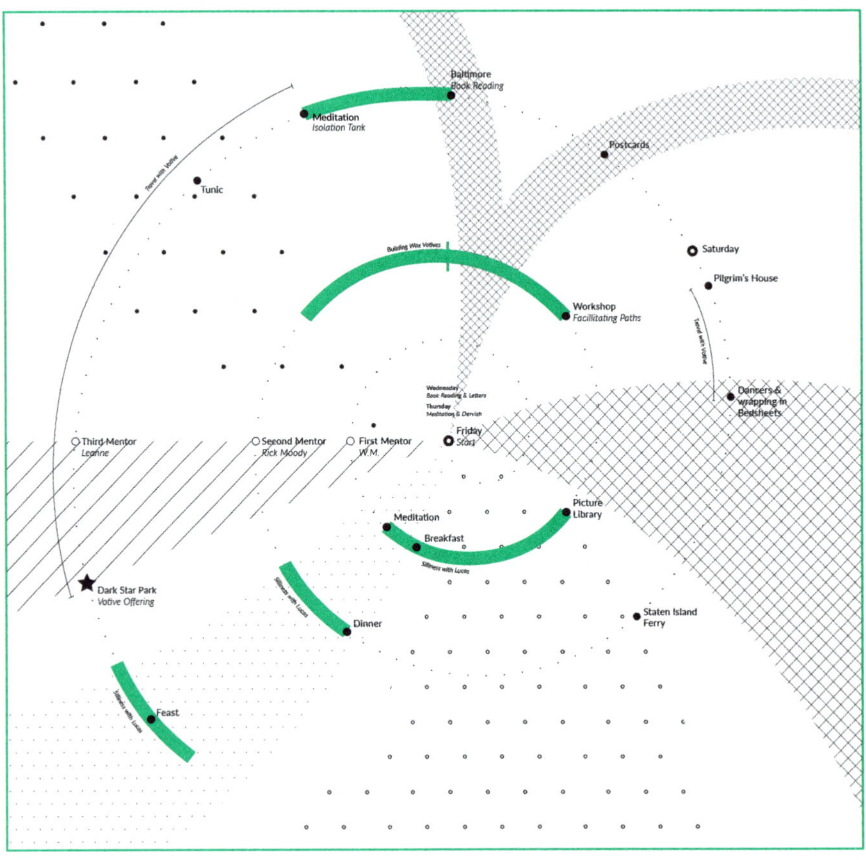

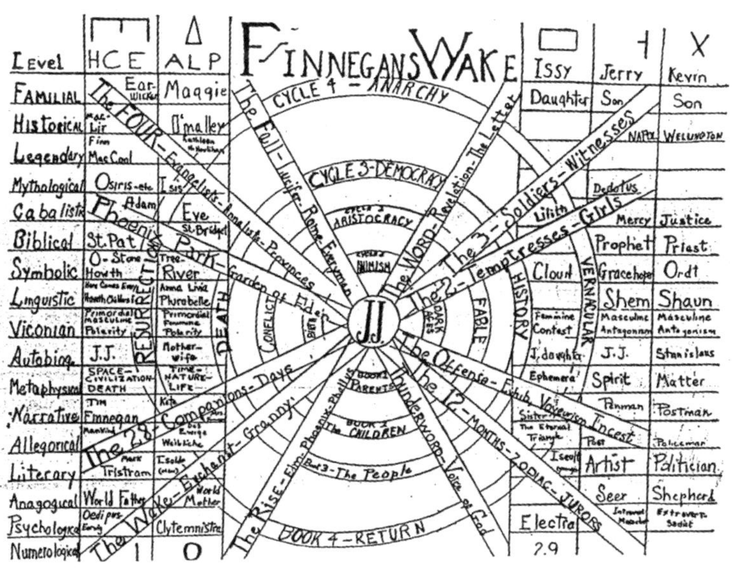

László Moholy-Nagy's diagram (*Motion Diagram of Finnegans Wake*, 1947) of James Joyce's novel *Finnegans Wake*. Here the radial design of the graph emphasizes the repetitions and cycles that organize the book.

The graph drives home the incredible capacity of diagramming to use the relationships between things as the compositional engine of a design. *The Book of Separation*, Odyssey Works' 2021 digital experience, was designed to create a new kind of closeness, possible only through a purpose-built platform (named OneThing). The piece was custom designed for pairs of people who would experience the journey together, though in separate rooms or in separate time zones.

The central compositional interest of the piece was this togetherness and separation, and a traditional script or a storyboard couldn't accommodate such a focus. So during phase zero, the piece was composed as a diagram. ⟶

The diagram moves from left to right, tracking the two participants as they progress through the video, audio, animations, and interactions of the piece, occasionally speaking to each other or receiving notes from one another, though never connecting by video. The diagram allowed for sculpting of that distance and testing of various elements that would bring the participants closer or push them farther apart. As the piece was developed, the diagram was reworked, each new iteration serving as a proposal for how to rewrite the text or the interactions. Later, the diagram served as a shorthand for the cast and for the OneThing digital platform development team to understand the big-picture experiential aim as each collaborator developed their portion of the piece.

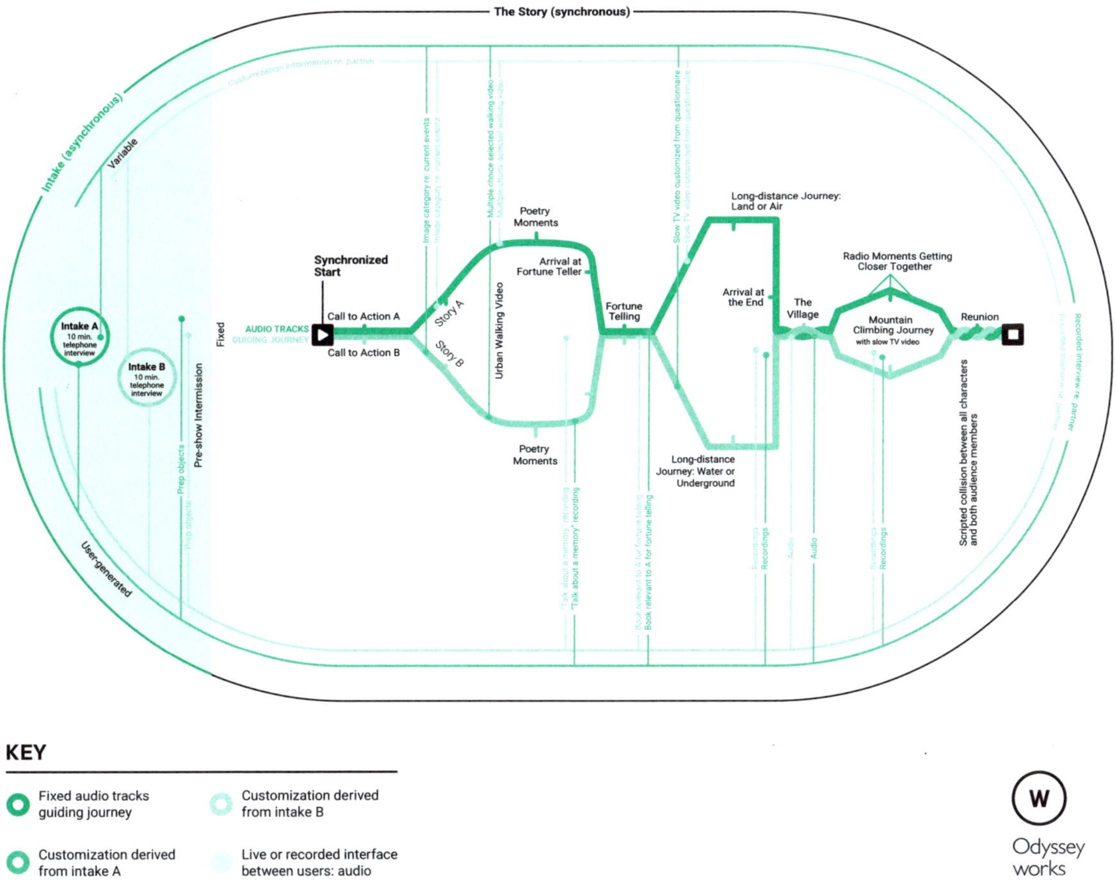

Abraham Burickson and Ana Tobin, Diagram of "The Book of Separation," 2020.

The Story (synchronous)

Intake (asynchronous)

Variable

Fixed

User-generated

Intake A
10 min. telephone interview

Intake B
10 min. telephone interview

Prep objects

Pre-show Intermission

AUDIO TRACKS
GUIDING JOURNEY

Synchronized Start

Call to Action A

Call to Action B

Story A

Story B

Image category re: current events

Multiple choice selected walking video

Urban Walking Video

Poetry Moments

Arrival at Fortune Teller

Poetry Moments

"Talk about a memory" recording

Fortune Telling

Book relevant to A for fortune telling

Slow TV video customized from questionnaire

Long-distance Journey: Land or Air

Arrival at the End

Long-distance Journey: Water or Underground

Recordings

The Village

Audio

Radio Moments Getting Closer Together

Mountain Climbing Journey
with slow TV video

Recordings

Reunion

Scripted collision between all characters and both audience members

Recorded interview re: partner

KEY

Fixed audio tracks guiding journey

Customization derived from intake A

Customization derived from intake B

Live or recorded interface between users: audio

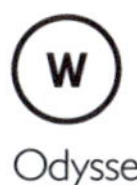

Maps

Maps describe a territory on the basis of a specific set of priorities. We can all be forgiven for thinking that maps are just there to tell you where you are and how to get from point A to point B; this is the set of priorities of the vast majority of maps we encounter in our daily lives, which says much about the nature of our world and little about all that maps can do for us. The elements of such maps—representation of travel, a trustworthy scale, place names, a uniformity of the built environment, and a sense of objectivity—are all choices. There are also topographical maps and weather maps and star maps, each addressing a different kind of territory with a different set of priorities. In the middle of the twentieth century, Guy Debord and the Situationists sought to subvert the capitalistic priorities of the standard map by piecing together their own maps that were based on a "mode of experimental behavior, . . . letting-go . . . of work and leisure activities [in order to] be drawn . . . by the city's psychogeographical contours."[2] The resultant maps, such as *The Naked City*, are both not to scale and highly subjective and personal, suggesting that the city might not be an objectively definable entity but something that emerges from personal experience.

Psychogeography is the practice of considering and mapping landscapes on the basis of personal and interpersonal relationships with places.

An architectural plan maps the territory of a house yet to be built, and its effectiveness depends on the proper prioritization of information. A plan that shows only the movement of light and shadow (as shown on page 176) would be useless to a contractor, but it might be an important first step in the architect's design process.

But a map may address even more abstract territories. The neurosurgeon Wilder Graves Penfield's *Cortical Homunculus* diagram (as shown on page 177) maps the human body with a scale representing not distance but the neuronal sensitivity of each part of the body.[3]

Guy Debord,
The Naked City,
1957.

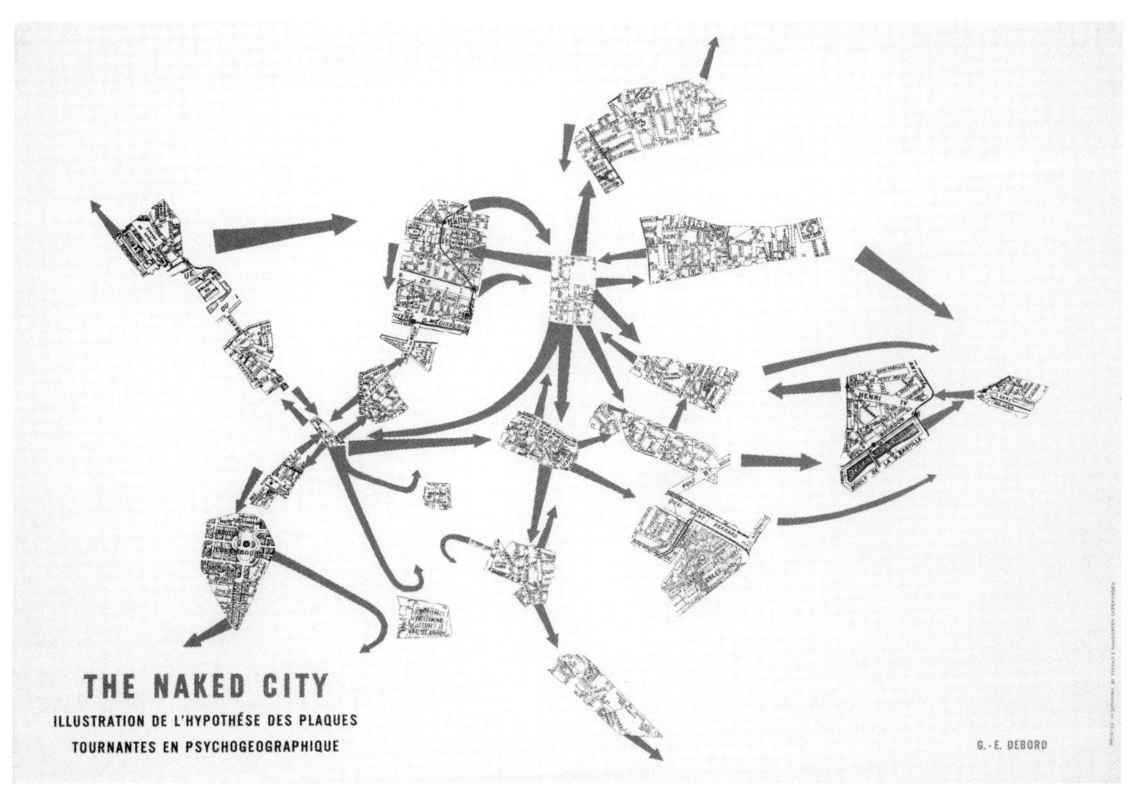

Abraham Burickson,
Qualities of Light,
2019.

Long Architecture Project image showing movement of light within a proposed house design.

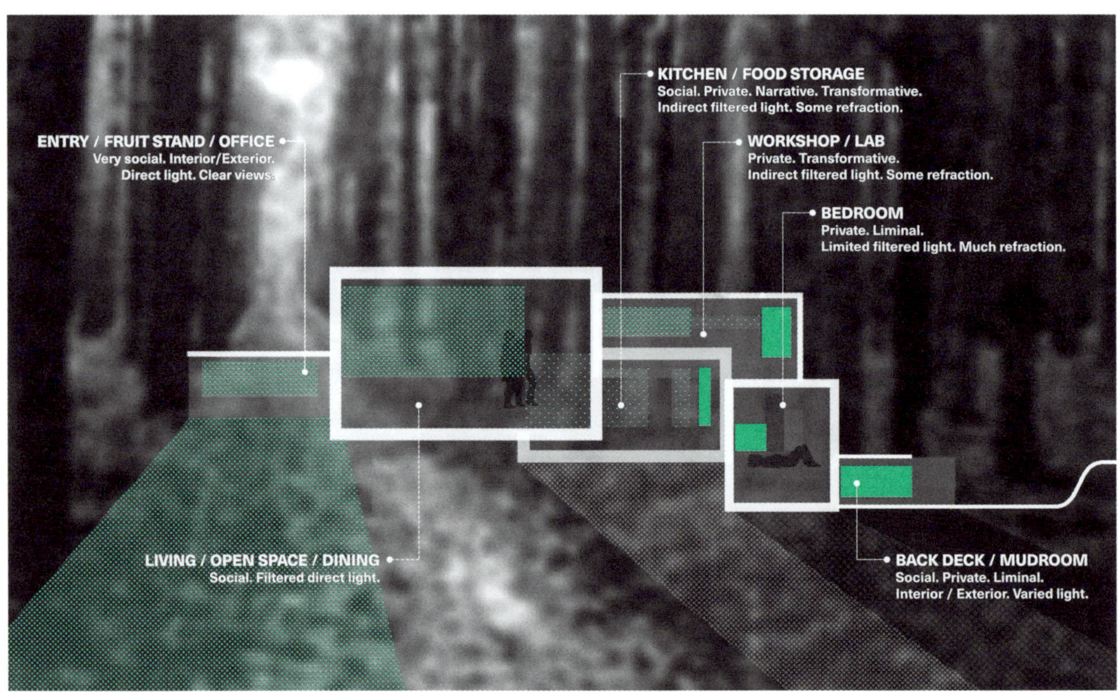

Adaptation of Wilder Graves Penfield, *Cortical Homunculus*, 1950.

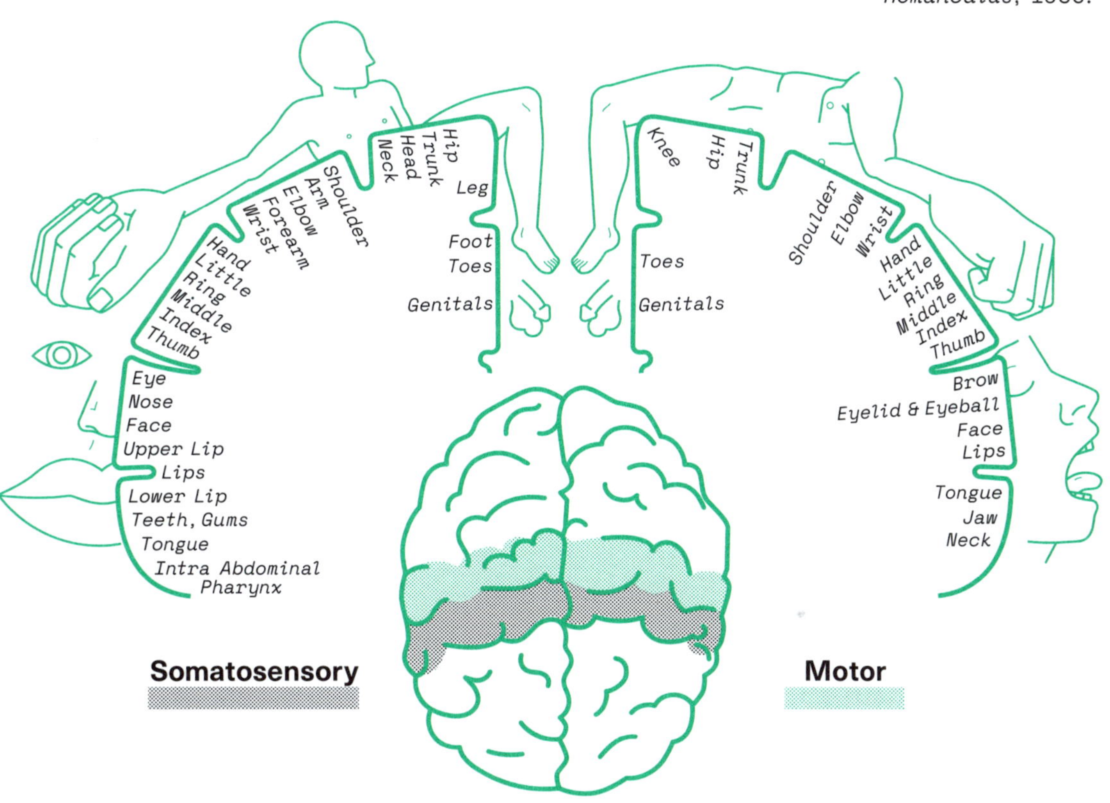

A mind map charts the relationship of thoughts within the territory of an idea. An organizational chart maps authority in the relational territory of a community. The table of contents of this book maps a journey across the territory of its pages. The musician and composer Ellen Fullman plays an instrument—the long string instrument—consisting of piano wire strung over great distances within a building. To play it, Fullman must walk alongside the wires, which she plays with her fingers. Thus, her scores cover a territory, mapping a choreographed movement over space that is also a movement through sound.

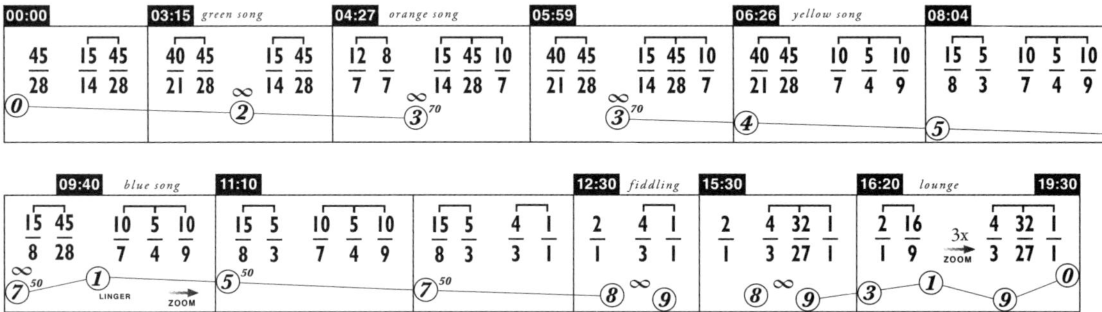

Ellen Fullman,
Four Colors Score, 2022.

"The instrument," she says, "is played by bowing strings with rosin-coated fingers while walking. Circled numbers represent distances in meters labeled on the floor beneath the strings, '*0*' being the bridge on the resonator. Diagonal lines show the motion of the performer along the string length, angling downward as the performer moves away from the bridge, and vice versa. Numbers in black boxes indicate a time line in minutes and seconds. 'Zoom' is a fast-paced walk."

Just as a world may be more conceptual than physical, so too may be the territory of a map. Maps are incredible tools for defining worlds and for helping us navigate them. *You are here*, says the map, and at once we both exist as a part of that world and have some idea of how to orient ourselves.

In 1869 Charles Joseph Minard drew a map of Napoleon's disastrous invasion of Russia. It is at once graph and map, overlaying distance traveled across territory and time, and representing the number of troops who survived to cross each part of the terrain and to return home again. He overlaid dates and temperatures on the map and the result is as elegant as it is horrifying.[4]

This is an infographic, used to analyze the past. But had such a diagram been used to plan the campaign before it started, might Napoleon have made different decisions?

Charles Joseph Minard's 1869 figurative map of the successive losses in men of the French army in the Russian campaign of 1812–13.

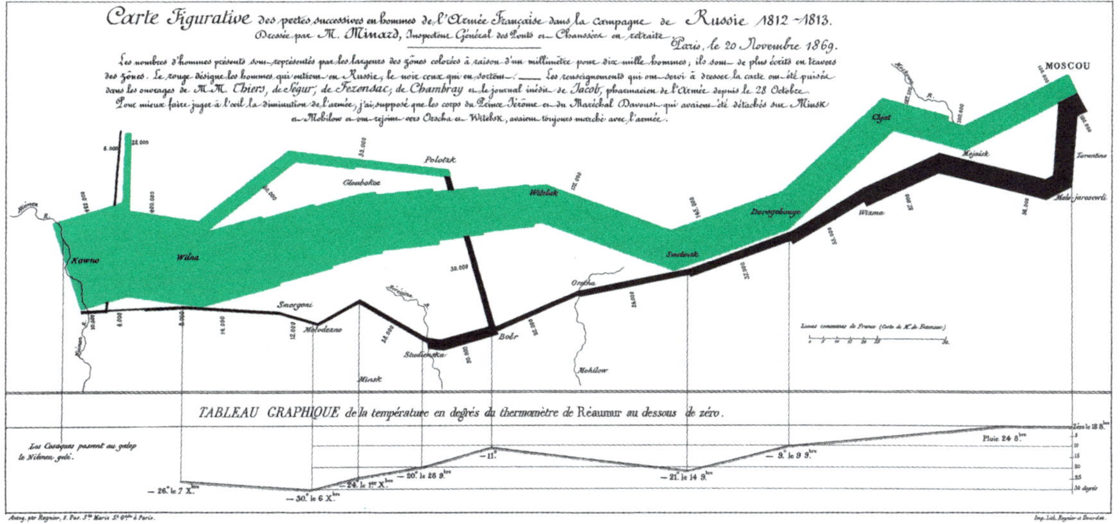

Symbols, graphs, and maps are not entirely discrete categories. Graphs are made up of symbols, some graphs are also maps, and many maps ultimately become symbols. Each, however, presents its own set of design possibilities, inviting the designer to restructure experiences in powerful ways. Maps invite us to clarify and specify what matters in the world of what we're making. Graphs focus the design process on the relationships and dynamisms that bring life to what we've made. Symbols offer us the opportunity to crystallize complex concepts in a shorthand that can define one's project, one's community, or oneself.

Making new diagrams for your work opens the door to wild possibilities. A professor might make a lesson plan that foregrounds states of receptivity in her students. An architect might design plans based on how storytelling would take place in a home. A festival organizer might arrange all experiences to build toward a moment of wonder or awe. The Google Map, the temperature graph, the road sign symbols are all great for what they do, having been relentlessly refined over long periods. But experience design is a wildly interdisciplinary practice, unifying often quite distinct activities under a single vision. The key to doing this effectively is designing the right diagram.

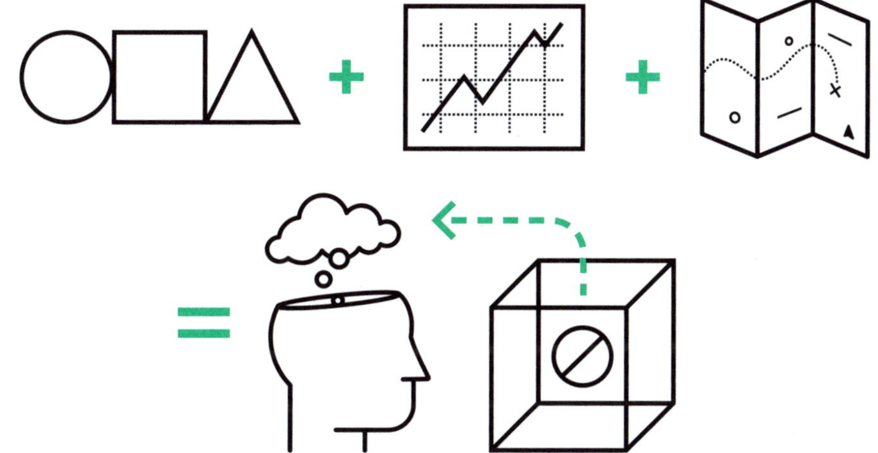

EXPERIMENT PART D

The Structure

Structure the time of the meal you will be having with your friend. Set the menu as a multisensory experience.

Consider not only the tastes, and the order of tastes, but sound, smell, visual elements, narrative elements, the symbolism of the food items, the timing of the food items, what else will be going on in the space of the meal, and so on. The food is just the starting point of the experiential elements of the meal. Nothing is off the table, so to speak.

The meal should have some eventness; what might the focal moment be? How will you mark the entry and the exit of the frame of the meal? Design some elements in minute detail, allow others to emerge from your interactions. Leave some things up to chance.

→ Use the following graph to design the composition of states of experience. Try to represent not just the food elements, but the narrative and experiential elements as they change over time. You may make your own diagram elsewhere if you think of a diagrammatic form more appropriate to what you are trying to design.

Meal Experience Diagram Template

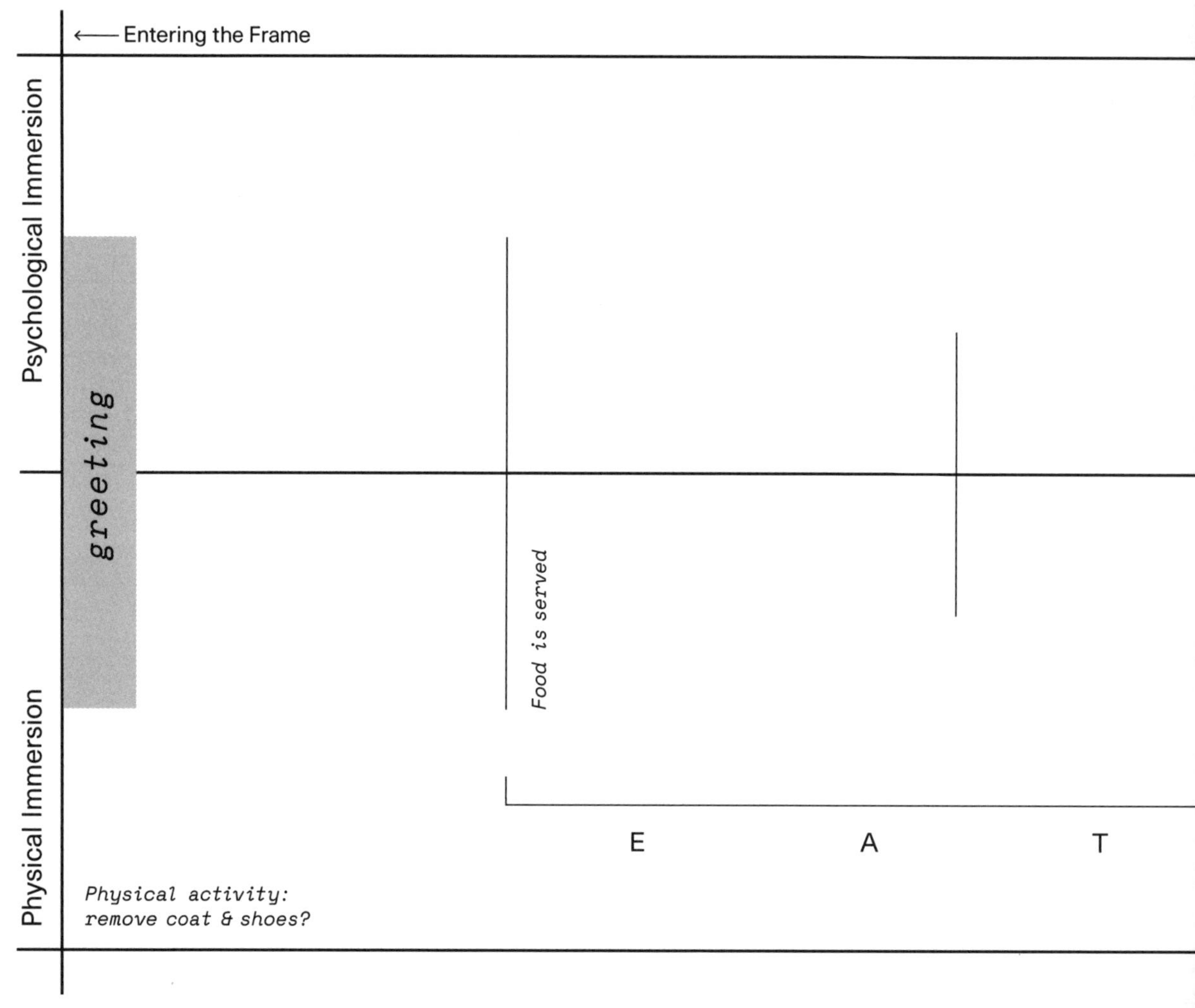

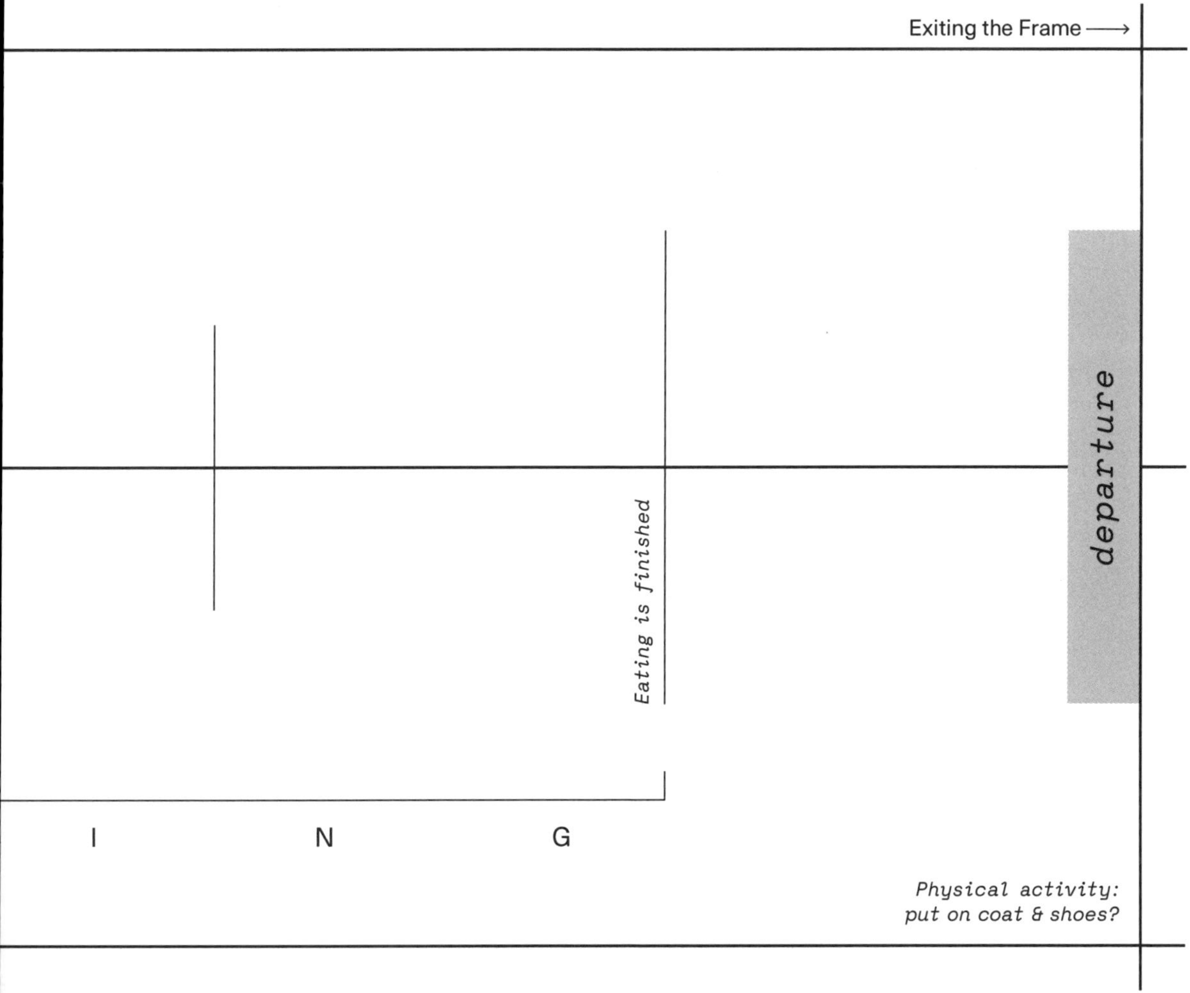

Exiting the Frame ⟶

Eating is finished

departure

I N G

Physical activity:
put on coat & shoes?

CHAPTER TEN

Make Work That Matters

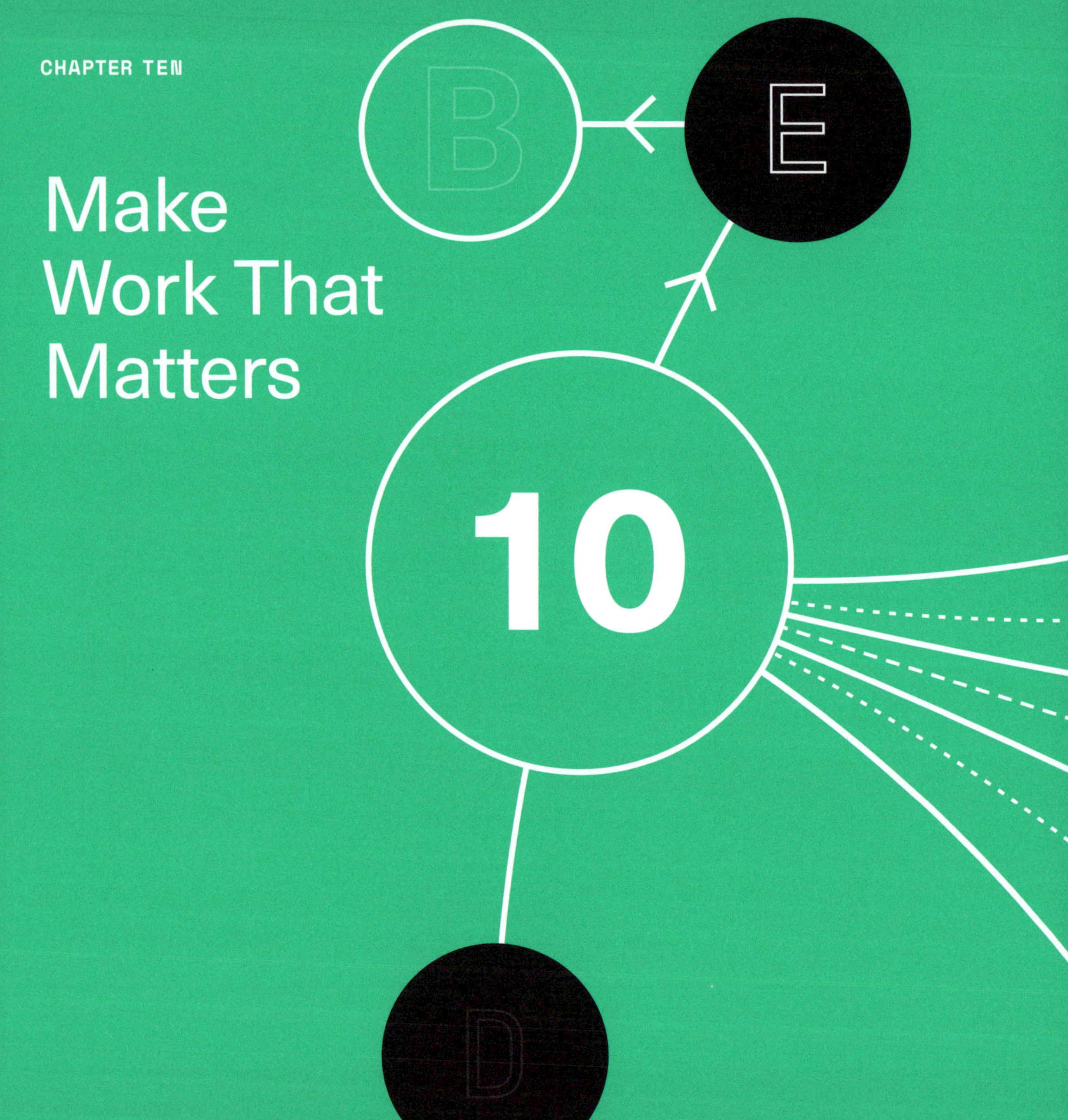

It was a warm New York day, an hour before lunch, and the attendees at the 2018 Future of Storytelling Summit were abuzz with the stimulation of trying out immersive technologies, witnessing performances, and meeting new people. They were artists and storytellers, technology innovators, filmmakers, AI engineers, experiential marketers, puppeteers, journalists, and a wide array of individuals exploring how they might rethink their fields.

At the windowed end of the great hall, a tall, tense man stood waiting for his group to straggle in. He was a lawyer for the American Civil Liberties Union, buttoned up and a little out of place. This was the only session at the summit dedicated to social good. It was to be a temporary think tank, and as the attendees sat down, a look of uncertainty passed across their faces. What would we possibly have to offer the ACLU?

"We need to fix voting," said the lawyer. Millions of people were choosing not to vote because they felt their votes didn't matter, because they weren't interested, or because it wasn't worth missing work. Canvassing and making phone calls was labor-intensive and not very effective. He explained that the organization was fighting to make Election Day a holiday so that people who couldn't afford to leave work could have the time off. But progress was slow. He was clearly not optimistic.

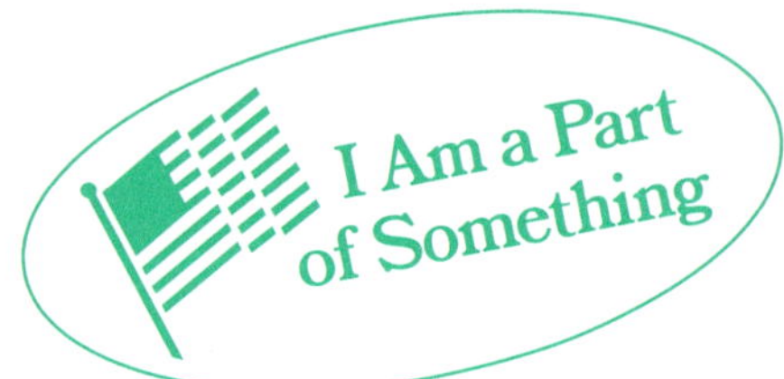

"The problem," somebody said, "is that voting is not a very *good* experience."

"I always vote. It feels like a sacred duty," someone else said, adding, "I really appreciate when I've done it, but I kind of have to guilt-trip myself into going."

"Honestly, the I Voted sticker is the best part," said another person. Though voting is a communal activity, it somehow isolates people from one another. Its appeal is being part of something, but the act itself offers little experience of that. Outside the middle school gym or community center where the voting happens, the world continues as normal. And voting spaces are stark and bureaucratic, focused on hiding people in their voting booths and moving them along quickly.

Piece by piece, the group outlined the strengths and the flaws of the experience design of the activity. Voting ought to have incredible *eventness*, being both highly anticipated and communally transformative, but the activity at its heart is anticlimactic. It is the primary action of democratic worldbuilding, but, other than the I Voted stickers, it hardly registers in the material culture of the community. And, other than a smile from the senior citizen volunteer who feeds the forms into the machines, there is little human interaction.

The analysis of the voting experience was revelatory by itself, both for the attendees and for the lawyer. An experiential understanding of the practice opened broad avenues for design experimentation. How might they turn the act of voting into a social occasion, a rare moment when strangers could connect? Could the I Voted stickers serve as entry passes to nearby gatherings? Could polling stations be redesigned? Could local third-place establishments such as coffee shops and gyms collaborate in programming activities for voters? In less than an hour, the group offered a torrent of ideas, and the lawyer, clearly surprised by what came his way, took furious notes. It was just a brainstorm, dipping the toe into Phase Zero, but people walked out energized. Think tank members had been able to use their experiential tools for something they cared about, and the lawyer was able to step outside the traditional, exhausting form of his practice and engage with a rare bit of divergent thinking. Despite having witnessed the spectacle of a projection mapping turning the enormous dining room convincingly into a ship at sea, and having sat down with famous directors and artists, many said that this event was the best moment of the weekend.

We long to make work that matters. Traditional practices generally ask us to constrain our sense of purpose to that which is understood to be part of the practice. A civil rights lawyer may have within his brief legal fights for voting rights, but not making voting a more meaningful activity. A marketer may have in her business model making a brand seem fun, but not making civic engagement fun.

Experience design begins with the question of purpose: *What experience are you trying to create?* There is a Phase Zero of a project, of a career, of a life. What experience are you trying to create for yourself and others? If we are to understand ethics as the question of our effect on others, then experience design, with its turn toward being intentional about that effect, is fundamentally an ethical activity. All design has an ethical dimension, of course. But when we step into the mode of experience design, we are forced, continually, to confront it. The design of a chair has ethical dimensions—in the choice of materials, in the labor that goes into it, in the way in which it alters the life of its users—and a designer must bear these in mind. The design of a house certainly has such dimensions. Even the design of a book jacket or a billboard ad has them, and good designers will consider these as a part of their process. But the chair designer's job traditionally ends when the chair is designed; they cannot account for the many lives it will lead. The graphic designer may design a new brand identity for a municipality's chamber of commerce, but the way that identity integrates with the life of the city is outside their job description. The designers may think about such things. They may be concerned with them, but those concerns are not part of a traditional design workflow.

When, during the construction of the new stadium for the 2022 World Cup in Qatar, the architect Zaha Hadid was asked whether she bore any responsibility for the deaths of numerous migrant Indian workers on the project, she replied: "I have nothing to do with the workers."[1] Understood through the lens of ordinary design practice, of course, she is correct; the architecture firm is responsible for the design of the building, not the management of the laborers or the conduct of the games. A Phase Zero process at the beginning of the project, however, would have brought stakeholders together to ask not just how they could make a great stadium, but what effect they hoped this project would have on everyone who touched it. Such questions draw a through line from the architects to the laborers to the players to the fans and, importantly, to the residents of Doha as they use the building in the decades after its brief moment as the home of the World Cup. It is impossible to cover every possibility, to anticipate every unknown, but a process that specifies the experiential aim and then shares that aim with all involved empowers individuals to respond to emergent situations.

Experience design is certainly not a new way of working; the designers of religious practices, the crafters of political movements, the visionaries of utopian communities, the masters of tea ceremonies and guild apprenticeships, the practitioners of traditional healing modalities, and so many others have refined many of the techniques in this book over centuries, even millennia. These practitioners understood their experiential work in a holistic way, placing well-honed craft in service of an experiential aim.

During a well-designed experience we may forget that it is designed, folding it into the moments of our lives, as in a great class when the ideas seem to flow without a lesson plan. Herein lies much of the power of experience design, and, like any powerful tool, it can be used for good or ill. A Nazi rally was a carefully designed experience, as was a slave auction, as were the attacks of September 11, 2001. Much of history can be understood through the lens of experience design: What narratives were Japanese kamikaze pilots in World War II participating in when they crashed their planes into enemy ships? What worldbuilding justified 918 cult members committing suicide together in Jonestown, Guyana? How did the storming of the Bastille become the event that galvanized the French Revolution?

We spend the entirety of our lives as participants in designed worlds, collaborating in the development of narratives and moving from frame to frame to frame. To take up the tools of experience design is both to try to understand the structure of our lives and to do something to shape it. How could life be? What matters? It may, in the end, be the disappointing experience designs, the ones that have lost their effectiveness or never had any to begin with that best illustrate the urgency of making experiences that matter. The West is largely bereft, for instance, of effective coming-of-age rituals. Those that do exist are generally remnants of a different world. A bar or bat mitzvah, much like a Catholic confirmation, is meant to mark the child's transition into adulthood, but for those embedded in contemporary secular society, this is far too early, as thirteen-year-olds are unlikely to be seen as adults. Holidays such as Memorial Day and Veterans Day fail to galvanize the majority of the community around their purpose, and while others, such as Secretary's Day and Commonwealth Day, are noted, if at all, only as trivia.

When ethically applied, experience design concepts can be revolutionary. This is the ACLU lawyer thinking about how to make voting fun; this is the filmmaker translating *Notes on Blindness*[A] into a VR experience that comes closer than anything before it to communicating the experience of going blind; this is safe spaces for needle exchanges; this is a college making bathrooms gender neutral so that portions of their population don't feel alienated; this is a turn-of-the-twentieth-century Italian woman[B] asking how she might redesign primary education to allow children to find what they are deeply interested in; this is a suitcase traveling around the world—a "grief case"[C]—as a means of connection between isolated mourners deep in unexpected grief; this is the Haudenosaunee Thanksgiving Address,[D] turning the minds of those present into conduits for gratitude; this is new approaches to higher education that do away with high price tags and replace the rigid lines between majors with the experience of developing ways of thinking; this is a composition[E] meant to be played "as slow as possible" so that each chord change becomes

A *Notes on Blindness*, adapted by Arte Experience from the memoir by John Hull.

B Maria Montessori, whose name still marks those schools following her teaching philosophy.

C Taouba Khelifa's *The Grief Publication*, designed in 2022.

D Delivered by Tom Porter, and discussed at length in the book *Braiding Sweetgrass*, by Robin Wall Kimmerer.

E This is still being performed. It is a composition by John Cage called "As Slow as Possible." The performance began in Halberstadt, Germany, in 2001. It will end in 2640.

an event in the community and a continuous reminder of the possibility of beauty; this is a watch[F] designed to encourage the wearer to be less concerned about time by being just a little bit imprecise; this is a human resources department recognizing that people need to be genuinely appreciated, and then creating systems[G] that facilitate appreciation within the workplace; this is a journalist launching a newspaper written by and for kids[H] as a way to give them a sense of community and purpose during the dark days of a pandemic; this is an immersive experience of life in a refugee camp[I] set up at the World Economic Forum at Davos to build empathy among economic leaders; this is the weekend retreat away from the internet; this is a liberal Christian youth group working together to redesign the Advent period[J] so that they might rethink how their faith functions in the world; this is a religious organization for people who don't believe in god;[K] this is an immersive "Recharge Room"[L] for first responders in the basement of a hospital during the height of the COVID-19 pandemic.

F
The Slow Watch has only one hand and is accurate to plus or minus two minutes.

G
As researched and implemented by the Workhuman company.

H
Six Feet of Separation, launched by Chris Colin and run by kids in the Bernal Heights neighborhood of San Francisco.

I
A Day in the Life of a Refugee, created by the Crossroads Foundation.

J
The Austin Presbyterian Theological Seminary hired Odyssey Works to help them rethink Advent in 2020, during the COVID-19 pandemic.

K
Alain de Botton talks about this in his book *Religion for Atheists*, and there are experiments afoot, notably the Formation Groups started by Casey Rosengren.

L
Created by Studio Elsewhere and EMBC.

Like so much design, experience design is inherently optimistic; it begins with the idea that we can make something good, or something better. It's a call to action, a balm for pessimistic times, and a demand for meaning.

The tools of experience design are individually radical and powerful; put together, they are revolutionary.

EXPERIMENT PART E

Event and After

Before you meet your friend for the experience, look over the diagram, the plan, the atom of food. What is the intention? Once the plan is clear and the materials are prepared, what do you need to do to be fully personally prepared for realizing that intention?

That's it. Go ahead.

→ Once you're done, take one last look at all your materials. How did the experience match up with the intention?

Now go design something else.

Back Matter

B

E

10

Notes

Chapter 2. Employ Empathy Rigorously

1. Empathy Museum, "A Mile in My Shoes," accessed June 9, 2022, https://www.empathymuseum.com/a-mile-in-my-shoes/.

2. Empathy Museum, "How Can We Improve Our Own Empathy?—Empathy Museum's 'A Mile in My Shoes,'" August 1, 2018, video, 1:41, https://youtu.be/A0_MFXUw10c.

3. Susan Lanzoni, *Empathy: A History* (New Haven: Yale University Press, 2018), 49.

4. Conflict Kitchen, "About," accessed June 9, 2022, http://www.conflictkitchen.org/about/.

5. Jon Rubin and Dawn Weleski, "Wm. O. Steinmetz '50 Designers-in-Residence: Conflict Kitchen Co-founders Jon Rubin and Dawn Weleski" (lecture, Maryland Institute College of Art, Baltimore, April 19, 2017).

6. Sean Illing, "The Case against Empathy," Vox, January 16, 2019, https://www.vox.com/conversations/2017/1/19/14266230/empathy-morality-ethics-psychology-compassion-paul-bloom.

7. Stephanie D. Preston and Frans B. M. de Waal, "Empathy: Its Ultimate and Proximate Bases," *Behavioral and Brain Sciences* 25, no. 1 (February 2002): 1–20, https://doi.org/10.1017/s0140525x02000018.

8. Cynthia L. Bennett and Daniela K. Rosner, "The Promise of Empathy," *CHI '19: Proceedings of the 2019 CHI Conference on Human Factors in Computing Systems*, May 2019, 1–13, https://doi.org/10.1145/3290605.3300528.

9. Lily Janiak, "Performance Artist Creates Theatrical Experience Just 'for You,'" SFGATE, April 3, 2017, https://www.sfgate.com/performance/article/Theater-made-just-For-You-11047155.php.

10. Helen Paris, "A Rhapsody for You," *Performance Research* 23, no. 6 (November 29, 2018): 7–11, https://doi.org/10.1080/13528165.2018.1533750.

11. Denise Shanté Brown, email to author, June 2, 2022.

12. Ibid.

Chapter 4. Powerful Experiences Engage the Whole Person

1. Martin Loiperdinger and Bernd Elzer, "Lumière's *Arrival of the Train*: Cinema's Founding Myth," *Moving Image* 4, no. 1 (2004): 89–118, https://doi.org/10.1353/mov.2004.0014.

2. These three levels of immersion were first outlined in Abraham Burickson and Ayden LeRoux, *Odyssey Works: Transformative Experiences for an Audience of One* (New York: Princeton Architectural Press, 2016).

3. *The End*, Swim Pony, October 30, 2017, https://swimpony.org/current-projects/the-end/.

4. Adrienne Mackey, "Immersive Experience Lab" (lecture, Maryland Institute College of Art, Baltimore, March 30, 2020).

5. Ibid.

Chapter 5. We Live in Many Worlds

1. John Wenzel, "Oscar-Winner Alejandro G. Iñárritu Debuts Powerful VR Experience at Stanley Marketplace," *Denver Post*, October 23, 2020.

2. Lesley Adkins and Roy A. Adkins, *Handbook to Life in Ancient Rome* (New York: Facts on File, 2004), 199.

3. University of Nottingham, Manuscripts and Special Collections, "Measurements," accessed June 10, 2022, https://www.nottingham.ac.uk/manuscriptsandspecialcollections/researchguidance/weightsandmeasures/measurements.aspx.

4. U.S. Metric Association, "A Chronology of the Metric System," August 3, 2020, https://usma.org/a-chronology-of-the-metric-system.

5. Tina Susman and Andrew Tangel, "Occupy Wall Street Marks 1st Anniversary with Marches, Party Hats," *Los Angeles Times*, September 17, 2012, https://www.latimes.com/nation/la-xpm-2012-sep-17-la-na-nn-occupy-anniversary-20120917-story.html.

6. Lisa W. Foderaro, "Privately Owned Park, Open to the Public, May Make Its Own Rules," *New York Times*, October 14, 2011, https://www.nytimes.com/2011/10/14/nyregion/zuccotti-park-is-privately-owned-but-open-to-the-public.html.

7. Carrie Kahn, "Battle Cry: Occupy's Messaging Tactics Catch On," NPR, December 6, 2011, https://www.npr.org/2011/12/06/142999617/battle-cry-occupys-messaging-tactics-catch-on.

8. Leigh Buchanan, "This Might Be the Most Whimsical Startup in America," Inc.com, June 22, 2016, https://www.inc.com/leigh-buchanan/leafcutter-designs-does-big-business-from-tiny-crafts.html.

9. Donnie Williams and Wayne Greenhaw, *The Thunder of Angels: The Montgomery Bus Boycott and the People Who Broke the Back of Jim Crow* (Chicago: Chicago Review Press, 2007), 48.

10. Kim Bellware, "Gender-Neutral Bathrooms Are Quietly Becoming the New Thing at Colleges," *HuffPost*, July 18, 2014, https://www.huffpost.com/entry/gender-neutral-bathrooms-colleges_n_5597362.

11. Cyril Lionel Robert James, *The Black Jacobins: Toussaint L'Ouverture and the San Domingo Revolution* (1938; repr., New York: Vintage, 1989), 45–46.

12. Ibid., 64.

13. Arika Okrent, *In the Land of Invented Languages: A Celebration of Linguistic Creativity, Madness, and Genius* (2009; repr., New York: Spiegel & Grau, 2010), 130.

14. David J. Peterson, *The Art of Language Invention: From Horse-Lords to Dark Elves, the Words behind World-Building* (New York: Penguin, 2015), 25, 90.

15. American Dialect Society, "2015 Word of the Year Is Singular 'They,'" January 8, 2016, https://www.americandialect.org/2015-word-of-the-year-is-singular-they.

16. Howard Schwartz, *Tree of Souls: The Mythology of Judaism* (New York: Oxford University Press, 2004), 124.

17. Martin Luther King Jr., "I Have a Dream" (speech delivered at the Lincoln Memorial, Washington, D.C., August 28, 1963), https://www.americanrhetoric.com/speeches/mlkihaveadream.htm.

18. Thomas Weber, *Gandhi as Disciple and Mentor* (New York: Cambridge University Press, 2004), 19–25.

19. Judith Margaret Brown, *Gandhi: Prisoner of Hope* (New Haven: Yale University Press, 1989), 26, 32, 44–50.

20. Margaret Kohn and Kavita Reddy, "Colonialism," in *Stanford Encyclopedia of Philosophy*, ed. Edward N. Zalta, August 29, 2017, https://plato.stanford.edu/entries/colonialism/.

21. Lisa Lowe, *The Intimacies of Four Continents* (Durham, N.C.: Duke University Press, 2015), 71.

22. P. J. Marshall, *The Making and Unmaking of Empires: Britain, India, and America, c. 1750–1783* (New York: Oxford University Press, 2005), 197.

23. Catherine Clément, *Gandhi: The Power of Pacifism* (New York: Harry N. Abrams, 1996), 45–47.

24. Ibid., 72–78.

25. Peter Ackerman and Jack DuVall, *A Force More Powerful: A Century of Nonviolent Conflict* (New York: St. Martin's, 2000), 83.

26. Jan Morris, *Farewell the Trumpets: An Imperial Retreat* (Boston: Faber & Faber, 1978), 5.

27. Frederick D. Lugard, *The Dual Mandate in British Tropical Africa* (London: Blackwood and Sons, 1922), 58.

Chapter 6. Narrative Is Everywhere

1. Jay-Z, *Decoded* (New York: Spiegel & Grau, 2010), 60–61.

2. Daniel Libeskind and Paul Goldberger, *Counterpoint: Daniel Libeskind in Conversation with Paul Goldberger* (New York: Monacelli Press, 2008), 10.

3. "The Libeskind Building," Jewish Museum Berlin, accessed June 11, 2022, https://www.jmberlin.de/en/libeskind-building.

4. Hidden in plain sight in our language is a wild directionality to everything we do. To go down that rabbit hole, open up George Lakoff and Mark Johnson's *Metaphors We Live By* (Chicago: University of Chicago Press, 1980).

5. Joseph Campbell, *The Hero with a Thousand Faces* (New York: Pantheon, 1949).

6. General Authority for Statistics, *Hajj Statistics 1440* (n.p.: Kingdom of Saudi Arabia, 2019), 12.

7. Adrian Snodgrass, *Architecture, Time and Eternity*, 2 vols. (New Delhi: P. K. Goel, 1990), 421.

8. Henry Corbin, *Temple and Contemplation*, trans. Philip Sherrard and Liadain Sherrard (London: KPI, 1986), 246–51.

9. Dale F. Eickelman and James Piscatori, eds., *Muslim Travellers: Pilgrimage, Migration, and the Religious Imagination* (1990; repr., Hoboken, N.J.: Taylor & Francis, 2013), 121.

10. Anank Nunink Nunkai, "Meeting Arutam," *Cultural Survival Quarterly* 32, no. 4 (December 2008): 18.

11. "Bing: Decode Jay-Z," DROGA5, accessed June 11, 2022, https://droga5.com/work/bing/.

Chapter 7. Design for the Unknown

1. Alex Marshall, Carlotta Gall, and Elisabetta Povoledo, "Four Months, 5,000 Miles: A Refugee Puppet Looks for Home," *New York Times*, November 10, 2021.

2. Steven Pinker, *The Language Instinct* (1994; repr., New York: HarperPerennial, 2007), 150.

3. Arika Okrent, *In the Land of Invented Languages: A Celebration of Linguistic Creativity, Madness, and Genius* (2009; repr., New York: Spiegel & Grau, 2010), 314.

4. Ibid., 105–7.

5. Amri Wandel, "How Many People Speak Esperanto? Esperanto on the Web," *Interdisciplinary Description of Complex Systems* 13, no. 2 (2015): 318–21.

6. Jeff Hull, "Nonchalance" (lecture delivered at Adventure Design Group, San Francisco, January 14, 2014).

7. Lydia Laurenson, "My Year in San Francisco's $2 Million Secret Society Startup," *Vice*, March 7, 2016, https://www.vice.com/en/article/xygykj/my-year-in-san-franciscos-2-million-secret-society-startup.

8. Geordie Aitken et al., *In Bright Axiom*, directed by Spencer McCall (Nonchalance/Pen and Banjo Films, 2019).

9. Muriel Garreta Domingo, "The Rule of Thirds: Know Your Layout Sweet Spots," Interaction Design Foundation, accessed June 15, 2022, https://www.interaction-design.org/literature/article/the-rule-of-thirds-know-your-layout-sweet-spots.

10. Atul Gawande, "A Life-Saving Checklist," *New Yorker*, December 3, 2007.

11. Atul Gawande, *The Checklist Manifesto: How to Get Things Right* (New York: Metropolitan Books, 2010), 48.

12. Will Hermes, "The Story of '4′33″,'" NPR, May 8, 2000, https://www.npr.org/2000/05/08/1073885/4–33.

Chapter 8. Transformative Experiences Work with Eventness

1. Daniel Sosnoski, ed., *Introduction to Japanese Culture* (Boston: Tuttle, 1996), 67.

2. Nele Bemong, Pieter Borghart, and Michel De Dobbeleer, eds., *Bakhtin's Theory of the Literary Chronotope: Reflections, Applications, Perspectives* (Gent: Academia Press, 2010), 39–40.

3. Mircea Eliade, *The Sacred and the Profane: The Nature of Religion*, trans. Willard Trask (New York: Harcourt, Brace, and World, 1959).

4. Daniel Kahneman and Amos Tversky, eds., *Choices, Values, and Frames* (Cambridge: Cambridge University Press, 2000), 676.

5. "The Nobel Prize Call," NobelPrize.org, accessed June 13, 2022, https://www.nobelprize.org/prizes/themes/the-nobel-call/.

6. Ellen Yard, Lakshmi Radhakrishnan, Michael F. Ballesteros, et al., "Emergency Department Visits for Suspected Suicide Attempts among Persons Aged 12–25 Years before and during the COVID-19 Pandemic—United States, January 2019–May 2021," *Morbidity and Mortality Weekly Report* 70, no. 24 (June 18, 2021): 888–94.

7. Lauren Camera, "College Enrollment on Track for Largest Two-Year Drop on Record," *U.S. News and World Report*, October 26, 2021.

8. Reuters News Service, "Tokyo Olympics Least Watched in History," *Cyprus Mail*, July 30, 2021.

9. Larry Buchanan, Quoctrung Bui, and Jugal K. Patel, "Black Lives Matter May Be the Largest Movement in U.S. History," *New York Times*, July 3, 2020.

Chapter 9. Use Diagrams

1. Lawrence Halprin, *The RSVP Cycles: Creative Processes in the Human Environment* (New York: G. Braziller, 1969), 7–11.

2. Elin Diamond, "Reactivating the City: A Situationist-Inspired Map of New York," *Theater Journal* 70, no. 3 (September 2018), 15–17.

3. Domenico Chirchiglia, Pasquale Chirchiglia, and Rosa Marotta, "Wilder Graves Penfield," *Lancet Neurology* 18, no. 2 (February 2019): 139.

4. Virginia Tufte and Dawn Finley, "Minard's Sources," Work of Edward Tufte and Graphics Press, August 7, 2002, https://www.edwardtufte.com/tufte/minard.

Chapter 10. Make Work That Matters

1. James Rich, "Zaha Hadid Defends Qatar World Cup Role Following Migrant Worker Deaths," *Guardian*, February 25, 2014.

Design Note

Erica Holeman

Typically, when designing a book, readability is my priority. You are here to read, after all. But this isn't a typical book. The text regularly calls attention to its design, asking you to notice the scale of the book, consider the frame it creates, or pause before turning a page. Rarely is a book so self-aware. Consideration of the experience of reading had to come before all else as I designed the book. Within the layout is a system of visual cues: black backgrounds indicate an experiment, chapters begin with monumental text to mark a new beginning, and large amounts of green punctuate the pages rhythmically. These decisions (among others) create a sense of place and pace, while allowing for easier recall and navigation each time you return to the book.

To support a simple, yet memorable, reading experience, the book's illustrations and typefaces reference language of manuals and guidebooks. The typeface used throughout is Neue Haas Unica. This 2015 design is a revival of Unica, a versatile and neutral sans serif released in 1980 as a hybrid of the classic sans serifs Univers and Helvetica. The illustrations are inspired by the work of Marie and Otto Neurath, who designed the Isotype system of simplified forms to quickly communicate complex ideas. The foreign text in many of the images is from a language called Siliconian, invented by Pragun Agarwal, Misha Gomez, and Katie Mancher.

Designing this book has been an enormous experience. In your hands is proof of the passage of time: illustrations born in the spring, chapters chiseled over autumn and winter. The book's design joined me on a cross-country move and a change in jobs. A large part of my life is represented within these seven compact inches. Concepts from this book seep into my teaching and infiltrate conversations with innocent, unsuspecting bystanders. It is a privilege to have this artifact of my time be part of your life as well.

Credits

Throughout the book, the invented language Siliconian is used in illustrations to represent generic text. Siliconian was created by Pragun Agarwal, Misha Gomez, and Katie Mancher in 2018.

p. 28: Denise Shanté Brown, *Beyond the Blues* box, 2017. Illustrated by Erica Holeman.

p. 48: James Hannaham, *Planet*, 2011.

pp. 50–51: Belina Costa, *Interiority/ Exteriority*, 2015. Illustrated by Erica Holeman.

p. 64: Abraham Burickson, *Layers of Immersion*, 2022. Illustrated by Erica Holeman. Sacred Heart based on the work of Joel Douglas Harrison.

p. 68: Adrienne Mackey and Swim Pony, cards from *The End*, 2017. Illustrated by Erica Holeman.

p. 91: *Che Guevara*, based on *Guerrillero Heroico*, 1960, photograph by Alberto Korda. Illustrated by Erica Holeman.

p. 159: Travis Weller, *Long Distance Duo*, 2017.

p. 161: Christian Nold, *San Francisco Emotion Map* (detail), 2007.

p. 164: Odyssey Works, Odyssey Works' Bologna/Baloney symbol, 2011.

p. 170: Miles Holenstein, Odyssey Works' *Pilgrimage* diagram, 2016.

p. 171: László Moholy-Nagy, *Motion Diagram of Finnegans Wake*, 1947; © 2022 Estate of László Moholy-Nagy/Artists Rights Society (ARS), New York.

p. 173: Abraham Burickson and Ana Tobin, *Diagram of "The Book of Separation,"* 2021.

p. 175: Guy DeBord, *The Naked City: Illustration de l'hypothèse des plaques tournantes en psychogéographique*, 1957, lithograph, ink on paper, 13.1 × 19.0 in. (33.3 × 48.3 cm). Collection Frac Centre-Val de Loire.

p. 176: Abraham Burickson, *Qualities of Light*, 2019.

p. 178: Ellen Fullman, *Four Colors Score*, 2022.

p. 179: Charles Joseph Minard, *Carte figurative des pertes successives en hommes de l'Armée Française dans la campagne de Russie 1812–1813*, 1869.

Acknowledgments

This book would not have been possible without the endless wisdom and patience of Dare Turner, who read and edited the text, and helped broaden my thinking about decolonization and what it means to change the world. It would also not have been possible without the intelligence and encouragement of Ayden LeRoux, alongside whom much of these ways of thinking were articulated and put to the test. I would like to thank Katherine Boller and Yale University Press for taking a chance on this book, and their anonymous peer reviewers for encouraging them to do so. Thanks to Ellen Lupton, such an inspirational human, teacher, and designer, for writing the foreword to this book, and to MICA for supporting me throughout this whole process.

So many of the individuals whose work is discussed or presented in this book have been an influence and a personal inspiration to me beyond what made it into the text, notably Travis Weller, James Hannaham, and Douglas Harrison.

Writing a book is an inflection point in one's journey of ideas, forcing one to go back and reexamine one's convictions; I feel such gratitude for those already mentioned who challenged my understandings as I wrote, as well as Lea Redmond, who pushed me in many ways, challenging my thinking about empathy. But a book is also the end point of a much longer journey, fueled by countless hours of experimentation and analysis, alongside fellow travelers. These include Matthew Purdon and Nell Waters and Shoshana Green and all my companions through the years at Odyssey Works. No idea is one's own alone; we stand on the shoulders of giants, and it's giants all the way down.

Finally, this book could never have happened without the brilliant vision and experimental spirit of its designer, Erica Holeman. What shall we make next?